Creativity, Spirituality, and Transcendence: Paths to Integrity and Wisdom in the Mature Self

Publications in
Creativity Research

(formerly Creativity Research Monographs,
Edited by Mark A. Runco)

Joan Franklin Smutney, Series Editor
Robert S. Albert, Former Series Editor

Creativity, Spirituality, and Transcendence: Paths to Integrity and Wisdom in the Mature Self

edited by

Melvin E. Miller
&
Susanne R. Cook-Greuter

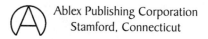

Ablex Publishing Corporation
Stamford, Connecticut

Printed in the United States of America

Library of Congress Cataloging-in-Publication Data

Creativity, spirituality, and transcendence : paths to integrity and wisdom in the mature self / edited by Melvin E. Miller, Susanne Cook-Greuter
    p. cm.—(Publications in creativity research)
    Includes bibliographical references and index.
    ISBN 1-56750-460-4 (cloth)—ISBN 1-56750-461-2 (pbk.)
    1. Creative ability. 2. Spirituality. 3. Maturation (Psychology)
    I. Miller, Melvin E. II. Cook-Greuter, Susanne R. III. Series.
BF411.C76   2000
153.3'5—dc21   99-29746
                                        CIP

Ablex Publishing Corporation
100 Prospect Street
P.O. Box 811
Stamford, Connecticut 06904-0811

To my parents, Mel and Roberta
—M.E.M.

To my spouse, Craig,
and to my children, Mariann and Matthew
—S.C-G.

Contents

Part III: Theoretical Approaches and Reflections

Figures and Tables

Figures

Tables

PREFACE

This collection has been developed by an interdisciplinary group of authors. They present a variety of new perspectives on creativity, spirituality, and transcendence in adulthood. The discussion in this volume is further deepened by chapters that address the interplay of these variables from theoretical, experiential, and clinical vantage points. Although written for academic and clinical audiences, this book should have great appeal to the general public and to all those interested in, and wrestling with, unexpressed aspects of their own creativity and spiritual yearnings. Some articles are primarily research based; most are theoretical. Together, they make a captivating collection of essays that challenges our thinking about what it means to be a creative adult striving toward personal integrity and wisdom.

The impetus for this book arose from the interplay of unmet academic needs and our personal interests in the underside, the less-often articulated side, of the creative enterprise. Gaps in the extant creativity literature, coupled with the degree to which mainstream creativity researchers have tended to neglect the role of inspiration in creativity, seemed to require that this book be written.

In addition to addressing this void in the academic literature, we hope this collection of essays will have a personal impact on both academic and lay readers who venture into its territory. As we approach the new millennium, there appear to be many who wrestle with their own creativity and spiritual yearnings as witnessed in the popular literature, in developmental studies, and in reports from therapeutic consulting rooms. There is a buzz in the air; there is a sense of urgency among many to understand and express hidden aspects of self—particularly among those who are moving into the second half of life. Perhaps this book will serve to ignite the creative fires of some readers, instill them with courage to create, and with the determination to take risks, and possibly invite them to explore their own creative self-expression on the path to personal integrity and wisdom.

In this stimulating and thought-provoking volume, we have gathered together developmental and clinical psychologists, psychoanalysts, educators, scientists, writers, and artists who are passionately interested in probing the depths of, and fostering, the creative urge. They strive to push the limits of their own thinking on creativity and spirituality from their respective areas of expertise. Furthermore, each hopes to foster an ongoing dialogue on these topics. In short, these writers are convinced that the creative and spiritual dimensions are natural aspects of what it means to be a fulfilled, actualized human being. The authors are dedicated to removing impediments to creative expression while, at the same time, promoting expansive, transcendent forms of adult development.

No project of this scope can be brought to completion without the assistance and advice of many people. Although it is impossible to thank everyone who has helped, we would like to express formally our appreciation to a special few. First, we thank Gladys Agell, Loren Miller, and Ken Smith for reading and giving feedback and editorial advice on various portions of the manuscript. Second, many thanks go to Alan Stubbs for his generous help with the photographic displays that appear in Chapter 6 on Edith Kramer, and to Milton Hammond and Mahri Jennings of the Norwich University Department of Psychology for their technical assistance with photographs used throughout the remainder of the volume. And third, heartfelt thanks and praise are extended to Sharon Dickinson, administrative assistant to Mel Miller, for her extensive and cheerful assistance with so many facets of this project, including: the coordination of mailings, extensive photocopying, disk formatting, software synchronization, and her overall bountiful support of this project. Finally, we thank Kim Burgos, former Acquisitions Editor, Laura Specht Patchkofsky, Meredith Phillips, and the entire staff at Ablex Publishing Corporation for their patience, support, and suggestions. Without the help of all these wonderful people, this project would not have materialized.

From the bottom of our hearts, we also want to thank our families for the encouragement and backing they have shown us throughout the various phases of this process. Our spouses, Loren Miller and Craig Cook, and our children (Melissa and Aaron; Mariann and Matthew), have patiently, creatively, and good-humoredly supported us throughout this and other projects over the past few years. To them we are sincerely grateful.

Melvin E. Miller
Susanne R. Cook-Greuter

Introduction: Creativity in Adulthood: Personal Maturity and Openness to Extraordinary Sources of Inspiration

Susanne R. Cook-Greuter

Melvin E. Miller
Norwich University

Extraordinary human achievement is awe inspiring. It fascinates. It challenges our assumptions. It elevates and inspires us toward transcending our own preconceived limits. Greatness in any domain shines like a beacon and illuminates the realm of the possible for all of us.

In an earlier book collaboration, *Transcendence and Mature Thought in Adulthood* (1994), Miller and Cook-Greuter focused on theories of development that describe the complex, mature ways some adults view reality. The achievement of these postconventional stages of development seems to be a fruit of both life experience and mental and emotional maturation. It is statistically rare[1] and generally does not occur before middle age. It is in this sense that it can be considered extraordinary in terms of human achievement.

This book continues to explore extraordinary achievement and grew out of the following observations. First, despite recent attempts to explain all such achievement in rational terms, some scientists and creators maintain that their creations are not only infused and nurtured by nonrational sources, but that they have entirely transpersonal, or transcendent origins. This view, to say the least, is unpopular. Second, adults at later stages of development generally hold broader, more complex perspectives on reality. They seem to be more open to recognize and welcome nonrational input—from body awareness to dreams to primary process thought—as legitimate sources of information in living their lives. Moreover, because of the broader base from which they can consciously draw, their artistic and intellectual products are potentially more creative in a profound, culture-altering way than those of their more conventional peers.

Thus, this book follows two threads in the discourse on creativity that are underexplored elsewhere. First, we reopen the case for extra-ordinary sources of creativity, whether they come from archetypal material, the classical muses, or divine inspiration. Second, we wish to introduce the notion that the developmental maturity of the creator may have a positive effect on the quality of the creative output and its potential to transform society as a whole.

MAPPINGS: BELOW AND ABOVE; INSIDE AND OUTSIDE

Problems of definition regularly emerge when we address the transpersonal dimension of experience in normal adults. The literature often confuses the terms *stages* and *states* of experience; it also obfuscates necessary distinctions that need to be made among different levels of the transpersonal. Ken Wilber has termed this confusion the pre-trans fallacy in several of his recent works (1995, 1997, 1998). In order to assist the reader with an understanding of how these concepts are generally used by the authors of this book, some points of clarification are in order.

Altered *states* of consciousness (daydreams, flow states, peak experiences) are *altered* in the sense that they are different from what is considered to be the normal, waking awareness. By definition, such altered states are temporary, fleeting, and lead the experiencer back to his or her ordinary, everyday view of reality. *Stages*, on the other hand, are the more permanent positions from which different people view, explore, and interpret experience from different perspectives. They constitute our preferred ways of making sense of reality. Developmental theory holds that these stages follow each other in an invariant sequence of greater and greater differentiation and integration. At the highest stages of consciousness development, individuals transcend the personal, rational perspective and permanently enter ego-transcendent, higher consciousness stages (Figure I.2). There are qualitative differences among those in the personal (rational) stages; the more evolved and mature individuals are, the more complex information (from more diverse sources, including transpersonal ones) they can meaningfully integrate and consciously use for their purposes. Thus, according to the developmental perspective, the degree to which individuals can profit from and integrate experiences and insights gained through contact with the numinous differs according to their existing view of reality and their developmental stage. The theory predicts that people at postconventional stages can more readily differentiate among transpersonal sources and make more deliberate use of the insights gained for the benefit of their quality of life. Moreover, how one uses the transpersonal realm also depends on one's developmental perspective. Below we share two different figurative renditions of the relationship between the personal and the transpersonal. These working models are equally useful in discussing the sources of creativity, but they are unequal, we suggest, in their explanatory, integrative power.

Figure I.1 shows a conventional, linear, rational perspective of the sources of creativity, which effectively splits the territory into three hierarchical layers. The prepersonal layer is at the bottom; the rational, language-meditated, and conscious egoic layer is in the middle; and the higher, transcendent layer is placed at the top. Input from the personal, egoic, or rational layer typically tends to reign supreme, while input from both prerational (prepersonal) and postrational sources is deemed irrational and outside the realm of science because the rational mind is appealed to as the final and only arbitrator in matters of truth.

Figure I.2 shows the unitary perspective on sources of creativity and places the whole personal trajectory of growth (from the preconventional, through the conventional [rational], to the postconventional, systemic view) within the transpersonal or the creative ground that enfolds the personal on all sides. The transpersonal, as a territory, covers every source of influence that is not mediated by, or under the control of, the conscious ego. Like the personal, the transpersonal also contains different levels of refinement. The pre-trans fallacy occurs when all undifferentiated prepersonal states and sources are deemed as equally powerful and illuminating as the transpersonal. See Chapters 4 and 11 by J. Funk and M. Boucouvalas (respectively), in this volume, for a more detailed discussion of this issue.

The unitary perspective takes the transcendent ground as prior to (and all-encompassing of) personal individuation and growth of consciousness. The creative sources are therefore accessible from all positions. Whereas in the early stages, the budding ego is confused between self and reality, it is over-differentiated in the conventional stages. Eventually, access to the transpersonal is regained once the rigid boundaries of the conventional worldview are loosened through continued individual differentiation and integration.

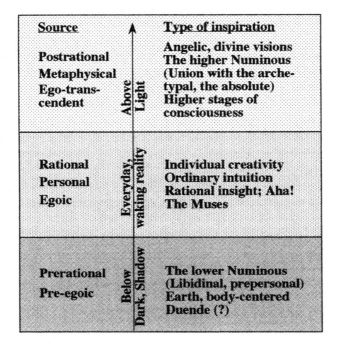

FIGURE I.1.   Access to Extraordinary Sources of Creativity: Conventional, Linear View

SUMMARY OF DEVELOPMENTAL THEORY

Because we emerge out of the ground of being, we have access to it in an unconscious, direct way. However, over time, normal maturation within a society leads to the development of increasing differentiation and control of the ego over what is (and what is not) defined as belonging to everyday waking reality, and what is considered real and important. In the West, this reality is generally defined as the rational, language-mediated set of concepts that constitutes the permanent object world and the permanent separate self. From the conventional, scientific point of view, any input from sources that are outside the rational—from dreams to daydreams, to drug-induced hallucinations, to flow states and peak moments—are deemed unreal, suspicious, potentially dangerous intrusions upon the sovereignty of the self. Such "intrusions" are therefore often vigorously defended against. Thus the adherence to a conventional, rational-linear view of reality, though implicitly required

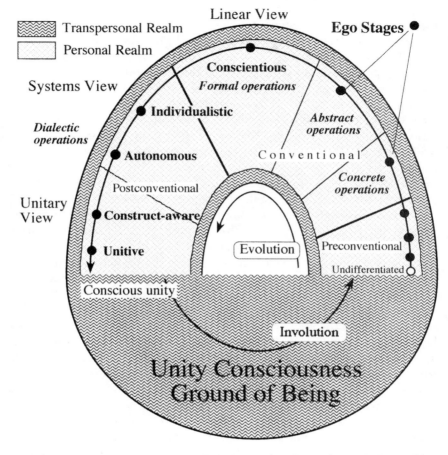

FIGURE I.2.   Access to Extraordinary Sources of Creativity: Unitary View

for best functioning in a modern society (see Kegan, 1994, *In Over Our Heads*), makes it harder for individuals to draw from the rich nonrational sources of knowing.

Most traditional Western psychology sees the realization of a separate, autonomous self with clear boundaries and a rational, objective stance toward life as the goal of development. According to Piaget (1954), this particular stance toward reality is reached by early adulthood and remains operative throughout life once achieved.

With increasing self-differentiation and understanding beyond conventional views of reality, the rigid compartmentalization between waking and other realities softens. Unlike at the earliest stages of development, the self can now consciously choose, direct, and integrate experiences from other sources.

Only recently have psychologists studied how some individuals continue to develop according to different, more comprehensive models of reality at postconventional stages of adult development (see Basseches, 1984; Cook-Greuter, 1990, 1994; Kegan, 1982, 1994; Koplowitz, 1984; Loevinger, 1976; Miller, 1994). Individuals at these stages become intrigued with what lies underneath or behind the particular constructions they unconsciously absorbed from their cultural surround as children. They explore questions of how we know what we know. Yet, unlike the postmodern approach to epistemology which *logically* exposes and de(con)structs the false premises of the mechanistic modern stance (without offering an alternative position upon which to stand), many researchers in postconventional adult development observe that mature insight and access to the metaphysical or transpersonal can support people's continuing sense of connection and meaning.

Researchers in adult development characterize the most mature stance as one's capacity to simultaneously use and enjoy the rational mind and to be mindful of its limits and trappings. They expose the costs of our automatic habits of the mind (e.g., dualistic splitting and relentless streams of thought and judgments) while at the same time, they look beyond the individual to transcendent, nonmaterial forms of understanding and insight (Fingarette, 1963; Wilber, 1996, 1997, 1998). In summary, the potential growth trajectory of the self can be described as one of increasing differentiation toward the rational, conventional view of reality from birth to early adulthood, and then one of a growing and conscious deconstruction of boundaries and increasing reintegration with the ground of being at later stages of differentiation.

As people become more self-actualized, they start to appreciate transpersonal input in a qualitatively different way. The uses made of numinous sources depend on the discriminating powers of the registering individuals as much as on the sources themselves. Given that only mature adults seem to have a relationship to the transpersonal that is simultaneously accepting and discriminating, we find it fruitful to approach the themes of creativity, spirituality, and transcendence in this volume from a developmental perspective.

As in our previous collaboration, this book continues to stretch the boundaries of what has been conventionally considered the proper domain of psychology. We do this in part because we believe that a critical, yet open-minded, voice is needed to counterpoint both the current vogue in the social sciences (namely, explaining mental phenomena predominantly within the rational domain), and the proliferation of untested claims about spiritual influences propagated in the New Age literature.

A BRIEF OVERVIEW OF MAJOR APPROACHES TO CREATIVITY

Within the last 20 years, the list of authors of books on creativity reads like a *Who's Who* in psychology. Many well-known psychologists have explored various aspects of creativity as well as the lives and characteristics of creative people. To our way of thinking, this multifaceted literature deserves to be taken seriously if we are to have a rich and meaningful dialogue on the topic of creativity. The following is a brief overview of some of the approaches that are currently being pursued, though the list is not meant to be comprehensive.The first prominent group of researchers believes that creativity is merely a fascinating puzzle or problem to be solved, not a mystery. The proponents of this popular *cognitive approach* attempt to "demystify" the creative process and its mechanisms by showing that it is nothing more than problem solving at its best. They look at the human brain as a complex computational device whose internal goings-on can be studied and clarified. David Perkins (1981), *The Mind's Best Work;* Howard Gardner (1982), *Art, Mind and Brain;* and Margaret Boden (1991), *The Creative Mind: Myths & Mechanisms* advocate this stance. Indeed, they demonstrate that in many cases the steps of the creative process can be reconstructed and made explicit.

Boden makes a powerful and lucid argument that we do not have to appeal to transcendent sources to explain creativity. Her research with artificial intelligence, for example, shows that some computer-generated art, from story writing to figure drawing, is close enough to human-made products to satisfy even a knowledgeable audience as to its aesthetic value and impact. According to Boden, the creative process can be explained by careful analysis of the complex underlying mental procedures. She shows how creativity occurs across domains based on similar cognitive devices, heuristics, analogical capacities, and mental maps. Even randomness has its function in her scheme. What's more, these mechanisms can be successfully imitated by machines. In turn, the computer is seen as a model system for human beings and their behavior. In general, proponents of the cognitive approach clearly favor rational explanations and actively dismiss romantic notions of divine or superhuman inspiration.

Not surprisingly, the truly formidable advances that have occurred in computer technology, artificial intelligence, and information processing, as well as in the biomedical sciences, strengthen the conviction that most aspects of the mind can be scientifically researched and eventually explained. We can study brain development and activity with computer-aided technology such as CAT scans and MRIs, and explore neurochemical and neuroelectrical differences among humans through advances in genetic manipulation and sophisticated chemical analysis. Indeed, new discoveries about the evolutionary substrates, cell biology, the growth and mechanics of individual mental processes—normal, abnormal, and extraordinary—are being made at a staggering rate. All of these, of course, seem to vindicate the rational position. Moreover, they also add weight to "nature" in the ongoing debate over the relative roles of nature and nurture in influencing the development of human mental capacities.

Rather than trying to explain how creativity and creative minds work, another group of researchers has investigated what nurtures creativity. They explore the personal, contextual, and social factors that influence its development and expression. Robert Sternberg (1988), in *The Nature of Creativity*, is concerned with mapping the conceptions and definitions used to study giftedness, while Feldman's (1986) *Nature's Gambit*, and Ericsson, Krampe, and Tesch-Römer's (1993) "The Role of Deliberate Practice" add to our understanding of the development of expert performance and mastery in given artistic domains.

Psychodynamic approaches investigate personality traits, the unconscious, and psychological defenses to account for differences among individuals in the type and quality of creative output. Freud (1958), *On Creativity and the Unconscious;* David Storr (1993), *The Dynamics of Creation;* and George Vaillant (1993), *The Wisdom of the Ego,* have researched aspects of adult creativity from this perspective. Ernst Kris (1952) and Lawrence Kubie (1961) have also contributed to our understanding of the role of psychopathology in both releasing and constricting/distorting creativity. See Chapter 3 by C. Goldberg in this volume, for an illustration of the psychodynamic approach.

Many researchers have studied creativity from a *personality* or *traits* perspective. Teresa Amabile (1983), in *The Social Psychology of Creativity,* as well as the dialogue between Herbert Simon (1988) and Mihaly Csikszentmihalyi (1988a) in *New Ideas in Psychology,* point to intrinsic motivation as a vital characteristic of creative people. Other personality traits mentioned in the literature as aspects of the creative personality are: physical stamina and mental persistence; curiosity combined with an ability for sustained, focused attention on the object of curiosity; a passion for one's work while remaining critical about it; a capacity to fully experience the emotional highs and lows of the creative process; flexibility and a childlike openness to experience; and the capacity to distinguish between important and unimportant aspects of puzzles. Additional traits mentioned as typical of great creators are: tolerance for ambiguity and uncertainty; an attraction to paradox and process; the capacity to work alone; the ability to work without constant external validation while simultaneously being aware of one's need for others in forming ideas and for critical feedback; a powerful combination of high self-regard, based on an accurate appreciation of one's giftedness, and a genuine humility that comes from knowing the depth of human ignorance. This latter set of traits is often associated with mature, postconventional stages of development. Whether and to what degree personality traits are inherited or acquired and how much they are changeable is part of an ongoing debate in psychology. The correlation between high ego development and extraordinary creative or scientific achievement is yet to be empirically tested.

A more complex framework for understanding creativity and creators comes from Csikszentmihalyi and Gardner who promote a *systemic view* in their more recent writings (Csikszentmihalyi [1988b], "Society, Culture, and Person"; Gardner [1993], *Creating Minds: An Anatomy of Creativity*). The systems view tries to elucidate which aspects of both nature and nurture are relevant to great art, in what sequence (and to what degree) the different parts of the system relate to, enhance, or constrain each other. Thus it seems that psychology is starting to acknowledge that broad approaches that place the individual into a personal, cultural, and historical context are necessary for both describing creativity and for producing deeper insights into such a complex and intriguing subject.

What then, we ask, weighs more heavily today, nature or nurture, evolutionary forces or social conditioning, in explaining the phenomenon of creativity? Due to the mass of interesting research findings arising from the hard sciences, the tide seems to favor nature with some currency given to culture and conditioning. On the other hand, a synergy of many sources, that takes into account genetic predispositions, historical context, in combination with individual and cultural factors, will more likely lead to a fuller understanding of creativity than any single-focus method or "either/or" approach (Csikszentmihalyi, 1996).

What is striking to us is that the transpersonal (outside nature and nurture) as a potential explanatory principle for certain aspects of creativity is absent in all of the approaches mentioned above, even in the most broadly conceived.[2] Csikszentmihalyi's (1996) *Creativity: Flow and the Psychology of Discovery and Invention* does seem to be an exception to this trend. Here he discusses such concepts as the "contemplation of infinity," "witnessing," and "spirituality" as powerful ingredients in creative people's lives. He describes his concept of "flow" as a state of consciousness that has many attributes in common with those described in the transpersonal literature. A profound absorption into the subject of inquiry, accompanied by self-forgetting, timelessness, and the experience of a profound joy (a joy that is qualitatively different from everyday happiness), are among such attributes. Csikzentmihalyi's underlying research emphasis—and this ties in with our own concerns—explores what great creators can teach us about those factors, traits, and variables that best foster the overall quality (and meaning-making capacity) in human lives.

It is precisely these concerns and how they relate to extraordinary creativity and mature science that we wish to expand upon in this volume. We advocate that the systems approach be broadened even further to include not just the rationally explorable domains of human creativity, but also the dimension of the mysterious. We have come to understand the "extraordinary" in extraordinary creativity to refer not only to the rare occurrence of great individual accomplishment that stands way above the commonplace, but also to the meaning of extraordinary (out of the ordinary) as coming from sources outside the individual.

DIFFERING BELIEFS REGARDING THE TRANSPERSONAL WITHIN THE SCIENTIFIC COMMUNITY

What researchers wish to study and what methods they believe are legitimate (and will get them results) seems to be a matter of their own basic beliefs about reality, an aspect of science-making often not consciously examined. Many scientists, including those in the social sciences, believe that the rational mind allows us to find out everything there is to know about the universe. They trust that if we do not understand something now, we will be able to explain it eventually—when the appropriate technology, procedures, and methods of scientific analyses have been developed. In light of the vast discoveries based on technology in all knowledge spheres, but especially in the domains inaccessible to our ordinary senses—the infinitely small (quantum physics) and the infinitely large (astronomy)—this trust in methods and instruments is most understandable.

Despite the many insights gained from the rational approach, other scientists feel that human life will never be explained completely. They sense that there will always be an element of mystery about the living universe, a realm that is inaccessible to scientific inquiry. In addition to explanations and ways to measure experience, these folks are also interested in exploring the question of what it means and feels like to be alive. They are actively engaged in asking epistemological questions. They explore how we know what we know and whether there are any inherent limits to the rational, scientific enterprise.

Thus, depending on whether researchers believe that reality is ultimately knowable in the long run or unknowable, they approach, define, and research human phenomena in different ways, consider data from different sources as legitimate, and apply different proofs to validate their inferences. Ken Wilber (1995, 1996) has written most eloquently about this topic in several of his more recent works and we refer the interested reader to his explications. There is some evidence to suggest that scientists' beliefs about these matters may also be related to their personal development.

When there is a change of heart within a researcher, it frequently seems to be in the direction of finding analytical science more limited and limiting. Such changes are often due to increasing age and insight. Albert Einstein (1950), Ludwig Wittgenstein (1935/1958), David Bohm (1987), and Stephen Hawking (1988), all report that they felt dissatisfied on some level with their youthful, purely linear-scientific approaches, because they believed, or came to believe over a lifetime, that there was more to human existence than their rational minds and methods could fathom.

Today, a spectrum of attitudes toward the mysterious or numinous is represented in science: There are the rationalists of both the modern and postmodern convictions who deny or doubt the existence of the transpersonal; and then there are those scientists who affirm its influence on their science-making in various degrees of certainty. Some in this group decry pure rationality while others acknowledge the rational mind as a valuable—even marvelous—but nonetheless a limited tool in the study of the human condition. This is so because every conscious being has to face anew: fate and free will, pain and joy, attachment and loss, birth and death, and the ebb and flow of one's awareness. No amount of "knowledge" created by rational science can help us forego the experience of these deeper realities of human existence.

Although representatives of the last group of scientists may employ the scientific method and appreciate its power, they are also aware of its profound limitations in answering existential questions. Thus, these scientists bridge the mental poles that Pascal so aptly described in *Pensées*. Humankind is both infinite compared to nothingness and nothing compared to the infinite (see Merlot, 1962, pp. 21–24). As mentioned earlier, both to be aware of one's greatness and remain humble in light of what one does not or cannot know, is one indicator of greatness.

Mel Miller invited me, Susanne, to coedit this volume and coauthor this chapter because I have an affinity for this latter stance. I also believe that conventional science and rational explanations are necessary and useful, but not sufficient to answer ontological aspects of human experience. Because we share this inclination, Mel and I included the voices of researchers at the opposite pole from the cognitive camp, those who see evidence for transcendent possibilities in their research. In addition, we invited chapters that reflect on how the postconventional thinking and integrative wisdom of the creator may enhance the quality and import of his or her creative output. To give the interested reader a taste of why I personally consider the transpersonal as a possible source in matters of research, a pivotal event in my own life is described in an endnote below.[3]

ORGANIZATION OF CHAPTERS

This book is comprised of a collection of chapters that explore the various ways creativity appears in and influences adult life. It examines creativity in both the arts and the sciences, and reflects on the ways in which certain forms of creativity can be understood best through an examination of their relationship with the numinous and transcendent.

The book is divided into three main sections: I: Creative Process, Inspiration, and the Muse in Writing and Composition; II: Personal Transformation and Integrity; and III: Theoretical Approaches and Reflections. Several authors have contributed to each topic. They offer contrasting views and perspectives, thus enriching the discourse and texture of the book. By focusing on mature creativity, creators, and the theories that aim to explain them, we hope that this volume adds a new dimension to the dialogue on creativity in adulthood.

Part I: Creative Process, Inspiration, and the Muse in Writing and Composition

This section includes four uniquely stated perspectives on the intrapersonal and extrapersonal influences that shape the creative process. The first of these chapters, written by Chris Edwards, is entitled "Creative Writing as a Spiritual Practice: Two Paths." Here Edwards discusses those forms of creativity that are presumed to derive from some form of contact with a divine force—during both the inception of the creative project and throughout the entire creative process. Edwards notes that there are at least two separate paths on the Via Creativa: one is the extroverted Via Positiva, and the other, the more introverted Via Negativa. Edwards argues that the Via Positiva is the more popular path in American society with its adherents deriving inspiration and a sense of spiritual presence from their observations of nature or society. The Via Negativa, on the other hand, describes an inner path that draws upon the deeper regions of the self for inspiration and creative images.

Edwards examines the writings from two contemporary authors—John Updike and Ursula Le Guin—to further clarify the two different sources of creativity.

In the second chapter, Verbena Pastor writes on "The Dark Side of Creativity: The Function of Duende and God-Battler in the Writings of Garcia Lorca and Kazantzakis." Pastor defines the concept of *duende* and characterizes it as the dark, suffering, and tormented aspect of the creative process. She explains the relationship of duende to the Spanish soul. Both duende and flamenco demand of the creator intense love, an emotional awareness of death, and a powerful, passionate struggle with the transpersonal from which the creator emerges victorious. Pastor argues that creativity generated through duende is an active battle in contrast to works of art passively inspired by the earthly, rational muses or divine intervention (see Chapter 4 by Funk in this volume on the role of passivity in inspired creativity). Pastor broadens her thesis by comparing Federico Garcia Lorca's struggle with duende with Nikos Kazantzakis's battle with God.

Chapter 3 presents three different approaches to writing and creativity. Carl Goldberg, a psychoanalyst, discusses how flaws or deficits in the artist's personality become "Limitations to Artistic Creation." Goldberg weaves his thesis around the personality and novels of Joseph Conrad. He posits that early object losses often result in character flaws, scarred personalities. The inability to mourn these losses turns into shame, self-contempt, and violent ideas that the creator unconsciously inserts into his characters and plots. Goldberg believes this is precisely what we witness in many of Conrad's written works, particularly in *The Secret Sharer*. He argues that the narrator of the story cannot acknowledge his actual inner feelings—not even to himself. Thus he becomes a prisoner of his recriminating past, mirroring Conrad's own dilemma. Both the narrator/protagonist of *The Secret Sharer* and Joseph Conrad are said to be contemptuous, destructive individuals because they have been unable to resolve critical personality conflicts. Goldberg suggests ways in which creators can avoid the limitations of unresolved material, gain insight, and begin to share more openly with others.

In Chapter 4, Joel Funk writes about "Inspired Creativity" from both the perspective of active musician and composer, and from the vantage point of developmental psychologist. He addresses the age-old debate in the field of creativity: whether extraordinary creativity is explainable by purely rational means (the "nothing-but" approach), or whether sometimes divine inspiration (or the influx from the transcendent or extraordinary states of consciousness) plays a role. Funk claims that mature, postconventional development more likely (and more often) contributes to the individual creator's access to both primary thought and the numinous, and thus to greater creativity. He offers two examples of inspired creativity, one from his own experiences as a composer, and the other from the life of the composer Iasos. Funk concludes with a list of "General Characteristics of Inspired Creativity," to help distinguish "inspired" creativity from other types. Having access to a superconscious state, the retention of ego capacities, a postconventional level of ego development, and the perception of "timelessness" and "mysticism" during the creative experience are among the characteristics listed.

Part II: Personal Transformation and Integrity

This section focuses on the lives of specific creative individuals. In Chapter 5, Carol Hoare writes about "Wisdom and Integrity in the Writings of Erik H. Erikson." Hoare, an Erikson scholar, explores the manuscripts, essays, and papers written by Erikson during the twilight years of his life. What can we learn from the fact that Erikson's mature writings do not seem to vindicate nor validate his own middle-age theory on the achievement of integrity (versus despair) in advanced age? Erikson, on the contrary, came to describe his old age as an "integrity crisis," a "daily dread," a "weakening of the will," and a period of "despair," rather than in the time-honored, popular notions of wisdom and integrity. Yet Hoare reminds us that Erikson's ultimate commitment—even in the face of despair—was toward personal integrity, ethical generativity, and a profound identification with humankind.

In Chapter 6, Miller and Cook-Greuter portray the life and "wisdom" of Edith Kramer, an outspoken, feisty, eighty-two-year-old maverick whom they interviewed to discover the secrets of her life. Kramer is an accomplished and still-active artist, teacher, scholar, and a pioneer in the field of art therapy; a woman who has created a good life for herself on her very own terms. What is more, she is an iconoclast who comments lucidly and unabashedly on the arts, the human condition, and the loss of soul and meaning in much contemporary life. The authors trace Kramer's development from childhood to maturity. They touch upon her upbringing in Europe during the 1920s and 1930s, her unique personal experience and background, her early and unquestioned talent and determination, as well as the most salient forces and people that contributed to who she became. They try to answer the question of what internal and external supports and challenges allowed Kramer to become the exemplar of mature creativity she is today. Supported by interview material, Miller and Cook-Greuter evoke her extraordinary and lifelong passion for beauty, integrity, and truth.

John McKenna wrote Chapter 7 entitled "Healing Images: Art and Meditation in Recovery from Cancer." McKenna offers a deeply intimate account of his cancer diagnosis, and his all-consuming struggle for survival. He believes that supportive talk therapy (psychotherapy) and art-making, coupled with a strong religious faith, were the catalysts to his recovery. This chapter describes the phases of his healing process through the shifting meanings and symbolism of the mandalas he created. McKenna's courageous account exemplifies the potential for personal growth through creative expression in all of our lives.

Part III: Theoretical Approaches and Reflections

This section includes chapters that examine creativity from many angles. All four authors in this section investigate a unique dimension of the transformative power of creativity in adulthood. They approach the topic from widely dissimilar perspectives that include the personal, the practical and/or experiential, the empirical, and the philosophical.

In Chapter 8, Ernest Zebrowski, Jr., discusses dynamics related to the integration of the artistic and scientific worldviews from personal and theoretical perspectives. Since Zebrowski is a scientist as well as an artist, he writes from experience and with a sense of conviction as he demonstrates to the reader the manifold ways that science and art overlap, as he outlines the commonalities shared by these ostensibly disparate disciplines. For example, Zebrowski spells out how the beautiful is part of science and art alike. He suggests that scientists and artists often strive to achieve an aesthetic quality in their products. Thus, the creator of a landscape painting and the author of a mathematical formula may aspire to reflect balance, symmetry, and elegance in their endeavors. Zebrowski also argues that science and art have more in common than is evident from their historical treatments and comparisons. He carefully outlines the "methods" of science and art, revealing similarities and differences along the way. Both disciplines value orderliness; both evidence objective and subjective attributes; both attempt to impact the human condition. In sum, he argues that we are all scientists *and* artists, and that it is the integration of science and art—both personally and collectively—that contributes to the acquisition of wisdom.

Michael Commons and Linda Marie Bresette take on an especially interesting challenge in Chapter 9, "Major Creative Innovators as Viewed Through the Lens of the General Model of Hierarchical Complexity and Evolution." Over the years, Commons has performed extensive research on complex levels of postformal adult cognitive development, and has articulated the findings (both quantitative and theoretical) gleaned from this research in his formulation of the General Model of Hierarchical Complexity. In this chapter, Commons and Bresette articulate the kinds and qualities of complex cognitive functioning that are required for high-level innovations and creations. They also discuss the requisite personality traits of creative innovators and the dynamic interplay (and fit) that needs to exist between the high-level innovator and his or her culture. The authors ground this research-based—and highly theoretical—discussion in the research of Charles Darwin. They posit that circumstances, culture, personality variables, and levels of cognitive complexity necessarily interface to produce a major creative innovation. They conclude their essay by pondering the potential consequences resulting from the contemporary value placed by some on higher stage development and complex thinking abilities.

In Chapter 10, Stephanie Glass-Solomon and Cheryl Armon write about "Lifelong Learning and the Good Life: Reconceiving Adult Education for Development." Glass-Solomon and Armon begin this chapter by voicing their dismay at the findings of the Commission for Life-Long Learning, a consortium of national organizations recently formed to investigate the requirements for adult vocational satisfaction through educational and related means. The authors are particularly troubled by the consortium's "agenda for lifelong learning." It was an agenda that emphasized vocational "adaptability"—the adaptation of individuals to global market forces. Lifelong learning was consequently framed in too narrow and too restrictive a context. The national policymakers, according to the authors, failed to look at other critical developmental variables as they formulated their agenda for the future of adult education. For example, they paid little if any attention to how values and philosophical perspectives affect lifelong learning and life satisfaction, nor did they heed adult learners' conceptions of the Good Life. Adult notions of the Good Life, according to the authors, must be included in any project of this sort. The Good Life includes perspectives on how to enhance the quality of individual and collective life. Glass-Solomon and Armon argue that we all (policymakers, developmental theorists, and educators alike) must consider a new agenda for the 21st century—one that will promote adult development in all its essential dimensions. Most importantly, lifelong learning should include, among other values, opportunities for creative and aesthetic expression, and not merely "vocational adaptability." It should be an agenda that includes the pursuit of the Good Life, not only for individuals, but for all humanity.

In the last chapter, Marcie Boucouvalas, in the spirit of the previous chapter, continues to argue for the ongoing promotion of enlightened individual and collective adult development. Her chapter is entitled "The Transpersonal Orientation as a Framework for Understanding Adult Development and Creative Processes." Boucouvalas writes from the perspective of transpersonal psychology. She begins by offering definitions of the transpersonal and a historical overview of the transpersonal field which has its roots in both Eastern and Western thought. Boucouvalas is an important voice in the transpersonal movement. Her summary of recent developments in transpersonal philosophy, psychology, and human development provides a background for some of the notions taken up in other chapters. The author, for example, highlights the unique ways that transpersonal theory offers a strategic platform for the integration of science, humanities, religion, and the creative process. Her argument brings to mind many of the issues articulated by Funk in Chapter 4. The author concludes by advocating for increased, respectful dialogue among the various disciplines that attempt to unravel the mysteries of human existence.

NOTES

1. Depending on the measurement instrument, the figures range from 10 to 15 percent of adults. (See Miller and Cook-Greuter, 1994, pp. xv–xxxiv.)

2. Another proponent of the demystifying school is K. Simonton. In his 1984 book on genius and greatness, Simonton originated the *historiometric, statistical approach* to find the commonalities that made past creators great. Simonton employed his findings from this investigation to help define the future predictors of greatness.

3. In 1987, I attended a three-day symposium on adult development in Cambridge. After the second day I came home to my family to receive the news of my father's death in Switzerland. I lay awake at night, wrestling with his death and the aftermath of our lifelong struggle for mutual understanding. I wondered what it might signify for him to have died at just this juncture in my life. Since I could not get a flight home until after the weekend, I decided to go ahead with my plans to give my conference presentation the next day. I thought of ways I could acknowledge my father's lifelong misgivings about the life of the mind in a creative and positive way.

As I lay awake, mentally and physically exhausted from the previous two days of intellectual stimulation and the unsettling news, I started to wonder about whether I could make coherent sense of anything in my life, let alone the conference contributions. Except for one talk by W. Hoyer and S. Clancy (1987) entitled "Age and Knowledge Representation in Medical Laboratory Decision Making" that used color slides to illustrate the research described, the presentations had been heady and abstract and the topics too varied for me to feel I could integrate them.

I lay awake for hours, agitated and confused. Flashbacks of life with my father, images from the medical slides with strains of bacteria invading human cells, abstract words and concepts from the talks, all paraded in front of my mind's eye. As I tried to make rational sense of all the stimuli, the visual images merged into a primordial soup that was boiling and bubbling in a huge caldron. Initially I could make out various kinds of shapes and words, but then I became absorbed by the vista of primitive organisms reminiscent of the swirls, chains of balls and squiggles seen on the medical slides. As if stirred by a spoon, the irregular roiling and foaming movement of the stew began to move in one direction. To my amazement the various ingredients arranged themselves with increasing speed, first into concentrical rings, then into a spiral. The spiral emanated from a shape like an embryo in the middle of the caldron. As I kept watching, the whole scene transformed itself into the simple, abstract black outline of the multichambered nautilus on a piece of white paper.

I "realized" that this was to me a whole novel metaphor for human development. It was one that could illustrate many more aspects of the theory I was to explain the next morning than the metaphor of the vertical spiral staircase—the most prevalent visual representation in our research field. It also went further in integrating two different theoretical approaches to adult development. It showed that one type of theory could be seen as a special case or a subset of the other. Contemplating how the nautilus is surrounded by the ocean, and how the last chamber always remains open to the surround, was a way to understand the difference between states and stages of higher consciousness.

The suddenness of the insight and the sense that it was a gift from a source outside and beyond my own capabilities was frightening enough at first for me to wonder whether I'd gone momentarily mad, anguished and stressed as I was. Yet the insight was so clear and simple, I decided to expose it to my peers the next day at the symposium, instead of presenting on the announced topic. I continue to use the nautilus metaphor in my work as a visual model to explain the progression and expansion of stages and the possible relationship between each individual as s/he is embedded in and nurtured by the primordial creative ground.

I did attempt to explain the experience of this minor but gratifying and useful insight with conventional theories. Neither Freud's notion of day residue nor Perkins careful deconstruction of the steps leading to the moment of epiphany provided satisfactory answers. I readily concede that many of the ingredients of the experience were present at the start. However, the experience itself, how the insight emerged as a transformation of strange images, simply felt too fantastic, too out-of-the-ordinary, and too discontinuous to be just an elaboration or integration of previous knowledge. Thus, I am attributing it tentatively to a transpersonal source, while I am still seeking a more logical explanation for it. If nothing more, this experience has made me more open to consider the possibility that the transpersonal or numinous may sometimes enter into the equation of human knowledge and creativity.

REFERENCES

Amabile, T. M. (1983). *The social psychology of creativity.* New York: Springer Verlag.

Basseches, M. A. (1984). *Dialectical thinking and adult development.* Norwood, NJ: Ablex.

Boden, M. (1991). *The creative mind: Myths & mechanisms*. New York: Basic Books.

Bohm, D. (1987). *Science order and creativity*. New York: Bantam.

Cook-Greuter, S. (1990). Maps for living: Ego-development stages from symbiosis to conscious universal embeddedness. In M. L. Commons, C. Armon, L. Kohlberg, F. A. Richards, T. A. Grotzer, & J. D. Sinnott (Eds.), *Adult development, Vol. 2: Models and methods in the study of adolescent and adult thought* (pp. 79–104). New York: Praeger.

Cook-Greuter, S. R. (1994). Rare forms of self-understanding in mature adults. In M. Miller & S. Cook-Greuter (Eds.), *Transcendence and mature thought in adulthood: The further reaches of adult development* (pp. 119–146). Lanham, MD: Rowman & Littlefield.

Csikszentmihalyi, M. (1988a). Solving a problem is not finding one: A reply to Simon. *New Ideas in Psychology, 6*, 183–186.

Csikszentmihalyi, M. (1988b). Society, culture, and person: A systems view of creativity. In R. Sternberg (Ed.), *The nature of creativity* (pp. 325-39). New York: Cambridge University Press.

Csikszentmihalyi, M. (1996). *Creativity: Flow and the psychology of discovery and invention*. New York: Harper Collins.

Einstein, A. (1950). *Out of my later years*. New York: Philosophical Library.

Ericsson, K. A., Krampe, R. T., & Tesch-Römer, C. (1993) The role of deliberate practice in the acquisition of expert performance. *Psychological Review, 100*, 363–406.

Feldman, R. (1986) *Nature's gambit*. New York: Basic Books.

Fingarette, H. (1963). *The self in transformation*. New York: Harper and Row.

Freud, S. (1958). *On creativity and the unconscious (collected writings)*. New York: Random House. (Original work published 1908)

Gardner, H. (1982). *Art, mind and brain: A cognitive approach to creativity*. New York: Basic Books.

Gardner, H. (1993). *Creating minds: An anatomy of creativity*. New York: Basic Books.

Hawking, S. (1988). *A brief history of time*. New York: Bantam Books.

Hoyer, W., & Clancy, S. (1987, June). *Age and knowledge representation in medical laboratory decision making*. Unpublished manuscript presented at Symposium for Research in Adult Development.

Kegan R. (1982). *The evolving self: Problem and process in human development*. Cambridge: Harvard University Press.

Kegan, R. (1994). *In over our heads: The demands of modern life*. Cambridge: Harvard University Press.

Koplowitz, H. (1984). A projection beyond Piaget's formal operations stage: A general system stage and a unitary stage. In M. L. Commons, F. A. Richards, & C. Armon (Eds.), *Beyond formal operations* (pp. 272–295). New York: Praeger.

Kris, E. (1952). *Psychoanalytic explorations in art*. New York: International Universities Press.

Kubie, L. S. (1961). *Neurotic distortion of the creative process*. New York: Noonday Press.

Loevinger, J. (1976). *Ego development: Conceptions and theories*. San Francisco: Jossey-Bass.

Merlot, A. (1962). *Précis d'histoire de la littérature française*. Paderborn, Germany: Ferdinand Schoningh.

Miller, M. (1994). World views, ego development, and epistemological changes from the conventional to the postformal: A longitudinal perspective. In M. Miller & S. Cook-Greuter (Eds.), *Transcendence and mature thought in adulthood: The further reaches of adult development* (pp. 147–178). Lanham, MD: Rowman and Littlefield.

Miller, M., & Cook-Greuter, S. (1994). From postconventional development to transcendence: Visions and theories. In M. Miller & S. Cook-Greuter (Eds.), *Transcendence and mature thought in adulthood: The further reaches of adult development* (pp. xv–xxxiv). Lanham, MD: Rowman and Littlefield.

Perkins, D. N. (1981). *The mind's best work*. Cambridge: Harvard University Press.

Piaget, J. (1954). *The construction of reality in the child*. New York: Basic Books. (Originally published in 1937)

Simon, H. (1988). Creativity and motivation: A response to Csikszentmihalyi. *New Ideas in Psychology, 6,* 177–181.

Simonton, D. K. (1984). *Greatness: Who makes history and why.* New York: Guilford.

Sternberg, R. J. (1988). A three-facet model of creativity. In R. J. Sternberg (Ed.), *The nature of creativity* (pp. 125–147). New York: Cambridge University Press.

Storr, D. (1993). *The dynamics of creation*. New York: Ballantine Books.

Vaillant, G.E, (1993). *The wisdom of the ego*. Cambridge: Harvard University Press.

Wilber, K. (1995). *Sex, ecology and spirituality: The spirit of evolution*. Boston: Shambhala.

Wilber, K. (1996). *A brief history of everything*. Boston: Shambhala.

Wilber, K. (1997). *The eye of the spirit*. Boston: Shambhala.

Wilber, K. (1998). *The marriage of sense and soul: Integrating science and religion*. New York: Random House.

Wittgenstein, L. (1958). *Philosophical investigations*. Oxford: Basil Blackwell. (Original work published 1935)

Part I

Creative Process, Inspiration, and the Muse in Writing and Composition

chapter I

Creative Writing as a Spiritual Practice: Two Paths

Christopher G. Edwards

Spiritual and creative passions have converged in the lives of some of our best writers, leading to the development of literature that asks the deepest questions about life. The works of Dostoevsky, Shakespeare, Kafka, Dickinson, Whitman, and Yeats, among many others, reflect fervent quests to discern the nature of human identity, its source, its purpose, and its place in the universe. This chapter explores two ways in which the process of creative writing can be considered to be a spiritual practice. I examine the historical context by which creative writing as a spiritual practice has become prominent in scholarly, religious, and artistic circles in contemporary America. I argue that the sources, intentions, and goals of this practice can be mapped on a continuum. At one pole of the continuum, writers work to complete an internally derived inspiration, which is considered to be a source of both spiritual and creative energy; for these writers, the internal completion of the task may be more important than the sharing of a finished product. At the other pole, writers seek creative and spiritual inspiration from observing events in the external world, and they intend their work to be a gift to that world. I examine these two poles by exploring examples from the lives and works of Ursula Le Guin and John Updike, respectively.

Although intellectual life in the 20th century has evolved largely with increasing secularization and the suppression of the transcendent, certain writers have discovered sources of inspiration that lie beyond the banality of contemporary life. Because these writers each see their vocation as an essential aspect of their spiritual journey, their pursuit of art as part of a spiritual journey has been referred to as the *Via Creativa* (Fox, 1983; Metzger, 1992). The Via Creativa entails living the funda-

3

mental questions of life so seriously that they permeate and motivate one's artistic endeavors. For writers on this path, creating can be a form of meditation or prayer, whereby the creative process becomes a vehicle for entering into a deepened religious consciousness.

The Via Creativa is a way of life in which a person creates in order to discover a deeper sense of self in relationship to the cosmos. This path is distinguished from the merely self-conscious aesthetic that predominates in contemporary artistic circles, one in which an artist creates largely to explore questions of identity as a psychological or social being. For the purposes of this chapter, I define creating in the broadest sense. Creating can refer to the forming of new bonds between people, the shaping of artistic works, or the formation and expression of new ideas, concepts, or fundamentally new perceptions about how nature, people, and the self are connected. A process can be defined as creative only insofar as one participates in a rearrangement of raw materials under the operation of unknown rules or powers, resulting in a work whose novelty is more than a reshuffling of pieces. To paraphrase the philosopher Margaret Boden, a creative act is not defined by the novelty of the product but by the impossibility of anticipating the product's existence by the mental rules or methods previously used by the artist (Boden, 1991).

A new form of spiritual aesthetic in American culture, distinctly different from either the modernist or more traditional versions of the postmodernist aesthetic agendas, has arisen in the past forty years. This path, the pursuit of the Via Creativa, can be discovered in the field of literature, humanistic and psychotherapeutic contexts, mystical theological scholarship, the field of writing pedagogy, and popular culture. By its presumption of contact with a divine force during perception and creation, it resembles aspects of the American transcendentalist movement, especially characterized by Emerson and Thoreau, and the literary mysticism of Whitman.

This chapter argues that there are at least two major paths on the Via Creativa in contemporary American culture. These paths can be distinguished by the trajectories of a creator's activities, beginning from the source of inspiration and continuing into the life and work of each artist. The forms are characterized by intense attention to either the external, physical world or the internal, mental world as primary sources of energy and insight about human identity in the cosmos. The extroverted path of the Via Creativa is a more common one, especially among contemporary American writers. Hence, I will refer to it as the Right-Hand Path, a term also used in Tantric spiritual practices to designate the most popular path. Followers of this way derive inspiration and a sense of spiritual presence from the close observation of nature or society. They resemble, at least in one respect, kataphatic mystics, who have classically devoted intense attention to spiritual presence in the natural realm while pursuing the *Via Positiva*. Classically, followers of the Via Positiva emphasize those aspects of the divine that resemble objects of human experience, such as trees, rocks, and other things, or human thoughts, images, feelings, and works of art and culture. The less travelled, introverted form, or Left-Hand Path, of the Via Creativa primarily relies on the deeper, unknowable regions of the self for both spiritual refreshment and creative images. Disciplined attention to this realm by devoted mystics has been classically related to the *Via Negativa* in apophatic mystical theology. (The Via Negativa stresses aspects of the divine that are completely unlike objects of human experience.) As I describe, people who pursue the Via Creativa are not necessarily mature mystics, but they draw upon the same sources of inspirational energy as the mystics. The choice of an introverted or extroverted journey plays a decisive role in spiritual and professional formation for creative writers who pursue this path, influencing style, imagery, and narrative in the author's work. In reality, writers can find themselves at either end of these two poles or somewhere in between at any given time in their lives.

Using two authors, John Updike and Ursula K. Le Guin, I give a brief account of the two polar forms of the Via Creativa. The work of Updike provides a basis for beginning to understand the Right-Hand Path, while the writings of Le Guin help illuminate the Left-Hand Path. My analysis is based on a holistic, ecological methodology combining biographical and autobiographical material; essays and interviews by the writers about their own experiences of creativity and spirituality; and analysis of their creative works for evidence of how these spiritual influences are evident in their art. This method makes it possible to describe the path traced by each writer beginning with the focus of his or her attention. The observations of Wilhelm Reich and subsequent measurements of how energy travels through biological systems offers another perspective on this path (Lowen, 1972, 1976; Reich, 1970, 1973). This route can be seen as a pathway of energy— the movement of energy in and through people and other natural objects in the physical world, as well as energetic changes represented in thoughts, images, and feelings in the mental world. On the Via Creativa, imagination is crucial because it mediates between chaotic forces inside the brain (or other unknowable realms), the conscious mind, and the external world that envelops the writer.

FURTHER ASPECTS OF THE VIA CREATIVA

The term Via Creativa refers to a spiritual path in which creativity becomes a focus for experiencing and forming relationships with a divine entity, entities, or the universe itself. Alternatively, the Via Creativa can be defined as a creative path that recognizes the role of spiritual relationships as a driving force in the production of an artistic work. Under either definition, the essential interplay between art and forces outside the body and the ego are recognized as vital elements in the creative process. On the Via Creativa, the artist's identity is somehow linked to an identified cosmos and both are explored through creative work. The imagination becomes a type of theater wherein the aspirant can minimize the experience of his or her habitual self-image in order to encounter a creator, a deeper self, an absolute mind, an angel, a teacher, or the full presence of the cosmos. A person living on the Via Creativa conjoins his/her aesthetic and spiritual intentions, although s/he may experience artistic and spiritual aspects of creativity in many different ways during the course of his/her life.

The concept of the Via Creativa used in this article is synthesized from considering diverse biographical, autobiographical, theoretical, and empirical studies in the psychology of religion and creativity, and selected spiritual readings in the mystical traditions of Christianity, Buddhism, and Taoism. As such, it treats spirituality as an experiential phenomenon distinct from, but often associated with, the dogmas, convictions, and traditions that characterize membership in religious groups. A constellation of characteristics can be used to determine whether an artistically or spiritually inclined person is on the Via Creativa. No single characteristic in itself defines whether a person is on this path, but one can pursue the Via Creativa without embracing all of these elements. Some defining qualities for such a creator include: the intention behind creating, in particular an attitude that views creation as an end in itself rather than as a path to fame or commercial success; an understanding of vocation, or the sacred dimension of work; a high degree of awareness of the emergence of novelty while creating; substantial reflectiveness about the creative work; a belief or perception that how an individual creates is related to the process of creation occurring throughout the cosmos; the existence of a highly individualized spirituality, which in its extreme forms approaches a mystical consciousness; a high degree of integration of diverse symbols derived from the natural and social environment; and a faith in one's own inner, personal knowledge, as well as the willingness to use it while creating despite the inability to define this knowledge.

The Via Creativa might best be understood in terms of the common ground acknowledged by advanced artists and mystics who feel compelled to seek or express ever more exquisite realities. Evelyn Underhill understood this idea, writing that: "the artist is no more and no less than a contemplative who has learned to express himself, and who tells his love in color, speech, or sound: the mystic, upon one side of his nature, is an artist of a special and exalted kind" (Underhill, 1915, p. 27). Their common ground is a state or states linking the artistic with the religious imagination through an experience of power that can be understood as either artistic or religious inspiration, depending on the context of the experience.

This common ground has been explored and understood in different ways throughout recorded history. Plato believed that poets were intoxicated with divine madness. Greek and Roman artists turned to the Muses, the nine daughters of Zeus, for guidance and inspiration in their work. Writers and other artists since then have "called upon" their muse for inspiration in one way or another. In his poem about John Berryman, "Berryman," W. S. Merwin recalls, "He suggested I pray to the Muse/get down on my knees and pray/right there in the corner and he/ said he meant it literally" (qtd. in Metzger, 1992, p. 182). Artists and poets alike report experiences of inspiration as highly energized states of engagement that motivate their greatest insights and works. The content and interpretations of guiding images discovered during inspired states vary greatly among and between artists and contemplatives; however, the images and the sense of power behind them seem mysterious and transcendent in both cases. The quality of the experience of inspiration varies greatly. It may seem peaceful, or it might be felt as a great urge to have an impact on the world, whether this is translated into prophecy, commitment, or composing or performing a work of art. In any case, the inspired state is one of extraordinary energy. This power can move artists and seekers to exert themselves far beyond their normal physical capacities. Reductive attempts to explain such states in terms of neurotransmitters or brain functions ignore the novelty of the created product. From where did the artistic work come? If you ask the artist, s/he is unable to answer the question. Even the atheistic writer must agree with the believer that the source of his/her creativity, in terms of both its felt power and the spontaneous emergence of the images, seems mysterious. In order to understand how the power of spiritual/creative inspiration manifests itself in contemporary American culture, it is helpful to examine the historical background of this phenomenon.

THE VIA CREATIVA IN HISTORICAL CONTEXT

The use of the imagination in conjunction with spiritual realization has been recorded in the world's great religious literature, long before the relatively recent discovery that each person is a center of consciousness apart from one's position in the tribe (Jaynes, 1976). The connection between experienced states of religious inspiration and the creation of literature is evident in traditional revelatory works, such as the Koran, the Psalms, and the Book of Revelation in the Christian Bible. All of these writings are creative, in both form and content, offering evidence of new ways to form relationships with the divine, with people, and with nature. These religious traditions also make explicit theological links between creativity and the divine; God, like an artist, creates the world *ex nihilo*, then creates Adam out of the potter's clay. All three monotheistic traditions stress that humans were modeled in the image of God.

Traditional religious writing, such as the Hebrew and Christian Bibles, did not focus on the writer. S/he tended to view him- or herself as either a scribe or a witness to events, which were the proper focus of the work. Mystical experiences, common then as now, were described in terms of the divine source, not the humble recipient. Oral transmissions, which formed the basis for Christian and Jewish literature as well as some seminal texts of Buddhism and Taoism, are even less likely to focus on the teller because the purported originator of the tale would tend to be forgotten or accorded a mythological status. Highly creative spiritual writers such as Hildegard of Bingen, Rumi, and St. John of the Cross, did not conceive of the imagination as a type of distinctly human cognition, as people in our current society do. These writers had visions, not images, and the visions themselves were considered to be divine. The increasing availability of books following Gutenberg's invention of the moveable press helped create a greater sense of individuality for both readers and the writers. This growth of individualism and literacy made it possible for highly self-conscious spiritual writers such as John Donne and the metaphysical poets to appear. Their contemplative and deeply intellectualized creative renditions of religious experience resulted from intensive study of religious and philosophical texts in an increasingly individualized post-Reformation culture. Later writers who lived the Via Creativa, such as Blake, Whitman, Wordsworth, and Coleridge, were influenced by a romantic sensibility that focused on the artist as a type of hero of near-religious dimensions. The emphasis on the writer as an individual made it possible and desirable for authors to examine in detail their own states of mind while creating. In the 20th century, the psychospiritual poetry of Wallace Stevens and Rainer Maria Rilke, as well as their essays about the nature of imagination, show that these authors would consciously access inspired metaphysical states while writing poetry. Their novelty of perception, as expressed in their poetry, offers evidence that they were able to train themselves to suspend the operations of their normal waking egos in order to enter into a state of expanded consciousness.

The current status and locus of the Via Creativa in America can be understood in terms of the decline of institutional religion as a source of mystical insight, the development of a secular capitalist world culture, and the changing status of art in American life. The spreading interest in Oriental mysticism since the 1950s may imply that Catholic, Jewish, and Protestant institutions are not generally regarded as the best places to develop the mystical tendencies that had been cultivated in earlier ages.

Americans, searching for a place to develop the inner life, have gone elsewhere. New religious movements and missionary branches of established Eastern movements have become a refuge for spiritual growth since the 1970s, developing business institutions and ashrams that have strongly affected the American landscape in many ways. Yoga and meditation, mainstays of Eastern esoteric spirituality, have now become highly popular offerings in such standard institutions as hospitals, universities, and fitness centers. At the same time, the translations of Eastern texts and the teaching of world religions on a more scholarly level has improved the status of Eastern mystical traditions in the United States, which has stimulated a market for more popular texts and practices. These practices and ideas continue to influence millions of Americans who suffer from the spiritual and social isolation that defines post-Protestant American culture in public and private life, a malaise described in detail in Robert N. Bellah's study, *Habits of the Heart* (1985) and Christopher Lasch's *The Culture of Narcissism* (1978). An inward, highly individualistic, and sometimes narcissistic spirituality has become popular as both an escape from secular culture and a haven for self-discovery and self-creation. In this sense, the imagination itself has become an ashram.

IMPETUS FOR THE VIA CREATIVA FROM WRITERS AND WRITING TEACHERS

In a popular culture that pays scant attention to literature as an avenue for self-understanding, subcultures have developed for writing (if not reading) to be honored as self-exploration. Three writers in particular have attempted to elucidate a type of Via Creativa to be followed by educated lay people. In 1992, writing teacher and film writer Julia Cameron published a highly popular, self-described "course in discovering and recovering your creative self" titled *The Artist's Way: A Spiritual Path to Higher Creativity* (1992). She describes the Artist's Way as:

> In essence, a spiritual Path, initiated and practiced through creativity. . . .
> an induced—or invited—spiritual experience. I refer to this process as

spiritual chiropractic. We undertake certain spiritual exercises to achieve alignment with the creative energy of the universe. . . . What you're doing is creating pathways in your consciousness through which the creative forces can operate. Once you agree to clearing these pathways, your creativity emerges. In a sense, your creativity is like your blood. Just as blood is a fact of your physical body and nothing you invented, creativity is a fact of your spiritual body and nothing that you must invent. (pp. xi, xii, xvii)

In the same year, poet, novelist, and therapist Deena Metzger articulated her vision of writing as a spiritual practice in her book, *Writing for Your Life: A Guide and Companion to the Inner Worlds*. In a chapter titled "Writing as a Spiritual Practice," her understanding of the Via Creativa corresponds closely with the working definition of this chapter:

Buddhism, Christianity, Judaism, Native American religion, and paganism are all paths; each in its very own way, takes one to the same depths and summits. Creativity is also such a path, writing is one of its practices, and the muse with her sweet breath or fiery torch stands in the dark place and lights our way. . . . There is a fundamental difference between the creative practice and other spiritual disciplines. Following the creative is a path, but it is not a known path. It has to be carved out by each individual practitioner. There is a practice, but its particular rituals are mysterious and unique, and again each practitioner must discover them for herself. . . . Of course, not every writer looks at creativity as a spiritual discipline, and indeed, not every person or artist is interested in such a practice. But for those who are, writing becomes another kind of activity altogether, and its effect depends not upon the product—the finished piece—or on the consequences—accomplishment, recognition, remuneration—but upon the process with which the written word is pursued. (1992, p. 187)

These works follow the publication of Natalie Goldberg's highly influential book, *Writing Down the Bones*, where she applies her studies of Zen Buddhism to writing as self-discovery. In her introduction, she recalls when her Zen master told her "Why do you come to sit meditation? Why don't you make writing your practice? If you go deep enough in writing, it will take you everyplace" (Goldberg, 1986, p. 3). Her series of books about the spiritual side of writing are based upon the roshi's assumptions.

In addition to these writers, other writers have founded popular seminars, written best-selling books, and touted variations of the notion that creative writing can lead to healing and spiritual growth. Kathleen Adams, author of *Journal to the Self* and director of an organization called the Center for Journal Therapy, has developed numerous writing techniques aimed at developing self-knowledge and has marketed her approach nationwide (Adams, 1990). Similarly, poet and lecturer John

Fox has developed a system intended to help students to discover themselves through the use of poetry writing (Fox, 1995). His recent book is titled *Finding What You Didn't Lose: Expressing Your Truth and Creativity Through Poem Making*. Programs have even sprouted that train people to teach these methods, such as one for Certified Poetry Therapists sponsored by the Association for Poetry Therapy. Regardless of whether these organizations or individuals help people to cultivate their spiritual nature in any genuine way, they testify to the popularity of the idea of the Via Creativa as a spiritual path.

CONTRIBUTIONS FROM HUMANISTIC PSYCHOLOGY

Humanistic psychologists have played a significant role in proclaiming and promoting forms of the Via Creativa as feasible avenues for spiritual development. These psychologists, building on the work of scholars such as Carl Rogers, Rollo May, and Carl Jung in the 1950s and 1960s, have reacted against disciplines and institutions that supported the mainstream social values considered to alienate humans from their understanding of their positions in the cosmos. Jungian psychologist Ira Progoff, for example, opposed the culture of behaviorist psychology in the 1960s that discounted internal sources of human knowledge and studied rats as definitive models for understanding humans. He and others believed, like Jung, that lack of awareness of the spiritual nature of life accounted for much of the meaninglessness and mental illness that characterized contemporary life.

Beginning in the 1960s, Progoff examined the major characteristics of creative individuals in order to determine the directive forces in human beings. Subsequently, he created journal-writing methods to help people become more familiar with those forces, which he felt were essential elements in the human personality and the human soul.

Progoff (1992) states the importance of his spiritual/creative training as follows:

> Many persons have found that as they involved themselves in the Intensive Journal process to resolve the immediate problems of personal life, they have inadvertently opened awarenesses that are trans-personal in scope. Without intending it, they find that they are drawn beyond themselves in wisdom to levels of experience that have the qualities of poetry and spirit. (p. 7)

He claims that the "Intensive Journal" work is

indeed a type of prayer and meditation, but not in isolation from life and not in place of active life involvement. Rather, it is meditation in the midst of the reality of our life experiences. It draws upon the actualities of life for new awarenesses, and it feeds these back into the movement of each life as a whole. The fact is that the fundamental process in Process Meditation is each life itself. (p. 8)

A large part of the Intensive Journal training involves writing imaginary dialogues with real or imagined wisdom figures, historical figures, one's own body, significant others, and with key events and society itself. According to Progoff's philosophy, such creative use of the imagination promotes deeper awareness of the soul, deepens relationships between the soul and other souls at the level of spirit, and allows one to fulfill one's spiritual purpose while enhancing the growth of the soul.

This system relies on Jung's concept of Active Imagination, a method Jung used with his patients to help them integrate fragmented parts of their psyches. Jung used many techniques to elicit Active Imagination. For example, he encouraged his patients to draw mandalas, artistic renderings of spiritual journeys as well as snapshots of the soul. Both Jung and Progoff understood images generated by Active Imagination techniques to be sacred objects. They assumed a mystical understanding of the *Imago Dei*, believing that images contained within the human soul could be reflections of God. Thus, these images can be doorways to the soul and potential doorways to God.

DEFINING THE VIA CREATIVA IN CONTEMPORARY WESTERN THEOLOGY

Spirituality was once cultivated in Christianity and Judaism by teaching esoteric doctrines and linking them to specific types of prayer, meditation, and contemplation. Lack of interest in mysticism within Christianity since the 1960s has developed in reaction to two antimystical trends: rigid orthodoxy in both Protestant and Catholic circles, on the one hand; and the loss of concern by "secularized" liberal and radical Christians for some aspects of their traditions that could have led them back to classical mystical practices. While mysticism continues to thrive in Eastern religions and forms the foundation of religious experience, the mystical basis of Western religions has withered.

One significant response to antimysticism in the field of Christian theology comes from Matthew Fox (Fox, 1983), a Meister Eckhart scholar who proposes the Via Creativa as an important Christian path. He describes it within the context of his theology of Creation Spirituality, which he considers to be the authentic basis of Christianity. The creation tradition, he claims, emphasizes that humans live more fully in the image of God when they are creative. People find their fullness as cocreators with God on earth and as part of the energy of creativity that exists on earth. Fox's emphasis on creativity is reminiscent of the thinking of Alfred North Whitehead, who asserted that creativity is the prime source of the universe, and that God draws upon it in actualizing his own reality as pure potential in bringing the world into being (Whitehead, 1978). For Fox, as for Whitehead, God is the divine poet. In contrast to Whitehead, Fox grounds his theology in the Judeo-Christian tradition. However, he retains a sense of Whitehead's mysticism. Fox cites the existence of elements of Creation Spirituality in Taoism, Buddhism, Sufism, Native American spirituality, Celtic religions, African religions, and even the Wicca traditions. He includes the Via Creativa as one of four spiritual paths that can nourish each other:

> Path I, the Via Positiva of Befriending Creation, cannot be fully experienced without Path II, the Via Negativa of Befriending Darkness and Letting Go, Letting Be. This path in turn finds its fulfillment in Path III, the Via Creativa of Befriending Creativity, since all creativity—as distinct from reshuffling—is ex nihilo, from nothingness and darkness. Path IV, the Via Transformativa and the Befriending of New Creation, fulfills Path III, for the direction of increased compassion as celebration and justice is the direction our creativity needs to take us. (Fox, 1983, p. 23)

According to Fox, the Via Positiva teaches us to trust the cosmos, including our bodies and passions, while the Via Negativa teaches us to trust darkness and nothingness. In contrast, the Via Creativa teaches us that our images are trustworthy. These images reveal truths about ourselves and the cosmos, since both are inextricably linked together. For Fox, human images are reflections of the divine. Fox's views draw upon the work of Meister Eckhart, who wrote: "An image receives its being immediately from that of which it is an image. It has one being with it and it is the same being" (Fox, 1983, p. 184).

Fox distinguishes between the more traditional, introverted, and psychological type of meditation developed by St. Ignatius of Loyola with the extroverted type that is realized by creating art.

> Art as meditation is not meditation without form, but it is meditation wherein the form serves the inner truth and not the other way around . . . only art as meditation allows one to let go of art as production a lá capitalism and return to art as a process, which is the spiritual experience that creativity is about. (Fox, 1983, p. 192)

TWO AMERICAN LITERARY JOURNEYS: URSULA LE GUIN
AND JOHN UPDIKE

John Updike and Ursula Le Guin can be seen as examples of two polar extremes of how the Via Creativa can be lived in contemporary American society. While both authors are aware of convergences between their own spiritual and creative experiences during the act of composition, they rely on different sources of inspiration, and the spiritual/creative goals of their works differ as well. Updike draws inspiration from the energy of the external world, closely observing people and the ironic juxtaposition between their divine spark and the suffering that results from unfulfilled, egotistical desires. Updike views the goal of his work as the creation of a "sacred book," which he offers to the world through his novels. Describing his adolescence, he states: "The idea of writing a novel . . . presented itself to me, and still does, as making a book. . . . My early yearnings merged the notions of print, Heaven, and Manhattan" (1989, p. 8). Thus, his journey begins and ends in the world outside of his skin. Updike connects his post-Protestant religious consciousness with the search for truth in the external world. He describes it is follows:

> The religious faith that a useful truth will be imprinted by a perfect artistic submission underlies these Rabbit novels. The first one, especially, strives to convey the quality of existence itself that hovers beneath the quotidian details, what the scholastic philosophers called the *ens* (underlying being). Rather than arrive at a verdict and a directive, I sought to present sides of an irresolvable tension intrinsic to being human. (1990, p. xiii)

His creative process is an attempt to examine his observations of people using the internal world of the imagination, a self-enclosed cosmos whereby he can meld the truth of his insights with the invention of narrative and characters.

> When you write, you do feel you're functioning by laws that aren't entirely human. They're somewhat absurd and otherworldly. The notion of the other world certainly figures in each time you write a novel, or an even briefer flight. You are trying to create another world. (Plath, 1994, p. 252)

This fictional world, for Updike, reflects the *ens* of human existence in the real world. By relating these basic truths in the novel, he relates himself to the divine. "My theory was that God already knows everything and cannot be shocked. And only truth is useful. Only truth can be built upon. From a higher, inhuman point of view, only truth, however harsh, is holy" (1989, p. 231).

FIGURE 1.1 John Updike

The depiction of truth is, in fact, a form of worship for Updike. As he states, "The Old Testament God repeatedly says he wants praise, and I translate that to mean that the world wants describing, the world wants to be observed and 'hymned.' So there's a kind of hymning undercurrent that I feel in my work" (Plath, 1994, p. 252).

However, Updike sees these truths as being too painful for people to accept directly. In investigating the nature of the truth of the world while writing, Updike manages to lighten the burden, for himself as well as his readers through artistic deception. He states that "Even the barest earthly facts are unbearably heavy, weighted as they are with our personal death. Writing, in making the world light—in codifying, distorting, prettifying, verbalizing it—approaches blasphemy" (Plath, 1994, p. 258). This type of writing is a way to fend off the writer's own thoughts of the truth of death; it serves as a type of therapy and religion at the same time. He describes writing as "an addiction, an illusory release, a presumptuous taming of reality" (Updike, 1989, p. 228). Updike has called it an effective religion, like all work, that enables him to ignore nothingness and get on with the job of living. Thus, Updike's writing process is a struggle between accepting the harsh reality of the world and making it livable through the deceptions of fiction. Through an imaginative self-examination of memory and desire he notes faint glimmers of a hidden God in the world and thus in his life. As he writes, "There's something in what the fiction writer attempts, of searching out . . . it's almost a scientific attempt to find those spots where a [God] shines through" (Plath, 1994, p. 258). His cyclic fictive journey begins in the external world with his search for the hidden God and ends in the world with his "sacred" fiction. Thus, he exemplifies the extroverted, Right-Hand Path of the Via Creativa, the type most commonly found among fiction writers.

Le Guin, in contrast, exemplifies the Left-Hand Path, since she uses the less common strategy of seeking truth first in her internal world and orienting her work primarily toward internal integration. Like Updike, her search for truth connects her to the divine. However, she believes that the external world is in such a state of disarray due to disharmony in people, that truth can be found more accurately within the terrain of the psyche; here lies the naked self, unpolluted by society. As a Taoist, she seeks this natural self, which is indivisible from nature and nature's ways. The natural self is woven into the fabric of reality; it cannot be known by any method that pretends to maintain a viewpoint outside of that interwoven reality. The experience of the sacred is thus the experience of the natural self in its true, seamless integration into the rest of nature's movement, always according to the principles of Yin and Yang.

Le Guin's encounter with this truth, a means of embracing the Tao, is a sacred vocation. As she states, "The writer's job, as I see it, is to tell the truth. The writer's truth—nobody else's" (1979, p. 200). Le Guin writes that she lives her life most fully while writing, and her writing is a way of embracing the Tao. "To me, writing is my central way of being. It's the best way I know how to be, how to live my life. My life is my writing" (Broughton, 1990, p. 334). Writing is amenable to discovering the hidden laws of nature, the Tao, in part because it is a concrete activity, like any other activity. Unlike religions that stress their absolute or universal principles in terms of a transcendent entity or being, the Tao is eternally present, always manifesting itself throughout all phases of everyday life.

FIGURE 1.2   Ursula K. Le Guin

For Le Guin and any other Taoist, creation is possible only by getting out of the way, by not interfering with the creative power as it moves through one's life and work. This is the meaning of *wu wei*, actionless action. Enlightenment, for a Taoist such as Le Guin, is self-creation, an unfolding of one's inner nature through embracing the Tao. From a Taoist viewpoint, the movement of Heaven's energy, via the human imagination, through the writer's body and into the earthy substance of the printed page, might be seen as the union of essence (*jing*, the essential components of the physical body), energy (*chi*, the energy that flows through all bodies), and spirit (*shen*, the mind of the Tao)—the Three Treasures of the Tao. The Three Treasures and how they are united might be summarized in the following way:

> The body is the temple of life. Energy is the force of life. Spirit is the governor of life. If one of them goes off balance, all three are damaged. When the spirit takes command, the body naturally follows it, and this arrangement benefits all Three Treasures. When the body leads the way, the spirit goes along, and this harm's all three treasures. (Reid, 1995, p. 6)

This movement, a regulated creative energy, is Le Guin's Via Creativa. Often it is best approached through the unconscious, using writing or meditation.

Le Guin incorporates three major principles of Taoism into her process of composing: following the model of nature; letting things be themselves through *wu wei*; and accepting change as a timeless concept. She follows nature in two ways: by her use of dreamlike states for composing, and by choosing naturalistic metaphors such as forest, water, and earth to express her awareness in her novels. Her cultivated capacity to be receptive to her unconscious and her acceptance of the autonomy of her characters can be seen as examples of *wu wei*, actionless action, in practice. Finally, her philosophy of writing as an interior, active dynamic between the inner and outer worlds, and her expression of this philosophy in her tales, are witness to how she follows the Tao.

Le Guin's acceptance of Taoism is illustrated by the manner in which she conceives of her novels. Upon awakening, she rests in bed for 10 or 15 minutes to solve the problems of her story and see where to go with the next chapter. As she explains it, "Between sleep and waking you're between the two worlds, and that's a really good time for me. It's not the dreaming. It's the coming up between. You're still in touch with your unconscious" (O'Connell, 1987, p. 20). This technique could be labeled the "one-eye-open" method since it combines aspects of dreaming and waking consciousness. It helps her to validate and honor the dark, mysterious world of the unconscious, where dreams and internal experiences arise, transporting its contents into the world of waking consciousness—like the mythical boatman who ferries passengers across the Ganges or the Styx. She also resembles, in this respect, the shaman who brings information from an altered state of mind back into ordinary reality. The resemblance is evident in her works. As she states it, "I am perpetually attempting by one metaphor and device or another in my books to re-establish the connection between dream-time and waking-time, so that one depends on the other absolutely" (Wickes & Westling, 1982, p. 154). In line with her exposure to different aboriginal cultures that honor the validity of dream-time, her essays explicitly reject the decision made by the Western world to declare that the only true reality is the one described by science. Her approach to writing as self-discovery expresses the maxim: "I learn by going where I have to go" (Le Guin, 1979, p. 139).

Her writing process thus serves as a spiritual journey for her, and reading her works can spark a similar journey in her readers. Her work uniquely combines fantasy and science fiction. The fantasy element evokes unconscious, archetypal symbolism. Science, as the predominant way of explaining the world, contains its own mythical elements, while it provides a context for making Le Guin's stories seem more realistic. By drawing the external, scientific universe into her state of mind while composing, she makes it part of her cosmos, transforming it into a make-believe universe that she can interweave with the characters of her inner life. (She once stated: "If science fiction has a major gift to offer literature, I think it is just this: the capacity to face an open universe. Physically open, psychically open. No doors shut" [Le Guin, 1976, p. 5]). The result is the cosmos as she mythically imagines it. These inner (mythical, archetypal) and outer (science fictional) worlds, both held in her mind, are complementary and interdependent for Le Guin, in line with Taoist teachings. By fictionalizing these worlds during composition, and plotting themes about how these two worlds get into and out of balance with each other, Le Guin is re-playing her perception of how her own inner and outer worlds relate—her own personal interpretation of the Tao in working in her life.

Le Guin has stated that all storytellers and their readers share common religious aspirations, whereby composing becomes a type of religious experience in a secular culture. She believes that stories are told and accepted because of the sense of immortality they create, tying a fictional world together from beginning to end. In this sense, all creative writing is a sacred activity, regardless of whether the novelist is aware of it or not. For Le Guin, "the novel is the descendent of the myth," helping people to feel a sense of cosmic unity and order. She quotes Eliade to support this:

> The tale takes up and continues 'initiation' on the level of the imaginary. . . . Believing that he is merely amusing himself or escaping, the man of modern societies still benefits from the imaginary initiation supplied by tales. . .

. Today we are beginning to realize that what is called 'initiation' coexists with the human condition, that every existence is made up of an unbroken series of "ordeals," "deaths," and "resurrections." (Le Guin, 1989, p. 28)

Unlike most contemporary people, however, Le Guin firmly believes the imagination is a sacred place, the bridge between mind and body, and a realm where the truth of ultimate things can begin to be revealed to the writer.

COMPARING THE JOURNEYS OF UPDIKE AND LE GUIN

A close comparison between writers who journey on the Right-Hand Path and the Left-Hand Path helps to illustrate their essential differences as well as their common ground. Le Guin and Updike share some similarities in their approaches to the creative imagination. Most importantly, they create images that represent, for themselves and their readers, their perceptions of basic truths of human existence in relation to the cosmos. However, their differences in approaching this task are immense. Updike relies on personal memories of events from the outer world to craft realistic narratives. In contrast, Le Guin uses voyages into the depths of her inner world to create fantasies that are often embedded in scientific realities or possibilities. While Updike's work reflects the influence of Protestant Christianity and its decline, Le Guin's approach is imbued with her lifelong devotion to Taoism.

Both authors consciously connect their art with their spirituality through the concept that writing is a vocation that has sacred dimensions. Updike's central value, pursued at the writing desk and throughout his life, is the hope for a hidden God, an idea lodged in the back of the mind that softens the pain of the decaying secular world. Le Guin, without pretense of ceremony or preoccupation, seeks to embrace and conform to the Tao, which the mature mind discerns throughout the natural world. Updike details the foolishness of the human ego through his hopelessly immature characters who are mysteriously redeemed by the nature of the life they have been given. In contrast, Le Guin features the hero who searches for self, resulting in a mature ego that accurately reflects his position in the cosmos. For Updike's characters, the world is absurd, but human beings can be reasonable by learning to recognize their own absurdity as part of the gift of their lives. Le Guin's characters discover the subtle and inherent reasonableness of nature and its complementary forces through becoming one with the Tao. As a result, they become fools in the eyes of ordinary men and women, yet they fully express the energies of the cosmos.

The two authors' approaches to religious intellectual history are also worth noting, since their views of history helps form their personal identities and are manifested in their characters. Updike is deeply interested in Anglo-American history and the development of Christian theology. Le Guin's intellectual passions move toward anthropology, including the study of storytelling and religion in cultures that do not frame reality in linear, historical terms. One of Updike's central themes is the decay of relationships, embodied in the decay of the church-related institution of marriage and the erosion of the belief in God's presence in the world. His writing often centers on male characters in varying states of physical or moral depravity who feel inadequate and out of place with women and society. In contrast, Le Guin uses characters, usually male, that reject sexual conquest and anxious competition in favor of the relatively feminine approach of Taoist thought. Cosmic marriage is a basic theme of all her works: the marriage of male and female, inner and outer, light and dark, individual and culture, and all seeming opposites; these marriages—natural, holistic, and dynamic—are the primary order of all things. As Bucknall points out, the interrelated themes of marriage and encountering the Other are inextricable elements of Le Guin's novels, and these themes are both resolved in Taoist consciousness (Bucknall, 1981). The route to the self is through the Other. In Le Guin's world, decay is bound to be followed by renewal because it reflects the rhythmic, cyclical pattern of nature.

Updike and Le Guin characteristically have developed styles that express their orientations to truth and their understandings of where deeper truths can be found. However, they use very different stylistic tools to create their effects. The narrative in Le Guin's stories consists largely of action, thought, or dialogue. The author wastes few words on the descriptions of things. Her novels are archetypal; the details of behavior are only important insofar as they reveal these archetypes in a way that points to the psyche's expressions in the external world. For Updike, in contrast, the characters are formed out of the details, in keeping with their conviction that truth lies in perceiving the minutiae of the external world. Their thoughts and other vestiges of the inner life are often trivial, and their actions are soulless.

Le Guin and Updike approach images in some strikingly different ways, as expressed in their creative works and in their autobiographical texts. Le Guin feels most alive when she is composing, and she seems awakened by the images of the characters who walk out of her unconscious. In her works, most notably *City of Illusions*, the revelations of the unconscious as expressed in dreams are truer than facts and have a guiding power over reality. Updike, in contrast, compares artistic and religious experience to sleep rather than wakefulness, since they give the mind a rest from self-consciousness. His characters reflect this philosophy of "sleep." Stumbling around with unexamined fantasies in their minds, they fog their perceptions and get into trouble by projecting these unfulfilled wishes onto reality. A central image in all of Updike's works is the fragile and somewhat helpless antihero who is indecisive and highly impulsive. Rabbit, whom Updike considers to be an alter ego, epitomizes this self-image. Le Guin's central image, in contrast, is the Taoist seeker who learns to live like water, flowing into the right places and never opposing the reality of the situation. Updike believes that his images express basic truths about the world, which he derives from memory and interprets with Kierkegaardian Christian theology. Le Guin instead treats her images as truths in themselves, apart from any consideration of their basis in sense perception, common sense, or history.

The pervading philosophy of Updike includes the notion that life is inherently empty, and that we must make meaning through those hopes and fantasies that stand in tension with the harsh reality of the world. Le Guin would see emptiness as opportunity, since out of emptiness comes all that is created. Life, art, and reading are meaningful in the balance that comes from embracing the interdependence of emptiness and the world, both of which are one as an emanation of the Tao. For Updike, the method for achieving the truth of the world is to explore self-consciousness, examining memory and desire. For Le Guin, truth is always present, appearing in its fullness as one walks the Wayless Way.

Both writers, by using the creative process to examine and extend their relation to the cosmos, are journeying along the Via Creativa. As polar opposites along a continuum of possible ways, they show how the energy of inspiration and the *telos* of creation can be focused primarily on a self-contained internal field of the imagination or on the world outside the writer's skin. In the skin or out, the writer creates the path he treads upon, and the journey knits the external world with the inner one. The Via Creativa thus proves to be a viable path for spiritual maturity. It draws upon direct, mystical experience to taste the divine through the process of creation.

REFERENCES

Adams, K. (1990). *Journal to the self: 22 paths to personal growth*. New York: Warner Books.

Bellah, R. N. (1985). *Habits of the heart: Individualism and commitment in american life*. Berkeley: University of California Press.

Boden, M. A. (1991). *The creative mind: Myths and mechanisms*. New York: Basic Books.

Broughton, I. (1990). *The writer's mind: Interviews with American authors.* Fayetteville: University of Arkansas.

Bucknall, B. J. (1981). *Ursula K. Le Guin: Recognitions.* New York: Unger.

Cameron, J. (1992). *The artists way: A spiritual path to higher creativity.* New York: Putnam.

Fox, J. (1995). *Finding what you didn't lose: Expressing your truth and creativity through poem making.* New York: Putnam.

Fox, M. (1983). *Original blessing.* Santa Fe, NM: Bear & Company.

Goldberg, N. (1986). *Writing down the bones: Freeing the writer within.* Boston: Shambhala.

Jaynes, J. (1976). *The origin of consciousness in the breakdown of the bicameral mind.* Boston: Houghton Mifflin.

Lasch, C. (1978). *The culture of narcissism: American Life in an age of diminishing expectations.* New York: Norton.

Le Guin, U. K. (1967). *City of illusions.* New York: Harper & Row.

Le Guin, U. K. (1976, July 30). Out of the ice age. *The New York Times Literary Supplement.*

Le Guin, U. K. (1979). *The language of the night: Essays on fantasy and science fiction.* New York: Putnam.

Le Guin, U. K. (1989). *Dancing at the edge of the world: Thoughts on words, women, places.* New York: Grove Press.

Lowen, A. (1972). *Depression and the Body; the biological basis of faith and reality.* New York: Coward, McCann & Geoghegan.

Lowen, A. (1976). *Bioenergetics.* New York: Penguin.

Metzger, D. (1992). *Writing for your life: A guide and companion to the inner worlds.* San Francisco: Harper.

O' Connell, N. (1987). *At the Field's end: Interviews with twenty Pacific northwest writers.* Seattle: Madrone.

Plath, J. (Ed.). (1994). *Literary conversations series: Conversations with John Updike.* Jackson: University Press of Mississippi.

Progoff, I. (1992). *At a journal workshop: Writing to access the power of the unconscious and invoke creative ability.* New York: Putnam.

Reich, W. (1970). *Character analysis.* New York: Farrar, Straus and Giroux.

Reich, W. (1973). The function of the orgasm: Sex-economic problems of biological energy. In W. Reich, *The Discovery of the Orgone* (Vol. 1). New York: Farrar, Straus and Giroux.

Reid, D. (1995). *The complete book of Chinese health and healing.* Boston: Shambhala.

Underhill, E. (1915). *Practical mysticism: A little book for normal people.* New York: Dutton.

Updike, J. (1990). *Rabbit angstrom.* New York: Knopf.

Updike, J. (1989). *Self-consciousness.* New York: Knopf.

Whitehead, A. N. (1978). *Process and reality: An essay in cosmology.* New York: Free Press.

Wickes, G., & Westling, L. (1982). "Dialogue with Ursula Le Guin." *Northwest Review, 20*(23), 147–159.

chapter 2

The Dark Side of Creativity: The Function of *Duende* and God-Battler in the Writings of Garcia Lorca and Kazantzakis

Verbena Pastor
Vermont College of Norwich University

GARCIA LORCA AND DUENDE

> Oh city of the gypsies!
> Who, having seen you, can forget you?
> Let them seek you on my forehead.
> A play of moon and sand.
> —F. G. Lorca, "Romance of the Spanish Civil Guard"

The conflictual, "dark" aspect of creativity finds a convincing proponent in Federico Garcia Lorca. His theory of inspiration, expressed in his 1928 essay on the theory and play of *duende*, "*Teoria y juego del duende*"[1] (Garcia Lorca, 1960, pp. 36–48), presents a challenging and useful foundation for my task. I say "challenging" because, as physicist David Bohm observes in "The Range of Imagination," (Bohm, 1998b), there is often ambiguity in definitions of creativity. In this context, by creativity I intend not only the potentiality or ability to create, but also the creative process itself.

As a poet, musician, and playwright deeply interested in the origins of inspiration, Garcia Lorca (1898–1936) extracted the concept of *duende* to explain the suffered aspect of creativity from his familiarity with flamenco music and Spanish folklore.

25

Duende is a term of debated etymology, believed to originate in the Spanish abbreviation of *duen de casa,* "master or dweller in the house." The *Diccionario de Uso del Español* (Moliner, 1984, p. 1043) defines it as a poltergeist-like goblin that causes *"trastornous y ruidos"* (disturbances and noises), while the *Diccionario Crítico Etimológico Castellano y Hispanico* (Corominas & Pascual, 1984, pp. 528–529) also connects it with the Roman household spirits Lares and Penati, giving the English translation as "house-fairy." Possibly related to this etymology are the Germanic *Dwerg* (familiar spirit), and the Arabic *dwar* (a dwelling, and presumably the spirits inhabiting it). In any case, the duende of folklore is a capricious imp whose presence is occasionally felt.

In flamenco lore, duende is a feature of Ibero-Moorish flamenco song, dancing, and guitar playing, especially in its tragic *cante jondo,* or "deep singing" form. Duende parallels the state of divine possession identified by the Greeks as *enthousiasmos.* This "god within" power is recognized by Garcia Lorca as inconstant, powerful, dangerous; its entry into the body of the possessed effected "though the soles of one's feet" (Garcia Lorca, 1960, p. 37). It is a particular state of artistic grace, a passionate departure from rules and text, whose numinous arrival is greeted, as Garcia Lorca observes in his essay, by crying out the Arabic name of God, hispanicized into *"olé."*

For Garcia Lorca, duende is a familiar spirit, a fairytale ghostly goblin such as it had been for Calderòn de la Barca three hundred years earlier in his play *"La Dama Duende."* However, Garcia Lorca's duende is also the originator and catalyst of artistic inspiration, not only limited—as traditionally understood in Spain—to successful improvisation in folk song and dance.

Born in the Andalusian city of Granada, where Visigothic, Moorish, and Sephardic influences shape the landscape and the local character, throughout his immensely fortunate literary career, Garcia Lorca drew from his ethnically rich background as Granadino and descendant of converted Jews, or *conversos.* The poetry collections *Poema del cante jondo, Romancero gitano,* and *Diván del Tamarit (Poem of the Deep Singing, Gypsy Ballads,* and *Divan of the Tamarit)* reflect the powerful sway flamenco terminology and sentiment had on him. By the time of his brutal murder during the Spanish Civil War, Garcia Lorca had embodied the poetic voice of Spain as no one before or after him. His prolific production of verses, theater, and critical essays is marked by the constant themes that Italian commentator Claudio Rendina summarizes as *"L'amore come fonte di dolore e l'esistenza vista nel costante riferimento della morte,"* "Love as source of grief and life lived in constant reference to Death" (Rendina, 1993, p. 15).

FIGURE 2.1. Federico Garcia Lorca

Love and death are also at the foundation of flamenco poetics. Originally a body of popular songs rooted in the medieval culture of Moorish
seasonal workers (inspired by the more formal Arabic love poetry termed
ghazal), flamenco had become, by the 19th century, the characteristic
musical expression among Andalusian gypsies of East Indian origin.

Unrequited passion, jealousy, despair, and betrayal are often the subject matter of flamenco, as of Garcia Lorca's own works. An emotional
awareness of death is singled out by Garcia Lorca as essential to

flamenco and to the creative process as such. To this process he gives the name of duende, and in the numinous aspect of duende does his discourse on creativity find its beginnings.

Yet, there is an important difference between god-inspired frenzy and duende. Possession implies the temporary submission (and even momentary disappearance) of the subject's individuality, so that a god speaks in the place of the possessed. The "veracity" of oracles and divinations is predicated on this. There is no artistic choice in *enthousiasmos*: the spirit moves, and acts, and is heard. Garcia Lorca on the other hand hastens to explain that "every ladder that climbs the tower of its perfection does so at costprice of the struggle it engages with a duende" (Garcia Lorca, 1960, p. 38).

So, while *enthousiasmos* defines an "inspirited" (rather than inspired) artist, Garcia Lorca's duende resembles Lévy-Bruhl's *participation mystique*, "an original state of unconsciousness and therefore non-differentiation . . . [in which] there is no determining whether it belongs or does not belong to the self" (Jung, 1953, p. 204).

Usually applied by anthropologists and psychologists to preliterate cultures where group identification often supersedes individual development, Lévy-Bruhl's "mystic participation" has a strongly ethnic character, something which is very noticeable in Garcia Lorca's works, and, as we shall see later, this is also true for Kazantzakis' poetics.

A parallel view of nondifferentiation is described by Jung (1953) as "projective identification." This is a mechanism by which a part of the individual's personality is projected into another human being or an object (in this case the creative process), so that the object is then experienced as independent from the individual, and endowed with autonomous qualities (Samuels, Shorter, & Plant, 1986).

For Garcia Lorca, the artist must confront the Other, to the extent that conflict is fundamental to his theory of creativity. "The true struggle," he insists, "is with the duende"; "*La verdadera lucha es con el duende,*" (Garcia Lorca, 1960, p. 39); also,

> Manuel Torre [sic], great artist of Andalusian stock, told a singer, "You have voice, you know the style, but you'll never triumph, because you have no duende." . . . The wonderful singer El Lebrujano . . . used to remark, "Those days when I sing with duende, no one can compare with me"; the old dancer la Malena exclaimed once, having heard Brailowsky play a piece by Bach, "Olé! That has duende!" (Garcia Lorca, 1960, p. 37)

From the above quotations, the apparent capriciousness of duende's visitations is expressed by Garcia Lorca. Yet, as I understand it, lack of duende does not result in what artists usually refer to as a "block," where the creative tap is stopped, and one's creativity is altogether incapable of finding expression. In the absence of duende, an artist can continue to create and even be proficient, but the ability to go beyond, from ordinary to extraordinary art, is missing. This step is what David Bohm seems to refer to, when he calls the achievement of a "new basic order," as a prerequisite of originality (Bohm, 1998a, p. 6).

In fact, Garcia Lorca's view of the difference between technically proficient art and duende-inspired performance complements Bohm's distinction (based on Coleridge) between *rational/imaginative fancy*, based on known patterns and merely recombining them into higher degrees of order and harmony, and *creative insight*, where, according to the physicist, "a new totality of images [is] perceived as a single, harmonious whole, first implicit and enfolded, and then explicit and unfolded" (Bohm, 1998b, pp. 53–54).

That this insight has a numinous quality for Garcia Lorca, is illustrated by his definition of duende as "descendant of that merry Socratic daimon . . . and of Descartes' other little devil, small like a green almond," but also "obscure and shuddering" (Garcia Lorca, 1960, pp. 37–38).

According to biographer Ian Gibson, Garcia Lorca began developing his "dark" theory of duende in 1922, when his friend, flamenco artist Manuel Torres, observed while listening to de Falla's *Nights in the Gardens of Spain* that "whatever has black sounds has duende" (Gibson, 1989, p. 114).

By insisting that "duende is power, not work; it is a struggle, not thinking. . . . It is saying, not a question of ability" (Garcia Lorca, 1960, p. 37), not only does Garcia Lorca discriminate between technique and the more immediate impetus that typifies true creativity (Bohm's already mentioned "insight"); he also confirms the presence of conflict in the creative process.

Duende "speaks of blood; it speaks of an ancient culture, of creation in action" (Garcia Lorca, 1960, p. 37), and "Duende doesn't show up unless there's a possibility of death" (Garcia Lorca, 1960, p. 44). "It loves the fringe, the wound, and seeks the places where shapes melt into a desire superior to its visible expression" (Garcia Lorca, 1960, p. 45). More, its presence in the blood "smarts like ground glass" (Garcia Lorca, 1960, p. 39).

"Shapes" are here understood as archetypal mental images, whose affect is so powerful as to be ineffable ("superior to its visible expression" [Garcia Lorca, 1960, p. 45]). Because poets and other artists cannot be content with speechlessness, duende's role lies in urging them to attempt a description of that ineffability. For Garcia Lorca, this result can only come about after desire for expression is experienced, and the struggle initiated.

But why a struggle? Why not blissful surrender to inspiration? The image of the wrestling match with a stranger is well known in mythology and religion, where encounters with the higher self or the spirit of God in its many forms are well represented. I refer to them later. But for now I point out that David Bohm also mentions a struggle when he defines the conflict experienced by a creative mind at odds with a "mechanically imposed pattern," so that "what is called for in such a conflict is that the mind shall be able to see the irrelevance of all mechanical patterns as to what one should be, or think, or feel" (Bohm, 1998a, pp. 20–21).

Garcia Lorca says, "[If we wish] to find [duende,] there's no map and no exercise. We only know that it . . . drains, that it makes one forget all the lessons learned, that it breaks style" (Garcia Lorca, 1960, p. 39), and that "the arrival of duende always presupposes a radical change in all forms based upon old plans" (Garcia Lorca, 1960, pp. 40–41). This conflictual situation is defined by Bohm as being "painful," and leading to a "state of *confusion*" (original emphasis, Bohm, 1998a, p. 21).

Garcia Lorca insists that the real struggle is with the duende. If so, faced with the arrival of the daimon, the artist must wrestle with it in the arena of the mind, where shapes (images, metaphors) "melt" into desire. The dark spirit is the catalyst for the transformation of inner images into successful creativity (desire), a process typified by the alternate fortunes of the struggle: giving in, resisting, adhering to artistic rules, breaking them, losing oneself in the wounded place of the suffering human condition, becoming one with it. Thus, ensue *participation mystique* with the artist's ethnic group and humankind at large, and a projective identification with all.

To the outsider, the onset of duende is revealed by sudden, and sometimes sustained, sublimity of creative expression. The artist breaks the bonds of techniques and engages in a performance that draws in those in attendance (or the reading public) as participant observers. Awe, delight, and breathless participation result from it, and possibly the recognition of the sublime in action.

In his poem *"Café cantante"* (Garcia Lorca, 1960, p. 248), Garcia Lorca describes a singer's duende-laden performance in the typical atmosphere of subfuse expectation attending public flamenco performances.

. . . .
On the dark stage
Parrala begins
a dialogue
with Death.
She calls him,

he doesn't come,
still she calls him.
. . . In the green mirrors
long silken tails
vibrate.

In "Portrait of Silverio Franconetti" (Garcia Lorca, 1960, p. 247), he sketches the *aficionados'* reaction to duende, as witnessed in the fierce performance of a Spanish-Italian flamenco singer:

. . . .
His cry was fearsome.
Old men
say that their hair would stand
on end
and mercury burst out
of the mirrors. . . .

"Certain kinds of things," Bohm reflects, "can be achieved by techniques and formulae, but originality and creativity are not among those" (Bohm, 1998a, p. 26).

Although coming from very different premises, unrelated to science, Garcia Lorca would agree.

KAZANTZAKIS AND THE GOD-BATTLER

> The more I wrote the more deeply I felt that in writing I was struggling,
> not for beauty, but for deliverance
> —Kazantzakis (1965, p. 451)

In his posthumously published, poetic, autobiographic narrative *Report to Greco,* Nikos Kazantzakis referred again and again to the dark numinosity of creativity and the struggle he faced in confronting it. Like Garcia Lorca, Cretan-born Kazantzakis (1883–1957) was a poet, playwright, and essayist; like Garcia Lorca, he was immersed in his native culture and recognized its influence on his creativity.

Best known for his novels *Zorba the Greek, The Last Temptation of Christ,* and *The Greek Passion,* Kazantzakis also authored an epic retelling of *The Odyssey.* Having experimented with a series of ideologies and spiritual approaches, from Leninism to Catholicism, Kazantzakis was and remained a restless physical and spiritual wanderer whose "greatest benefactors [were] journeys and dreams" (Kazantzakis, 1965, p. 445).

Throughout the text of *Zorba*'s highly reflective fiction, and in the pages of his autobiography relating the gestation stage of *The Odyssey*, he repeatedly tells of the suffering undergone while struggling, not so much with the subject matter but the process of creation itself. He openly invokes a reified spirit he calls Grandfather (Odysseus? Dionysus? A Cretan *spiritus loci*?) as taskmaster and deliverer. Likewise, he sees the human condition, and the artist's role in relation to it, as darkly as Garcia Lorca.

In Kazantzakis' own words, "There is much darkness in me. . . . All my life I have fought desperately to transubstantiate this darkness" (Kazantzakis, 1965, p. 476). Using the imagery of the *nekuya*, or communion with the dead, as narrated in Homer's *Odyssey*, Kazantzakis further elaborates the point: "The human heart is surely a deep, closed, blood-filled pit. When it opens, all the thirsting, inconsolable shades we have loved run to drink and be revived; they grow continually denser around us, blackening the air" (Kazantzakis, 1965, p. 458).

At the core of the struggle between daimonic influence and artist, is a dangerous and difficult choice. Even in a state of creative "madness," the true artist retains voice and individuality, and recognizes the bounds of medium and style while no longer feeling constrained by them. In fact, the bounds recede in a landscape less and less familiar, until one has to grasp for them in order to retain coherence. What Bohm calls "an act of creative perception through the mind" (Bohm, 1998b, p. 41) is what victory an artist can snatch from the intimate struggle between self and inspiration.

When speaking of the first intimation that led to his retelling of *The Odyssey*, Kazantzakis admits both the intimacy and the difficulty of it, "The seed which entered me as a conqueror had to be united with me, so that both of us might become victorious and vanquished" (Kazantzakis, 1965, p. 460). This uneasy symbiosis complements Garcia Lorca's vision of artist vis-à-vis duende, a connection that "smarts like ground glass" in the blood (Garcia Lorca, 1960, p. 39). Again, Kazantzakis, "All hurt me and made me cry out, as though my body had been flayed by some god and could not tolerate even a breath of wind" (Kazantzakis, 1965, p. 464).

Indeed, Kazantzakis' images of the creative process resemble less a gestation than a heroic struggle, comparable to Jacob's nocturnal wrestling with the stranger who is the Shekinah of God. It is the combat between Menelaus and Proteus, the shape-shifting god who must be firmly restrained in order to obtain prophecy from him, just as Jacob's stranger must be held down to force him to identify himself (which he does obliquely by renaming Jacob *Israel*, or "God-battler"). It is also the wrestling match between Heracles and the earthy giant Antaeus, whose

FIGURE 2.2.   Nikos Kazantzakis

name means "he who is encountered": a chance event that demands immediate, forceful response.

Kazantzakis: "The invisible presence hovered everywhere in the air, everywhere and nowhere. . . . Man is able to bear working only in a fixed, circumscribed arena. I had to submit to this human incapacity if I wished to surpass it" (Kazantzakis, 1965, p. 469). Recognition of self and one's inner adversary is difficult: "Since I had no clear idea which my soul's countenance was, of how it looked, the struggle was a difficult and a desperate one" (Kazantzakis, 1965, p. 471). Unlike Garcia Lorca, the Greek author seems not to notice the numinous nature of the Other, but the theophany is not long in taking place:

> All my journeys had become a red line beginning from man and ascending in order to reach God. . . . On the fourth day, as I was fighting to see how far the line marking my ascension had reached up to now, I was suddenly overcome by sacred awe. This red line had not been inscribed by my blood; someone else was ascending . . . someone incomparably higher. . . . I would look around me then and see no one. But I felt his immense breath hanging over me." (Kazantzakis, 1965, p. 472)

Acute perception of the intrapersonal Other in Kazantzakis' autobiography, and the sense of powerlessness accompanying the recognition, are reminiscent of the *numinosum,* a term Jung borrowed from Rudolf Otto's *The Idea of the Holy,* and described as "either a quality belonging to a visible object or the influence of an invisible presence that causes a peculiar alteration of consciousness" (Samuels, Shorter, & Plant, 1986, p. 100).

It is tantalizingly unclear—and perhaps immaterial—whether Kazantzakis ascribes his adversary to heaven or earth, because he speaks of a "devil inside us," at once adding, "let us call him Lucifer, for he brings light—[he] kept urging us on. He it was who wished to overstep the limits in order to go we knew not where" (Kazantzakis, 1965, p. 496). What is certain, is that for Kazantzakis inspiration takes the artist beyond the allotted limits of convention. Bohm: "by becoming aware of preconceptions that have been conditioning us unconsciously we are able to *perceive* and to *understand* the world in a fresh way. One can then 'feel out' and explore what is unknown" (original emphasis, Bohm, 1998c, p. 39).

Divine or diabolical, the visitor is sacred. The following remarks so closely relate to Jacob's episode in Genesis 32:24–32 that it is impossible not to see Kazantzakis' awareness of the biblical passage. Addressing the numinous and contentious newcomer, he writes,

I see you on every side and struggle to compress you into a word, to immobilize your countenance and declare, "I've got you, you won't get away!" But you smash the word (how could you ever fit inside it!), slip out of my clutches, and I hear you laughing in the air above me. (Kazantzakis, 1965, p. 473)

And, revealing his knowledge of biblical as well as Dionysian texts, "What names did I not set as traps to catch you! I addressed you as God-swindler, God-battler, . . . seven lives, multiple mind, . . . house-closer, soul-abductor, soul guide" (Kazantzakis, 1965, p. 473). This awareness of the divine allows Kazantzakis to transcend the highly individual nature of his creative conflict, and to realize the potential implications of bringing forth original artistic expressions.

"I had been struggling for a lifetime to stretch my mind until it creaked at the breaking point in order to bring forth a great idea able to give a new meaning to life, a new meaning to death, and comfort to men" (Kazantzakis, 1965, p. 474).

This reference to the cosmic quality of creativity reminds me of Bohm's definition of theory as a "way of looking at the world through the mind, . . . a form of insight" aiming at "some universal sort of significance," (Bohm, 1998c, p. 43) and delivering a product "clear, simple, beautiful" (Bohm, 1998c, p. 47).

What the physicist defines as painful "confusion" in the mental conflict between the fetters of past knowledge and the desire to bring forth fresh insight, is to the Greek novelist (as for Garcia Lorca) a spiritual life-or-death fray. "It has been a harsh struggle without pity or respite. Had I tired for even an instant and allowed an interval in the hostilities, I would have perished" (Kazantzakis, 1965, p. 476).

In the end, David Bohm's initial warning about the ineffability of the creative process is echoed by Kazantzakis: "The creator wrestles with a hard, invisible substance, a substance far superior to him. Even the greatest victor emerges vanquished, because our deepest secret, the only one that deserves expression, always remains unexpressed" (Kazantzakis, 1965, p. 481).

DUENDE, ANGEL, MUSE, AND DEATH

An approximation of the ultimate mystery of creativity, whether understood as the ever-receding horizon of scientifc investigation, or as the most genuine and perhaps universal meaning of human experience, is all we can expect to achieve in our lives as researchers and artists. Federico Garcia Lorca and Nikos Kazantzakis were acutely aware of their finiteness, and therefore, possibly as a compensation, they believed in the infinite nature of their transcendent selves and the need to confront death through creativity.

The creative struggle—risky as always when one's own worth and sanity are at stake, dark because of the soul-suffering required—brought them as close to numinosity as they could experience while on Earth. Both recognized and honored the indispensability of maintaining freedom of choice in the struggle, forcing the inner stranger (duende, the God-battler) to grant coherence and harmony to their art.

In Garcia Lorca and Kazantzakis, the creative process carries a deep sense of the ancestral shadow. This made Garcia Lorca suggest that duende could only be Spanish, and Kazantzakis identify the God-battler with a Hellenic spiritus loci; thus both writers seem to confirm that Lévy-Bruhl's *participation mystique* and Jung's "projective identification" were at play.

In fact, given the strong cultural identification of the two authors in question, the dark nature of duende and God-battler affects them into producing agonizing ethnic metaphors. Garcia Lorca's cry in his "Lament for Ignacio Sanchez Mejías," written for the death of his poet/bullfighter friend, rises from cultural imagery: "Oh white wall of Spain! Oh black bull of grief! Oh, Ignacio's hard blood!" (Garcia Lorca, 1960, p. 470);

> His blood already comes singing:
> singing through marshes and prairies,
> slipping over horns rigid with cold,
> swaying without soul through the fog,
> stumbling over thousands of hoofs
> like a long, dark, sad tongue,
> to form a still pool of agony
> on the banks of the starry Guadalquivir.
> (Garcia Lorca, 1960, p. 469)

Speaking of Helen of Troy, Kazantzakis says,

> Thanks to this Spartan queen, sexual desires assume exalted titles of nobility; the secret nostalgia for some lost embrace sweetens the brute within us. When we weep or cry out, Helen throws a magic herb into the bitter dram we are drinking, and we completely forget our pain. In her hand she holds a flower whose scent drives off serpents. At her touch ugly children become beautiful. (Kazantzakis, 1965, p. 159)

The combination ethnicity/splendid metaphor is not only due to the strong cultural contents both writers project into their work, but also to their keen sensitivity to human mortality. Awareness of the latter over-shadows creativity, making the creator restless and self-conscious. This is not to say that duende-inspired artists need be negative or despondent. Indeed, from all reports, Garcia Lorca (and Kazantzakis' alter ego Zorba) were paragons of zest, energy, and of life fully lived.

Still, is a struggle the only model possible for a definition of the creative process? Anything short of inner conflict is dismissed by Garcia Lorca as inspiration by an angel or a muse. In his essay he defines the angel as a grace-dispensing catalyst of effortless art. The angel "gives . . . protects . . . and prevents," but also, "*commands,* and there is no way of resisting his light, because he flaps his steely wings in the face of the chosen one" (Garcia Lorca, 1960, p. 38, author's emphasis). No creative choice seems to be possible here, because surrender is the only option. The price of blissful creativity, is, in this case, the silence of the individual voice.

The muse, whom Garcia Lorca describes as "distant and weary," presumably because of her long flight from Mount Helicon and her attachment to technique, "dictates, and on some occasions, inspires. But she cannot do much. . . . [She] awakens intelligence . . . and intelligence is often the enemy of poetry, because it is imitative." Indeed, carrying "false taste of laurels," the muse "elevates the poet to a throne of sharp spikes of grain, making him forget that the ants could devour him at any time." (Garcia Lorca, 1960, p. 38).

For Garcia Lorca, angel and muse "come from the outside," while "duende must be sought in the deepest recesses of the blood" (Garcia Lorca, 1960, pp. 38–39). Clearly, Garcia Lorca's definitions of angel and muse are tongue-in-cheek. Still, they cut to the core of his struggle-based "no pain, no gain" theory of creativity. He views artistic outcomes through angel or muse as not original, because they lack what Bohm calls the "state of confusion" preceding insight (Bohm unequivocally points out the conflict between the stasis of the mechanistic and ordinary and the pull of the original and uncharted as prerequisites to originality).

Moreover, adumbrated in the dark numinosity of duende and the God-battler is Garcia Lorca's and Kazantzakis' sense of finiteness versus the infinite nature of art. Christianity, with its rigid dualism between Good and Evil, made numinosity coterminous with positive divinity. Both Garcia Lorca and Kazantzakis reclaim the dark side of God, as expressed in the Old Testament (especially the Book of Job), and as familiar to pagan antiquity.

"Art is long, life is brief," the Romans warned. From this paradox, a sensation of inner dualism arises, so acutely felt by the artist as to seem an intrusion by extraneous powers. Complexes and neuroses, as well as art, arise from the projection. In particular, the dark nature of the projection (duende, God-battler) in Garcia Lorca and Kazantzakis resembles Jung's collective shadow, affect-laden and in need of integration. Hence the two poets' insistence on the possessive, even obsessional contents of duende-like creativity. And because the collective shadow is often equated by Jung with the trickster-figure, dramatic circumstances are necessary for its rise to consciousness. "For the Trickster image to be active means that a calamity has happened or a dangerous situation has been created" (Samuels, Shorter, & Plant, 1986, p. 152). Jung's statement is analogous to Garcia Lorca's already quoted remark that duende does not show up unless there is a "possibility of death." As for Kazantzakis, he recognizes the Dionysian, mercurial nature of the God-battler by addressing him as "God-deceiver . . . crossroad mind . . . soul-abductor, soul guide" (Kazantzakis, 1965, p. 473).

So, how can we distinguish duende-inspired writing or visual art from the rest? Bohm and Garcia Lorca seem to agree that felicitousness, simplicity, beauty, the unexpected, daring, are telltale traits of originality. In Garcia Lorca, as in Kazantzakis, prose and poetry "work" quite independently of subject matter and plot, at the level of a language immediate and rich in powerful metaphors, pregnant imagery, not merely captivating but awe-inspiring, often producing in the reader the stunned suspension of judgment that is an effect of the sublime.

To make this distinction clear, let me draw upon another example from Garcia Lorca. In his late collection bearing the title *Sonetos del amor oscuro* ("Sonnets of Dark Love"), describing the agonies of homosexual love, he avoids all poetic commonplaces of unrequited or impossible romance:

> . . . .
> Oh bleating without wool, oh wound,
> needle of spleen, fading camellia,
> flux without water, city without walls!
> and,
> Oh dog in the heart, persecuted voice!
> Silence without end, mature iris bloom!
> (Rendina, 1993, p. 422)

For Garcia Lorca, duende functions also in the context of work already produced by others, so that the same song, the same dance, can be transformed by the arrival of the numinous. Duende's capacity to renovate existing material is illustrated on page 40 of his essay (Garcia Lorca, 1960), where we read an episode in flamenco history. The story revolves around the singer (*cantaora*) Pastora Pavón, performing in a small tavern in Cadiz. "She sang with her shadowy voice, her voice of molten tin, her voice covered with moss. . . . And yet, nothing. The public remained unimpressed." Despite her undeniable technique and immense effort, the knowledgeable listeners began to whisper and more and more chided her for her lack of duende, to the point that she stood up like a madwoman, aggrieved like a medieval mourner.

> Then, according to Garcia Lorca's narrative, she began to sing without voice, breathlessly . . . with a parched throat, but . . . with duende. She had succeeded in demolishing the entire structure of the song to make room for a duende furious and ablaze, friend of the silt-laden winds. (Garcia Lorca, 1960, p. 40)

So strong was the impact of her rendition, that the listeners responded in a frenzy, tearing their shirts, like the believers crowding in religious furor before the image of Saint Barbara. Garcia Lorca concludes that duende was finally compelled to wrestle with the enraged *cantaora*. "And how did she sing! Her voice . . . was a gush of blood ennobled by grief and truthfulness" resembling the image "with pierced feet, full of storm" of a Christ figure (Garcia Lorca, 1960, p. 40).

I already indicated that contact with duende, as with the God-battler, signifies for Garcia Lorca and Kazantzakis perils to sanity, health and life. Jung calls this risk "loss of soul," a dangerous state akin to shamanistic trance, and often the precursor to individuation, "the better and more complete fulfillment of collective qualities" (Samuels, Shorter, & Plant, 1986, p. 77).

CONCLUSION

Federico Garcia Lorca died young having, despite his premonitions and all warnings, decided to return to fascist-occupied Granada. An early death is the destiny often ascribed to those beloved by the gods, the *enduendados* among whom the mystic *conversos* John of the Cross and Teresa of Avila are also counted.

Nikos Kazantzakis reached old age, and was thus able to look back on art, life, and his own struggle with the numinous. Yet in her introduction to *Report to Greco,* his wife Helen describes how, wasted by disease and with eyes full of tears, he hoped for more time to complete it. "Oh, for a little time, just enough to let me finish my work. Afterwards, let Charon come" (Kazantzakis, 1965, p. 10).

It was not to be, and the Greek master's autobiography remains incomplete. "Did I win or lose?" he wondered about his long struggle with the dark spirit of his inspiration. "The only thing I know is this: I am full of wounds and still standing on my feet" (Kazantzakis, 1965, p. 512).

The strength to remain standing despite all suffering, fierce passion, and spiritual weariness is the essence of sustained creativity, as Garcia Lorca and Kazantzakis understood it. Their careers reflected a willingness to confront what was to them a tyrannical, inescapable, ecstatic relationship with the Other. Nothing less than suffering in the creative process seemed authentic or productive to them. In these hedonistic times, the concept is both obscure and attractive, adjectives well suited to duende.

NOTES

1. All translations from Italian and Spanish in this chapter are by the author.

REFERENCES

Bohm, D. (1998a). On creativity. In L. Nichol (Ed.), *On creativity* (pp. 1–26). New York: Routledge

Bohm, D. (1998b). The range of imagination. In L. Nichol (Ed.), *On creativity* (pp. 41–62). New York: Routledge.

Bohm, D. (1998c). The relationships of science and art. In L. Nichol (Ed.), *On creativity.* (pp. 27–40). New York: Routledge.

Corominas, J., & Pascual, J. A. (1984). *Diccionario crítico etimológico castellano y hispanico (Castilian and hispanic critical and etymological dictionary)* (Vol. 2). Madrid: Editorial Gredos.

Garcia Lorca, F. (1960). *Obras completas (Complete works)*. Madrid: Aguilar.

Gibson, I. (1989). *Federico Garcia Lorca: A life*. New York: Pantheon Books.

Jung, C. G. (1953). *Two essays on analytical psychology*. New York: Pantheon Books.

Kazantzakis, N. (1965). *Report to Greco* (1st English ed.). New York: Touchstone Books.

Moliner, M. (1984). *Diccionario de uso del español (Dictionary of Spanish usage)* (Vol. 1). Madrid: Editorial Gredos.

Rendina, C. (Ed.). (1993). *Federico Garcia Lorca: Tutte le poesie (All the poems)*. Rome: Grandi Tascabili Economici Newton.

Samuels, A., Shorter, B., & Plant, F. (1986). *A critical dictionary of Jungian Analysis*. New York: Routledge & Kegan Paul.

chapter 3

Limitations to Artistic Creativity: Joseph Conrad's *The Secret Sharer*

Carl Goldberg

> Nothing is as oppressive as a secret
> —Jean La Fontaine (1621-1695), French poet, orator, historian

Every day scores of men and women, by means of physical force or persuasive behavior, cause someone—even themselves—the outrage of undeserved suffering. Some of these acts are violations of conventional morality or statutes of criminality, while others are less easy to define as immoral or criminal, especially in regard to self-injurious behavior. Nevertheless, these acts have in common treating other people, or oneself, with a lack of respect and consideration for the victim's humanity.

Each act of destructiveness to which we are exposed contributes to a feeling of impotence, whether one is a victim or an observer; our resulting demoralization creates a vicious cycle in which destructiveness gains strength and reoccurrence. With repetition comes resignation. And from resignation, we too frequently have remained immobilized as a society; telling ourselves that our societal ills are too complex to solve.

An ability to deal efficaciously with destructiveness relies, of course, upon significantly grasping the roots of vicious behavior. Unfortunately, the causes of destructiveness—despite the pervasiveness of violence in contemporary American society—have been poorly understood (Goldberg, 1996). Charles Silberman (1978) in his sociohistorical account of crime in the United States, indicates that most of what is believed about destructive behavior is either false or irrelevant. He is referring to the knowledge of behavioral scientists, as well as that of the general public. With limited scientific data, how do we best come to a firm understanding of the factors that promote destructive behavior?

The well-told story is both the essence of captivating literature and the crucible for insights about human nature. The lessons of life always have come best from story, myth, and legend; concepts important to a life lived well—love, caring, compassion, creativity, decency, as well as the dark side of the human psyche—are understood more lucidly from the lives of particular individuals (real or fictionalized) than from generalizations based on the scientific investigation of large numbers of people.

> The true sign of (literary) genius is the ability to begin from the tensions of one's world, wherever and whenever it may be, or from one's personal experiences, and use them for creations that never lose their ability to speak to the future because they illuminate certain permanent aspects of the human condition. Such creators, as William Blake wrote, possess the capacity "To see a World in A Grain of Sand/ And a Heaven in a Wild Flower." (Joseph Frank, 1866/1987, pp. xxix)

In other words, in regard to the motif of destructiveness, great literature, by the acuity of its perspectives and the dexterity of its conceptualizations, liberates for inspection the ambiguities, paradoxes, and contradictions contained in society's various views of virtue and wickedness through the millennia. Moreover, it reworks the limited and misconceived threads of popular thought, turning conventional ideas upside-down about what is moral and desirable. The product of great literature offers us guidance and inspiration.

Virtually all great literary writers—from at least the time of Homer—have written about moral development, insightfully illuminating their characters' struggles with their dark side in ways that few others have been able to articulate. These master writers, like modern professional psychologists, have first been concerned with determining to what extent people have choice and responsibility for the acts they commit or influence, and second, the factors that—if recognized and competently acted upon—can change destructive lifestyles.

Obviously, some literary psychologists are better than others in articulating the factors influential in destructive behavior. The more perfect the artist, the more that artistic mind uses its creative work as a mirror to recognize and heal troubling, disavowed aspects of its inner conflictual life. But few writers retain an ever-reliable mirror throughout their careers. This difficulty speaks to the origins of the creative process itself. In an epigenetic sense, the limits of development and maturation are set at birth for all species except humans. Joseph Campbell (1968) tells us that myths from earliest times plainly show that, unlike other creatures, humans are born too soon; they are unfinished and unprepared to deal alone with the outside world. Our human condition requires a continuous personal journey of exploration to probe our psyches, developing and shaping our own destinies (Goldberg, 1987).

Creative people share, of course, the epigenetic, unfinished quality of selfhood with all humans. What differentiates them from others, however, is their active curiosity and passion for self-discovery which is often thwarted in less creative people.

FACTORS THAT KINDLE CREATIVE IMPULSES

There are a number of particular factors that appear to contribute to the creative person's curiosity and passion for self-discovery. Among them is a sense of being special. H. J. Kleinschmidt (1967) believes that "the childhood of creative people seems to be burdened by their awareness of being 'different' with all the implications of the guilt and ambivalence of being 'special'" (p. 100).

A second common factor in the lives of creative individuals is loss. For example, Freud (1910/1964) puts great emphasis on Leonardo da Vinci's early privation of his father. Psychoanalyst George Pollack (1982) confirms Freud's intuitive sense of the importance of the bereft in the lives of creative people, finding in his study that a surprising number of writers of all kinds had suffered a premature loss in their family.

The early losses of the master writer, however, are probably not as catastrophically traumatic as they are to those persons who do not seem able to achieve creative mastery. Generally, they involve a death of an important family member, a physical separation, or an emotional estrangement due to empathic failures. The loneliness of these privations leads to the development of fantasy as a mode of consolation and perhaps a form of play related to later creative activity. Here the denied aspects of self, impeding the sense of self-integration, are reworked in fantasy and daydream, and recast in the imagination of the writer-to-be in the form of a remade world.

By adulthood, the written form of expression becomes a primary source of personal satisfaction. In other words, for the less creative, hurtful experiences are events the sufferer generally tries to forget; for the artist, on the other hand, all experiences—no matter how painful—are grist for the mill for creative reworking.

A third factor helps us recognize that an artist's early losses are more complex than whether or not the representations of these losses find their way into a work of art. In short, the artist's inability to mourn early losses may impede his attempts at self-integration.

Clinically, we know that when a person mourns, powerful or loved aspects of the lost object are taken into the mourner's self; that is, internalized and made available for creative endeavors, as well as for satisfying interpersonal relationships. In contrast, failure to mourn important, personal losses results in a feeling of incompleteness; which, if unresolved through renewed efforts at integration, prevents a person's present world from the sense of a bright tomorrow.

These considerations have important implications for creative endeavors. Most creative people seek to match the concerns preoccupying them with the situations contained in their external occupation—their artistic works. As such, toxic and painful introjects that cannot be tolerated intrapsychically are expelled into the work of art. This work tends to be pessimistic, troubled, even violent.

Consequently, even the great literary masters—because of the nature of their own personal conflicts at certain trying times in their lives—have not sufficiently developed their intuitively brilliant insights in some of their writings. In short, although these writers have shown their psychological mastery in other of their literary creations, in at least one work, they demonstrate an inability to provide the protagonist with a deep understanding of his or her psychic conflicts, preventing us from recognizing the precise steps and the choices involved in the development of the story's destructive characters.

JOSEPH CONRAD

A notable example of the unexplained protagonist is found in the writing of Joseph Conrad, a master storyteller and a brilliant literary psychologist. Meyer's (1970) psycholiterary examination of Conrad shows that this eminent writer failed during certain trying times in his life to use his artistic work as a tool for dealing with troubling aspects of his inner life, "with the result that at such times his art declined, contaminated, as it were, by current personal distress" (p. 14).

In this chapter, I investigate the problem of destructiveness as depicted in Conrad's novel, *The Secret Sharer,* as I explore psychological explanations for the author's unwillingness or inability to clearly present the protagonist's emotional conflict. The thesis I examine—that human destructiveness is a product of unexamined self-contempt—is based on some of Carl Jung's notions (Campbell, 1976).

Jung claims that we deny our dark side at extreme risk, because that which we do not bring into consciousness appears in our life as fate. His idea is that a person's past inescapably clings to him or her, and if the shadow of some of its events are too terrifying to examine, the cast of

FIGURE 3.1.   Joseph Conrad

that shadow becomes one's eventual destiny. I show how this notion is illustrated in the literary work of Joseph Conrad.

Jung also contends that examining our vices is not necessarily a pessimistic venture. Such an investigation, which originates from our curiosity about what we do not understand in ourselves, can become a healthy exploration. In other words, by exploring our vices, we can locate the apprehensions, limitations and weaknesses that force us to live fearful and cloistered lives (Goldberg, 1996).

Conrad's *The Secret Sharer*

The story of *The Secret Sharer* concerns a young man who is given command of his first ship in the South Seas after the death of the ship's captain. The new captain, the narrator of the story, is a stranger to his crew. He feels strongly contemptuous and untrusting of his sailors, for reasons that Conrad does not make clear. On the first night on the ship, while on the deck alone, the narrator saves from the sea a young man, Leggatt, who is struggling to stay afloat. The rescued man, who physically resembles the narrator, tells the captain that he has fled from his own ship because he, an officer, killed another sailor, and was to be returned to England to be tried for murder. The narrator hides the young sailor in his own cabin for a couple of weeks while at sea. At the end, he enables Leggatt to abscond to a desert island undetected by the narrator's crew. In helping the runaway to escape, the narrator navigates his ship in a reckless manner.

While the protagonist of *The Secret Sharer* is the narrator, Conrad provides minimal explicit information about him. The question I address in this chapter is why Conrad doesn't allow us access to the biography of the novel's main character. What do we know about the narrator? In the novel, two overriding qualities are conveyed: one, that the narrator doesn't seem to know himself very well, admitting that "I was somewhat of a stranger to myself" (Conrad, 1910/1983, p. 21); two, that he appears to regard every other character in the novel with contempt and mistrust—with the important exception of Leggatt, a self-described murderer and opportunist, who apparently gained his officer position without merit. The narrator describes his experience with Leggatt from almost the very instant of encountering him as a "secret sharer of my life" (Conrad, 1910/1983, p. 38).

I make two assumptions based upon the above data: one, the narrator has a *secret* that Conrad doesn't want to convey directly to the reader; and two, the only sources we are provided for gaining insight into the character of the narrator is by focusing on his *actions* and observing what is reflected of the narrator in Leggatt.

Psychodynamic Explorations and Interpretations

For us to understand *The Secret Sharer* psychologically, my first task is to examine the concept of secrets. My thesis is that behind every disturbed life (the narrator's extreme guardedness, as well as his contemptuousness, is suggestive of a personality disturbance), resides a painful mystery.

Ironically, though as desirous as he is to confess and rid himself of his painful burden, no less urgent is the sufferer's need to guard against its revelation. There are inordinately powerful agents requiring his silence. These forces consist of loyalties to people from the past to protect them from disclosure of their shameful and incriminating involvements in his life.

It is dialogue with a responsive Other that serves as a mirror for oneself. In communicating with the Other we are enabled to see ourselves for who we are. In short, it takes another to know oneself (Buber, 1970). Finding a caring and wise Other with whom to dialogue enables the sufferer of the painful secret to rewrite what had been until then his secret narrative, and in the process to find a more viable and hopeful way to live. We find in *The Secret Sharer* far more secrecy than open dialogue between the characters.

Secondly, a hallmark of modern literature is the use of split characters or double selves to dramatize psychological conflict. From at least as early as Shakespeare, dramatists and novelists have tended to depict a major character's internal struggle by creating minor (in this novel, a major) character(s) who act out the contending sides of the protagonist's psychological conflict. The most concentrated intellectual attention to the phenomenon of "the double" probably occurred in Europe in the latter part of the 19th century (the period shortly before Conrad wrote this novel), when there was considerable speculation about the divergent makeup of the soul in terms of personality.

Psychology, at the time, recently separated from theology and philosophy, was making an exciting impact on the intellectual climate, as writers produced a spate of short stories and novels suggesting the possibility that each person houses a shadowy second self. Novels like Robert Louis Stevenson's *The Strange Case of Dr. Jekyll and Mr. Hyde*, Oscar Wilde's *The Picture of Dorian Gray*, and short stories such as Edgar Allan Poe's "William Wilson," can be regarded as literary experiments in the spirit of the new psychology. It is Dr. Jekyll, after all, who proposes the thesis that "man is not truly one but truly two." Herman Hesse elaborates on this theme in his novel *Steppenwolf* by going further in suggesting the possibility of multiple selves. Hesse writes:

> There is not a single human being . . . who is so conveniently simple that his being can be explained as the sum of two or three principle elements. . . . It appears to be an inborn need of all men to regard the self as a unit. However often and however grievously this illusion is shattered, it always mends again . . . the delusion rests upon a false analogy. As a body everyone is single, as a soul never. (Hesse, 1920/1963, pp. 77–79)

Typically, the 19th-century writers of double-self tales focused on the disquieting psychological conflict that prevents separate selves from functioning harmoniously. These literary works, particularly those of Wilde, Poe, Maupassant, Dostoyevsky, and Hoffmann, dramatically depict the suffering that emanates from the conflict of attempting to integrate the different selves within the personality (Goldberg, 1996).

Leggatt is the narrator's double self. What do we find in Leggatt's character that may provide information about the narrator's secret? Leggatt is a fugitive; he committed an impulsive and lethal act: he has killed another sailor during a furious gale at sea. The murder by Leggatt in the novel is based on an actual incident that Conrad heard about during his sailing days as a skipper in the Malay Archipelago (Meyer, 1970). It is noteworthy that for the purpose of the novel, Conrad

> made Leggatt a much more sympathetic character than the hard-fibered, despotic Smith (the actual sailor Leggatt represents), who killed his man with an iron capstanbar. Conrad's sailor is a younger man, son of an English parson, . . . and he kills in a desperate act of self-defense while trying to save his ship. (Walker, 1981, p. viii)

Presumably, Conrad was trying to render more acceptable the character and circumstances of Leggatt's destructive behavior. What does this "softening" imply about the character of the author?

Normally, it is unwise to interpret the meaning of a work of fiction from the contents of the author's autobiography (Conrad, 1912/1924). However, Conrad himself gives implicit permission to inspect his life story in order to more fully understand his creative fiction. He states, "A novelist lives in his own work. He stands there, the only reality in an invented world, among imaginary things happenings and people. Writing about them he is only writing about himself" (Conrad, qtd. in Meyer, 1970, p. 3). In this regard, the strong parallel between the sea experiences of Conrad, who took over his first command of a vessel as a young man after the death of the ship's captain (Walker, 1981), and that of the narrator in the novel is striking. It suggests that Conrad strongly identified with the character of the narrator and wanted to hide, suppress, or deny part of himself—presumably, some frightening destructive behavior he was party to as a participant or spectator (in reality, or even fantasy). Conrad indicates that although the author reveals his reality in his fiction, his revelation is incomplete: "He remains, to a certain extent, a figure behind the veil, a suspected rather than a seen presence" (Meyer, 1970, p. 3).

Joseph Conrad had been a frail and sickly child. Through strong will and persistence, he became robust (Meyer, 1970). He was assigned as a master-at-arms on the ships he served early in his career at sea. In the 1800s, the duty of a master-at-arms was to serve as a sort of chief of police, charged with maintaining order on the ship. The sailors were, for the most part, rough, uneducated men, given to brawling from minimal provocation. Conrad undoubtedly witnessed, if not participated in, numerous violent and destructive acts on ships and shore leave with men under the influence of drink—men who had been isolated for many months or even years from women and the constraints of polite society.

Aside from his experiences at sea, early in his life Conrad had witnessed the violence of revolution in his native land, as his Polish countrymen struggled to free themselves from the yoke of supplication to their Russian overlords. Indeed, Conrad's parents were active patriots, who were imprisoned for several months and then exiled (along with Conrad as a young child) from their native country for their anti-Russian activities. His parents died early in his life, as did a number of other relatives with whom he had close relationships. Conrad may be alluding in *The Secret Sharer* to one of these untoward experiences when the narrator describes himself in a process of psychological *splitting:* "Part of me was absent. That mental feeling of being in two places at once affected me physically as if the mood of secrecy had penetrated my very soul" (Conrad, 1910/1983, p. 46). Presumably, his second self represented his denied untoward experiences.

The psychodynamics of Conrad's denial may be described in still another way. Hamilton (1975), a psychoanalyst, suggests that Conrad, because of early losses of significant adults in his life, has many of his main characters undergoing a process of depersonalization, a psychologically defensive position in which what appears to be happening to the protagonist does not affect him. In other words, in this version of the doubling process, the protagonist, by separating himself into *experiencing* and *observing* selves, says to himself, in effect, "This isn't happening to me (the observing self). It is happening to the other person (the experiencing self). I'm just an onlooker."

The shameful quality of Conrad's real or fantasized events may have made it difficult for Conrad, the writer, to attribute these experiences to the character in the novel with whom I assume he consciously identified—the narrator. People who are vulnerable to feelings of shame and self-contempt tend to hide their feelings from everyone, including themselves (Goldberg, 1991). Consequently, Conrad may have tried to gain some psychological distance from his fantasies (or even actual experiences of acting destructively), by attributing those encounters to Leggatt, the character with whom he also unwittingly identifies.

We may regard Conrad's efforts to come to terms with his dark secrets to be a creative solution. This is to say, Conrad uses the written page as a mirror upon which he tries to reflect those psychic hurts and shames he has been unable to successfully grasp by other means. *The Secret Sharer*, a work that most critics regard as his last notable literary creation (Meyer, 1970) was written late in Conrad's life (1909). Consequently, *The Secret Sharer* may have unsuccessfully tried to capture the truths Conrad strived to articulate about himself.

Some support for my contention that the novel is at a psychological level an exploration of the dark side of personality comes from A. J. Guerard's (1983) notion based on Jungian psychology that *The Secret Sharer* concerns an "archetypal experience of the 'night journey,' of a provisional descent into the primitive and unconscious sources of being" (p. 9).

However, whether or not my speculations about Conrad's personal life are valid, we can see that because the narrator's inability to acknowledge his actual inner feelings even to himself, and because of his distrust of others, he is a prisoner of his recriminating past. I base this premise on the assumptions that a narrator's discourse in a novel represents his actual feelings, and secondly, that expressions of contempt for others are statements of distrust. In other words, contemptuousness—which, more often than not, is an expression of unexamined self-hatred—is a common vehicle for maintaining irrational views of oneself and others. People who are too fearful to examine unknown aspects of themselves frequently resort to magical thinking, which involves a suspension of their critical reasoning faculty. Elements of magical thinking are suggested in *The Secret Sharer* by the dreamlike quality of the narrator's story. One cannot be certain whether the narrator actually interacted with a person named Leggatt, or only imagined the events.

According to the child analyst, Melanie Klein (1960), magical thinking begins in the anxieties about annihilation by feared enemies. However, evidence suggests that it is the predilection of the child's psyche during the age of belief (ages four to eight)—the years that Conrad spent in deplorable conditions of exile with his parents—to trust innocently in the sincerity and benevolent intentions of those with whom they are significantly involved. These years (and these dynamics) are thus most crucial in determining the relationship of magical thinking and vicious behavior. Childrens' innocence during these years renders them vulnerable to betrayal.

Based on my 30 years of clinical experience with patients who have committed murder, rape, and mayhem in particularly heinous ways, I have formulated a theory (Goldberg, 1997) indicating that there are a number of specific destructive factors that take place during a child's age of belief, that, when found together, adequately explain why, as adults, they fail to develop a capacity for emotional connectedness and mutuality with others, and instead become involved in vicious behavior. I discuss here the possible presence of one of these five destructive factors in Conrad's life; namely, the inability to mourn hurts and disappointments.

The Inability to Mourn and its Consequences

To the extent that a child is unable to acknowledge consciously and give words to his/her inability to achieve or maintain a desired relationship with his/her parents, or someone else s/he regards as important, s/he is condemned to a world of pretense. In other words, children who cannot express their upset over a lack of control in their lives are compelled to find ways of pretending that they are not as helpless as they feel. Destructive behavior, in an important sense, is an attempt to show that the perpetrator has control over his life—that s/he can do whatever s/he pleases.

Meyer (1970) reveals Conrad as a secretive man who was reluctant to discuss, even with those closest to him, the painful events of his past; especially the loss of his parents at a tender age. The physical loss of his parents, and, presumably, an inability to grieve this major loss during his age of belief, may have served to insulate Conrad from feelings of trust and security in other people, compelling him to a world of fantasy in which he attempted to control the destinies of those in his psychic world in ways he could not with external reality.

Meyer (1970) provides clear evidence that Conrad was in continual struggle with family and friends over what he regarded as violations of trust. In fact, *The Secret Sharer* was written the same year as his breakup with Ford Maddox Ford, a literary friend whose support and inspiration, according to Meyer (1970), afforded Conrad "those introspective journeys into the self that constitute the greatest of the impressionistic art he created" (Meyer, 1970, p. 243).

After his parting with Ford, Conrad's writings greatly deteriorated. One critic (Guerard, 1958) goes as far as to judge Conrad's work in the last period of his life as no better than the then-popular romances written by far less talented authors. In other words, Conrad may have attempted to vivify in his writing that which he was not able to achieve in his own real life. He was unsuccessful because of failing health and the loss of a friend upon whom his sense of well-being depended at that time in his life.

What I mean by this is the following: children who learn during the age of belief that they cannot depend on their caretakers for compassion and security, decide early in life that they can survive only by not becoming overly dependent on other people. To compensate for the pain of the loss of caring and concerned others, these children frequently deny their wish for care and intimacy by acting as if they harbored the opposite desire. That is to say, they invest no effort in establishing satisfying interpersonal relations because they have decided that they are already very special and don't need anyone else. Their subsequent behavior, characteristically boastful and expansive, belies their fearful, shamed, inner lives.

Although Conrad in his personal life was a man who manipulatively demanded the attention of others for his care (Meyer, 1970), the protagonists of his novels are almost always outsiders from their societies. They go to considerable efforts seeking to prove their ability to survive valiantly alone. Their efforts to show the lack of need of others frequently results in acts of destructive behavior, as most poignantly shown in such novels as *The Heart of Darkness* and *Lord Jim*.

In other words, insofar as warm, caring, and trustful relationships with early caretakers are lacking, children develop magical thinking to compensate for their feelings of vulnerability and lack of self-worth. As adults they tend to transform the felt experience of being emotionally frail and vulnerable into a position of invincibility (Goldberg, 1996). Remember, Conrad had been a frail, sickly child.

In short, rather than making an effort to improve their characters, those who transform themselves from shameful and self-contemptuous selves by magical thinking to superior people, convince themselves that they are already perfect. One who is complete requires no self-improvement; narcissistically viewed, it is the Others' flawed perceptions that prevents one's superiority from its rightful recognition.

In the throes of magical thinking, destructive personalities use any means available to their imaginations to convince others of their inferred special status. The need to defend themselves from an awareness of vulnerability, unleashes a desperate delusion of superiority turned vicious; striking out at anyone who questions their entitlement to regard themselves as special. Their vulnerability fosters a state of permanent crisis. The extreme contemptuousness of Leggatt and the narrator in *The Secret Sharer* support this interpretation.

Could this—a pervasive sense of shame and self-contemptuousness—be the secret that Conrad privately shared with his characters? If so, I disagree with Guerard (1983), who contends that at the end of the novel the narrator is a mature man, having obtained wisdom. In my view, the narrator speaking of his experience with Leggatt, as he does from "this distance of years" (Conrad, 1910/1983, p. 39), appears to have no more insight into himself than he did during the earlier events. In other words, even at the end of the novel the narrator's secret remains undisclosed, just as Conrad's secret appeared to remain untold in his personal life.

CONCLUSION

What overall statement does Conrad's life provide us in trying to discover the contents of his protagonist's secret in *The Secret Sharer*? I offer this: the crisis of acute suffering can provide a crucible for the mysteries of life, involving, as it does, an encounter with forces that decay and destroy, together with those that resuscitate and inspire. Suffering can thus become a vehicle to a higher level of consciousness and self-awareness if the seeker has kept alive his or her inner fires, and used them as a means of directing his or her life. These inner fires, ignited from fierce passion of combat with illness and suffering, may be employed to inspire others as well.

Thus, if writers recognize the awesome impact of early losses on their creative endeavors, and this realization enables them to come to terms with their destructive shadows—their disavowed aspects of self—they may more successfully accentuate their creative efforts with intuitive insights and wisdom.

For some writers, however (even great ones like Conrad), the struggle with discordant aspects of the self have so overcompensated and exhausted their psychic energies, that at some point the work produced, as in *The Secret Sharer*, becomes secretive and ordinary, inspiring neither the writer nor his readers.

REFERENCES

Buber, M. (1970). *I and thou*. New York: Scribners.
Campbell, J. (1968) *The hero with a thousand faces*. Princeton, NJ: Princeton University Press.
Campbell, J. (Ed.). (1976). *The portable Jung*. New York: Penguin.
Conrad, J. (1924). *A personal record: An autobiography*. New York: Doubleday, Page. (Original work published 1912).
Conrad, J. (1983). The secret sharer. In J. Conrad, *The heart of darkness and the secret sharer*. New York: Penguin. (Original work published 1910).
Frank, J. (1987). Introduction. In F. Dostoevsky, *Crime and punishment* (pp. v-xx). New York: Bantam. (Original work published 1866).

Freud, S. (1964). *Leonardo da Vinci and a Memory of his childhood.* New York: Norton. (Original work published 1910).

Goldberg, C. (1987). A Psychological analysis of the myth of the remade world. In C. B. Yoke (Ed.), *Phoenix from the ashes: The literature of the remade world* (pp. 13–35). Westport, CT: Greenwood Press.

Goldberg, C. (1991). *Understanding shame.* Northvale, NJ: Jason Aronson.

Goldberg, C. (1996). *Speaking with the devil: A dialogue with evil.* New York: Viking.

Goldberg, C. (1997). Chautauqua institution lecture: The responsibilities of virtue. *The International Journal of Psychotherapy, 2,* 179–191.

Guerard, A. J. (1958). *Conrad the novelist.* Cambridge: Harvard University Press.

Guerard, A. J. (1983). Introduction. In J. Conrad, *Heart of Darkness & The Secret Sharer* (pp. 7–15). New York: Penguin.

Hamilton, J. W. (1975). The significance of depersonalization in the life and writings of Joseph Conrad. *Psychoanalytic Quarterly, 44,* 612–630.

Hesse, H. (1963). *Steppenwolf.* New York: Random House. (Original work published 1920).

Klein, M. (1960). *The psychoanalysis of children.* New York: Grove.

Kleinschmidt, H. J. (1967). The angry act: The role of aggression in creativity. *American Imago, 24,* 98–128.

Meyer, B. C. (1970). *Joseph Conrad: A psychoanalytic biography.* Princeton: Princeton University Press.

Pollack, G. (1982, July 11). Discussion of creative people. *New York Times Book Review.*

Silberman, C. E. (1978). *Criminal violence, criminal justice.* New York: Random House.

Walker, F. (1981). Introduction. In J. Conrad, *Heart of Darkness and The Secret Sharer.* New York: Bantam Books.

chapter 4

Inspired Creativity

Joel Funk
Plymouth State College

> The vision of the splendor of creation, like all kinds, lays a duty upon one
> who has been fortunate enough to receive it, a duty in his turn to create
> works which are as worthy of what he has seen as his feeble capacities will
> permit. And many have listened and obeyed. It has been, I am quite cer-
> tain, the initial cause of all genuine works of art, and, I believe, of all gen-
> uine scientific inquiry and discovery, for it is the wonder which is, as Plato
> said, the beginning of every kind of philosophy.
> —W.H. Auden

The belief in the inspired source of creativity expressed in the quote above is, today, a tenet not held by many. Most current literature contends that creativity can be more or less fully described and explicated by ordinary rational and environmental approaches (Gardner, 1993; Sternberg & Lubart, 1995; Weisberg, 1986). During my three decades as a student of transpersonal psychology and creativity, however, I have encountered numerous examples that question this premise (Funk, 1982, 1989, 1991). Even though inspired creativity seems rare, I advocate an open mind toward the phenomenon, one that allows for the influx of the numinous and for nonordinary states of inspiration.

In this chapter, I define and outline the rational versus inspired creativity debate, and show how inspired or transcendent creativity is underresearched and even dismissed in the current literature. I argue that constructivist developmental theory, both Eastern and Western, leaves room for considering that creators sometimes access a range of non-ordinary states of mind that, to varying degrees, can be ascribed to transpersonal sources of inspiration. This thesis is supported by a few examples of creative work that appear to have been derived from a transpersonal source; indeed, in the second example, the creator insists on the composition's divine origin! Following that, I offer a list of the phenomenological and related characteristics that characterize inspired creativity and distinguish it from other forms or levels of creativity.

To concretize the issue somewhat, let us begin by examing a slightly dramatized—but essentially real—debate between two leading psychologists, one representing the rational approach, the other the transpersonal perspective.

A DEBATE OVERHEARD

Several years ago at a conference on adult development I happened to be present during an informal debate between two well-known psychologists, both quite stimulating, innovative thinkers. The first, David Perkins, was a representative of the cognitive approach to creativity; in fact, he had authored a successful book (1981) arguing that creativity can be fully explained within the objectively known parameters of the mind. The findings of cognitive psychology, he explained, can account for *both* ordinary thinking as well as what he called "the mind's best work," i.e., problem solving and creativity. There is never a need, according to this view, to resort to esoteric or transpersonal explanations of creativity. In contrast, the other psychologist, the late Charles Alexander, was committed to a meditative discipline and had created a complex model of development that synthesized Eastern (Vedic) and Western approaches to transformation and creativity (Alexander, Heaton, & Chandler, 1994).

I eagerly awaited Alexander's rejoinder, for I had been struggling with the purely rational approach in my own reflection and teaching about the creative process. My belief to this point had been that genius always requires some measure of transcendence and that even lesser mortals are capable of moments of inspiration. But I could not help wondering: Is there really anything to such notions as intuition, inspiration, and transcendence? Or is creativity in principle explicable by contemporary (or future) theories of brain, mind, and social context, as most current theory would have it? Can contemporary models of the creative process truly explain such "sudden apparitions as the Gothic cathedrals, the four-part polyphony of Perotin, the works of Shakespeare and J. S. Bach, try as people will to interpret these as the effects of some known cause" (Godwin, 1987, p. 85)? On the other hand, could Weisberg (1986) be correct in declaring that genius is a myth, a best forgotten relic of romanticism, and that there is essentially no difference between routine problem solving and Mozart's composition of an opera? Are the "nothing but" theorists correct? Is the contrast between ordinary creativity and "genius" merely a difference in degree rather than in kind?

Alexander countered that at least the most exalted forms of creativity—what we typically call genius—*cannot* be explained without reference to inspiration and non-ordinary states of consciousness. Moreover, he cited research to support the contention that transcendental meditation, in enhancing the development of consciousness generally, *ipso facto* enhanced creativity to some extent in "ordinary people" as well (Aron & Aron, 1982). In short, the debate I overheard was the perennial one between materialism, broadly defined, and a worldview that allows for a nonmaterial, transcendent source of consciousness and creativity (Alexander, Heaton, & Chandler, 1994; Funk, 1982, 1989, 1994; Miller & Cook-Greuter, 1994; Wilber, 1980, 1996, 1997). Currently, materialism appears to have carried the day, as noted above. Due to recent pioneering research and theorizing on the cognitive, social/contextual, historical, and motivational/personological influences on creativity (Csikszentmihalyi,1996; Gardner, 1993; Simonton, 1994; Sternberg & Lubart, 1995), inspiration and transcendence seem to have fallen out of favor as sources of creativity.

THE TRANSPERSONAL RESPONSE

For transpersonal psychologists, however, the matter is not so easily settled. Transpersonal approaches to creativity postulate that just as different levels of consciousness are far from equivalent, *not all creativity is equal*. A creative product is assumed to reflect the level of consciousness that produced it (Funk, 1989; Wilber, 1998). If consciousness can be analyzed into more than a dozen levels (Wilber, 1980), and if adult consciousness alone can be divided into six or more levels of functioning (Cook-Greuter, 1990; Wilber, 1980), then one wonders whether a similar division can be applied to the creative works derived from these levels. Indeed, I have articulated previously some eight or so levels and sublevels in the evolution of the works of Beethoven and, to a lesser extent, other classical composers (Funk, 1982, 1989).

Here, though, a more parsimonious model will suffice. Miller and Cook-Greuter (1994) divide development broadly into four fundamentally distinct tiers: preconventional, conventional, postconventional (postformal), and transcendent. Psychologists have already documented the input from the first three levels. For example, numerous psychoanalysts have provided examples of preconventional (e.g., primary process) material in many forms of creativity (Kubie, 1958/1979). Many social, personality, and cognitive psychologists have contributed to an understanding of the conventional tier of creativity, as noted above (Sternberg & Lubart, 1995). Humanists, existentialists, and theorists of postformal operations have pushed the boundaries to include the postconventional tier (Abra, 1988; Funk, 1989). Csikszentmihalyi's (1996) concept of "flow" and Otto Rank's critique of the artist's solution to the existential dilemmas of life (Becker, 1973) reflect the workings of the third-tier mind.

The fourth, the transcendent tier, has been far more problematic for rational, scientific/materialistic approaches, for it requires a paradigm shift in one's conception of mind and reality. Leading transpersonal theorists like Wilber (1997, 1998), Alexander (Alexander, Heaton, & Chandler, 1994), and Washburn (1988) argue for a transcendent mode of consciousness or a "Ground of Being" that is ontologically prior to and qualitatively different from the ordinary egoic consciousness studied by mainstream psychologists. Moreover, this consciousness is said to coexist alongside ordinary consciousness even as the latter evolves ontogenetically, as described by Piaget, Loevinger, and others (Wilber, 1996). In the transpersonal view, people we label geniuses have the ability, some of the time at least, to access this transcendent consciousness.

This idea is not new; its roots go back at least to Plato. Over 150 years ago, the poet-scientist Goethe declared that, contrary to the reductionist belief that science and the arts were products of "mere human power," geniuses like Mozart or Raphael "exceeded human nature . . . and were . . . gifted by the gods" (cited in Lauer, 1989, p. 150).

It may be objected that access to the transcendent is possible from *all* developmental levels, even those characteristic of childhood. I have argued this myself elsewhere (Funk, 1994). Generally, however, transpersonal experiences are more likely to occur to those at higher developmental levels since one's ego boundaries become ever more permeable and open to the numinous once into the third and especially fourth tier of development.

The transcendent mode of consciousness is said to function at a level beyond that of the physical body/nervous system and the Newtonian conception of reality. A consciousness capable of transcending the limits of Newtonian reality would be capable of far greater knowledge and understanding than is normally possible. Greene (1996), writing of the "super-natural intelligence" he alleges was the source of Homer's poetry, observes:

> To this higher intelligence, existing in a more spacious present moment—that subsumes much larger portions of space and time together—. . . accessing information from different historical periods might be no more difficult than for us to glance back and forth at the objects on our living room table and the painting on the wall behind. (p. 245)

In other words, this transcendent or "super-natural" intelligence could perceive cosmic patterns existing beyond Newtonian space and time. Greene's idea might partially explain, for example, how Beethoven could compose his incredible, visionary, late string quartets (Funk, 1982). The *Grosse Fugue [Great Fugue]*, was not understood until at least three generations after its composition, and it seems barely comprehensible to many listeners today.

What actually does occur when we access higher levels of consciousness? Some would say that at these rarefied moments, we resonate to something much larger and greater, more intelligent and profound, be it a Platonic archetype, a luminous vision, a subtle sound, an experience of the numinous devoid of content, a revelation of a heretofore invisible structure of the cosmos, or "merely" felt contact with something beyond the ordinary, some hint of the infinite (Wilber, 1998). Characteristically, creators who have access to the numinous ground describe a realm of being transcending time and space. An entire work may appear all at once, or "holographically" (Funk, 1989), as in the examples below. Seen thus, concepts such as "grace" or "divine gift," usually reserved for religious phenomena, become increasingly appropriate as descriptions of the creative process.

This raises a somewhat sticky issue. Over the years, transpersonal psychology has been taken to task for smuggling theological, religious, and metaphysical beliefs and presuppositions into scientific psychology. To an extent, this charge does have some merit, although the arrow should point both ways. It would be helpful to all camps to be more explicit about their assumptions. What theological and metaphysical beliefs underlie mainstream psychology?

The author, for one, resonates with the Russian theologian Berdyaev (1965) who believes that

> Man is not the source of his gifts and his genius. He has received them from God and therefore feels that he is . . . an instrument of God's work in the world. . . . The genius feels that he acts not of himself, but is possessed by God and is the means by which God works His own ends and designs. (1965, p. 199)

These gifts include *both* the egoic as well as the transegoic or numinous (Funk, 1994); the everyday, ordinary, rational capacity as well as archetypal inspiration and apprehensions of Suchness, as they are commonly portrayed in transpersonal psychology. *Both* the egoic and the numinous, as explained later in the chapter, are essential to genius.

Precisely where is the original source of creativity situated according to the typical psychologist studying creativity? In most cases the question is never asked. Would mainstream psychologists agree with physicist David Bohm that the source of creativity lies *not* in thinking but in a much deeper, more subtle intuitive perception? Comparing the mind to a stream, Bohm maintains that thinking is located "fairly far downstream" (Bohm, 1991, p. 177).

Feldman (1994), for example, one of the more expansive writers on creativity, has intuited a "transformational imperative" in human consciousness, but, unlike Bohm and Berdyaev, is unclear about the source of this imperative. Most psychologists would probably ascribe creativity to materialistic evolutionary processes, whereby certain creativity-engendering routines are selected because they provide some advantage. Chronological evolution, from the lower to the higher and more complex, is acceptable to mainstream theorists, but ontological involution (Wilber, 1980), that is, the influx of the higher into the lower, is not seriously considered as a possiblity. To the transpersonalist, evolution is certainly not to be dismissed, but it is itself seen as part of the play of the divine—the outbreath that complements the involutionary inbreath.

One final digression: If we are "made in the image of God," then human creativity mirrors divine creativity. If the microcosm reflects the macrocosm, as esotericism maintains, then we as human beings must embody, to some extent, the characteristics of the divine as well. As Michael Grosso aptly summarized it, "If Mind at Large is an artist, and the forms of life are works of art, and if we are the clearest reflection of the work of Mind at Large, then the artist in us would reflect most clearly the meaning of life" (1985, p. 127).

EXAMPLES OF "INSPIRED" CREATIVITY

The reader by now might be eager to see a concrete example of the kind of creativity that current theories are hard pressed to "explain." The two following anecdotes illustrate the type of experience that lead me to ponder the "inspired creativity" question in the first place. To differing degrees, each anecdote involves extraordinary aspects of the creative process.

Dream Songs

During those infrequent periods when I have had the pleasure of becoming very involved in amateur songwriting, I often hear songs in my dreams. What strikes me as odd is not the mere occurrence of music during dreams, but the fact that the music seems qualitatively different from my waking output. Moreover, there is a strange feeling of passivity during such dreams, as if I were a mere witness to a performance put on by someone else. I have even felt a twinge of jealousy for the "dream songwriter," realizing only upon awakening that—surprise!—*I* wrote the song. Or at least it was in *my* dream, for it did not feel, as I have said, as if I had written anything!

Yet, there is an even more subtle point here that is easily overlooked. Consider a musical theater production. An actor feels some emotion and bursts into song. Obviously no one could improvise such a polished, tightly organized song spontaneously. The audience knows perfectly well that some composer/writer with years of experience labored for hours or months getting the music and lyrics just right; the last note of the song has already been composed (in the score) even as the first note bursts forth. The singing is *anything but spontaneous*. My dream songs work in an identical manner. As I sit and watch/listen to some song playing itself out in my dream, I realize—upon awakening, of course—that if the song has any organic quality at all, the entire piece from beginning to end *must have been already written from the start!* It is like playing a CD or tape for the first time. All the music to be heard is already there, it simply takes time for it all to pass through our waking consciousness, focused on moment-to-moment succession.

The Irish poet and visionary A. E. captured my experience perfectly, noting that there is a division of consciousness in dreaming, one part of us being the seer, another part the mysterious creator. The seer is *not* aware of the creative process, and thus the images in the dream appear to be not of one's own making. Upon awakening, however, the dreamer realizes that the creator of the dream "had a magical power transcending anything which he could do in his waking state. . . . The creator [of the] dream is swift inconceivably. What seems a long dream to the seer of dream often takes place in an instant" (1932/1991, pp. 23–24).

This is precisely how my own dreams appeared phenomenologically! It is possible that I may have partially deceived myself about the structural tightness of these dream songs. On the other hand, on the few occasions when I have been able to reconstruct them somewhat, they did not seem like "my usual style." If the dream songs were indeed true structured songs, then I am led to conclude that they are created timelessly, or very nearly so. I have referred to this process as "temporal holography," in that each moment of the work implies the rest. The ending is right there at the beginning (Funk, 1989).

Thus, these dream experiences made vivid and compelling to me the anecdotes about great composers who claim to experience works all at once. "Great masters of music have told us how they sometimes hear the whole of some grand [work] . . . in one resounding chord . . . though when they try to write it down in notes, many pages of music may be necessary to express it" (Leadbeater, 1912/1979, p. 37). Mozart, for example, noted that, at a certain point in composing a work,

> The whole, though it be long, stands almost complete and finished in my mind, so that I can survey it, like a fine picture, or a beautiful statue, at a glance. Nor do I hear in my imagination the parts *successively*, but I hear them, as it were, all at once" (cited in Ghiselin, 1952, p. 45)

It seems that most of us are potentially far more creative in the dream state than in our "normal" waking state, because access to transcendence—as well as to prepersonal material—may become less restricted as the ego relaxes its grip.[1]

"Angels of Comfort"

Some creators deeply believe that their inspiration is from a divine source. Consider the following abridged account, sent to me by a contemporary composer named Iasos,[2] of the purported visionary origins of a work entitled "The Angels of Comfort":

> I decided that I wanted to create music that had the energy of the HOLY SPIRIT[3] in it. So I went within, and silently but sincerely made a mental request: "Oh, Holy Spirit, I wish to create music that has your energy in it. Please assist me in creating music that has your essence in it." To my great surprise, as quickly as one week later, some musician friends allowed me to use a synthesizer that sounded like many violins (something I myself did not then have). I quickly went into their studio, set up my recorder, recorded feverishly for 2 and a half hours. . . . Went home to my studio with that recording. Experimented processing what I had recorded, and to my great surprise realized that a composition of great beauty and depth was emerging—"The Angels of Comfort." It sounded very "composed," although at the time I was recording, I was not thinking of any particular composition. After the piece materialized, it became abundantly clear that this was the answer to my request from the Holy Spirit. . . . You would be amazed at how many people have told me that, concerning "The Angels of Comfort," "This is the music I would like to be hearing when I die."[4]

The letter continues with a general description of Iasos' composing process.

> Sometimes a highly evolved being I work with . . . transmits musical ideas into my consciousness, for the express purpose of my manifesting this on our physical dimension. . . . When this occurs, usually the entire composition comes out in a very rapid and clear no-question-about-it manner. It comes through so rapidly, I don't even have time to write down the chords

as I go. . . . But they emblaze into my consciousness deeply enough, so I have no trouble remembering it long enough to write it down later.

Finally, reflecting the perceived all-at-once nature of higher creativity alluded to above, Iasos comments that, "Sometimes . . . a holographic image of the entire composition . . . [is present in] my consciousness. This is amazing when it happens, since it is much more of a 3-D picture and a feeling than it is a sound, but it does also have a musical . . . component" (Iasos, personal communication, November 17, 1989).

Compare Iasos' account of all-at-onceness to that of a better-known composer, Johannes Brahms:

> Contact with the source of our Being is a wonderful and awe-inspiring experience. . . . In this exalted state I see clearly what is obscure in my ordinary moods. . . . Straight away, the ideas flow in upon me, directly. . . . Not only do I see distinct themes in my mind's eye, but they are clothed in the right forms, harmonies, and orchestrations. Measure by measure the finished product is revealed to me when I am in those rare, inspired moods. (Shear, 1982, p. 163)

I have garnered some empirical evidence to support Iasos's claim (Funk, 1991). In a series of experiments, approximately 60 near-death experiencers—and 10 meditators—*did indeed* find Iasos's "The Angels of Comfort" a significantly better match to the sound and mood of their own transpersonal experiences than the works of Bach, Beethoven, Wagner, and many other New Age composers who deliberately tried to create "transpersonal music." Similarly, in another empirical study, Linda Melrose (1989) interviewed prominent creators about their experiences. One playwright in Melrose's study, for example, reported experiences of divinities, sometimes in dreams, on a number of occasions. Other creators reported insights in dreams, sometimes of a paranormal nature; that is, they seemed to exhibit some degree of extrasensory knowledge (ESP). Most felt that inspiration was a key element in their work, and there were a number of references to God or the divine.

More informally, I have also presented "The Angels of Comfort" to numerous "ordinary" listeners who also tell of being quite transported—even overwhelmed. One anonymous listener reported:

> To this day my "body" has not forgotten the impact of that music. I still yearn to hear it again. . . . To me the experience was a revelation. I had no other evidence of the realm of "heavenly" music, no connection to it. But once I heard it there was suddenly a *there* there. From then on I knew of a possibility (a whole category of experience) that didn't exist before. (personal communication, February 27, 1998)

What can we learn from these two cases? My dreamsong incident reveals, I believe, that even the extraordinary moments of ordinary creators can exhibit *some* of the characteristics (e.g., all-at-onceness) of inspired creativity. This is reminiscent of Maslow's (1971) claim that during peak experience one shifts to a mode of cognition he referred to as Being-Cognition, which is qualitatively distinct from more mundane Deficiency-Cognition.

The Iasos anecdote constitutes a more thoroughly transpersonal example: here is a musical opus that transcends the ordinary, both in its purportedly celestial source, in its revelatory method of composition, and in its impact on listeners.

GENERAL CHARACTERISTICS OF INSPIRED CREATIVITY

Neither example cited above is unique; scores of similar instances appear in the scattered literature of inspired creativity. At this point it would be valuable to examine the general characteristics of inspired creativity, the common denominators that appear repeatedly in the numerous cases studied. Later, this list is used to help the reader make decisions about whether a particular creative work is inspired, and to what extent.

Therefore, I now offer a brief delineation of a dozen key aspects of the kind of inspired creativity that I have tried to explore here, with a buttressing example or quote for each point. Note also that these characteristics may not be independent of one another.

Access to a "superconscious" state. Creators typically report entering an altered state—often at crucial periods in the creative process—during which new, previously unavailable capacities emerge. Although the qualities and intensities of these states may vary somewhat, the universal common denominator is the enhancement of creative ability. Brahms referred to this state as "superconscious" (Shear, 1982).

Sometimes, rather than a distinct altered state, a strong intuitive sense of "rightness" or directionality guides the creators, so that they know when they are heading toward something new and profound. Often this type of creator proceeds like someone walking at night, the darkness being periodically lit up by lightning. During those moments of illumination, the path is relatively clearly laid out, although once back in darkness, a good deal of groping about may still occur. Beethoven is reported to have operated this way.

Active passivity. There is often a sense of contact with what might be called the Dynamic Ground (Washburn, 1988) of Being. The creator apparently works in collaboration with a higher creative force, so that, *paradoxically*, one is both active and passive simultaneously. Actually, not quite simultaneously, for the activity arises during the earlier stages of preparation and (sometimes) struggle. Once the transcendent experience of creativity arises, the creator feels essentially passive, although active labor in articulating what has been revealed is necessary in some cases. As composer Alexander Goeher wrote, "The music writes itself. . . . There is no longer a composer who pushes the material about, but only a servant, carrying out what the notes themselves imply" (Storr, 1992, p. 97). Goeher adds that at such times he feels "overcome by an oceanic sensation of oneness with all around me (p. 97).

Perhaps surprisingly, some would argue that this higher creative force "needs" the participation of the genius as much as the genius needs inspiration! As Gowan (1975) writes:

> Because we have been conditioned to think of "God" . . . as perfected and completed instead of being in process, we find it difficult to imagine a numinous entity which changes and becomes more complete with our own developmental stages. Yet that developmental process in the individual is in one sense the effort of the numinous element to perfect and complete itself, rising to the level of rational will and consciousness through the developing life experience of each one of us. . . . Man is necessary for the evolution of the universe! (pp. 9–10)

Humility and self-importance. As Briggs (1988) observed, another paradox of inspired creativity, one that follows from active passivity, is that the creator feels both humble and self-important. When Bach dedicated his works "to the greater glory of God," he was both minimizing and drawing attention to his own significance simultaneously! Mozart, Brahms, Beethoven, Haydn, Stravinsky: they asked God to use them as instruments (Storr, 1992) or merely reported what a higher power "dictated"; yet, of course, they are among the elite few chosen for that task.

Retention of ego capacities. Egoic structures and capacities remain intact; for example, the ability to synthesize or evaluate a potentially overwhelming mass of input remains. In cases of transcendently creative dreaming, egoic capacities may be *temporarily* submerged to some extent, only to reappear after the dream. In fact, a fairly high level of ego development is more conducive to creativity that is open to the numinous.

Possession of requisite technical skills. Technical know-how is a *sine qua non* of creativity (Sternberg & Lubart, 1995). Otherwise, the creator would be unable to give form to the transcendent vision; thus, only a very few mystics and transpersonal experiencers are geniuses as well.

Simonton (1994), in a grand survey, claims that it takes a minimum of ten years' hard work to obtain the required mastery of a discipline, and often it takes much longer than that. Nevertheless, technique alone is quite obviously not sufficient for genius.

Postconventional level of development. A well-integrated structurization at a postconventional level of ego development is likely to facilitate inspired creativity and genius (Cook-Greuter, 1990; Gemant, 1961). Postconventional development is more likely to allow for non-ordinary sources to influence the creator, be they dreams, primary thought processes, transcendent states, and so on. This is so because the rigid boundaries of the conventional egoic stance have become more permeable. The subject/object distinction, so crucial to ordinary functioning as well as to scientific endeavor, becomes increasingly less powerful, more transparent as constructs, as development proceeds. Thus, the barriers to numinous experience become less defended, less rigid.

There *are* probable exceptions: Mozart certainly had the techncial skills and, many (including the composer himself) would assert that he experienced frequent contact with the numinous. His overall level of ego development, however, appears to have been fairly modest in some important respects. It is interesting to speculate on whether Mozart's childlike characteristics actually allowed him *easier* access to the the transpersonal than would otherwise have been the case (Funk, 1994).

Timelessness. As noted above, there is frequently a timeless, "all at once" quality inherent in transcendent creativity. At the very least, the speed of creativity in transcendent experience seems orders of magnitude beyond that of regular methodical thought, as evidenced in the two earlier musical examples.

True novelty. The more rational approach would characterize all creativity essentially as variation on what already exists, and therefore explainable. Although the outcome might not be entirely predictable, the steps are claimed to be understandable and perhaps predictable to an extent. In the transpersonal cosmic drama, however, *novel creations really do occur,* and these creations are often surprising and inexplicable to the creator as well as to observers and subsequent interpreters of the work. According to Jean Gebser (1949/1986), a scholar of the evolution of consciousness, the creative breakthrough is analogous to a biological mutation. He describes such creativity as "spontaneous, acausal, and discontinuous" (p. 313). Gebser argues that terms like "acausal" and "discontinuity" cannot be accommodated by the rational mind which inevitably seeks orderly explanations, predictability, and replicability. In Gebser's words, "Creativity is something that 'happens' to us, that fully effects or fulfills itself in us. . . . It cannot be adequately circumscribed by a psychological interpretation" (p. 313). It is only in *retrospect* that the rational mind can convince itself that such discontinuous creativity, for example, Beethoven's *Eroica Symphony*, is a more or less "predictable" outcome of what came before.

Transcendence of comprehension of creator. As Godwin (1979) observes, the creators themselves may not fully understand the significance of the transcendent revelation (or how it came about) with their everyday egoic consciousness. While composing *Porgy and Bess*, George Gershwin was described as dreamily playing the famous lullabye "Summertime," wondering how he could have written such wonderful music. Is this narcissism or could it be a true apprehension of the mystery of inspired composition?

Communal nature. The social or communal aspect of creativity should not be overlooked (Gardner, 1993). In Wilber's (1996) grand scheme, every psychological event has an individual as well as a cultural/social dimension; for every "I" there is a "we." All creativity is dependent on what Feldman (1994) calls "the crafted world," the symbol systems, artifacts, and memes that already exist in the world. Transcendent creativity, however, typically goes beyond the culture in which it originated. In fact, transpersonal creativity probably has been involved in *creating* many of the major changes in culture, for example, the music of Beethoven which opened the door to romanticism and even modernism in music (Funk, 1982). In short, from the transpersonal perspective, creative transcendence is a prime agent in cultural transformation.

Possession of other skills and characteristics. Genius requires more than the ability to access transcendent states of consciousness. As Gemant (1961), Simonton (1994), Sternberg and Lubart (1995), and others have noted, there are many other factors involved. We have already mentioned a few: advanced ego development and technical mastery are helpful, if not essential, to genius. Other prerequisites include independence of thought, motivation and perseverance, capacity for intense task absorption, prolificness, and willingness to risk, among others.[5]

Analogy to mysticism. If the genius sometimes experiences transcendence, is the genius actually a mystic? Perhaps the most appropriate answer is "yes and no." Briggs (1988) cites many points of similarity between creator and mystic. Both experience a drive to wholeness, insist on the *coincidentia oppositorum* (coincidence of opposites), keenly feel a sense of the omnivalence (sense of "moreness") of the universe, often seek a project to unify all diversity and thus "reveal the secret mind of God" (p. 120), relate to the mystery of being with a sense of awe, and often feel an evangelical need to share the omnivalent experience, even awakening a mystical feeling in others. However, despite these similarities, Briggs observes, creators are *not* truly mystics, because "creators believe that transcendental experience can be manifested in a physical form—in an artwork or scientific discovery" (p.121). Whereas mystics seek union in the spiritual realms, creators seek to manifest the spiritual in the sensory realms, leaving behind some record of their experience. Or as Fingarette (1963) observed, rather than transforming the self directly, the artist/creator shapes the self indirectly through the work of art. The integration achieved is "not one of the self but of a *separate*, autonomous entity. . . . This helps account for the fact that we expect that the artist will be open to experience, but not that he will himself be a Sage" (pp. 283–284).

CONCLUSION

I have been asked occasionally how one can determine whether and to what degree a work reflects inspiration. How does one know if there is a transcendent origin to the work? Given the general aspects of inspired creativity cited above (a few of which, like technical mastery, would apply to most other forms of creativity as well), the task becomes easier, although by no means clear-cut. Here are some key criteria to consider; if each of these is met, then there is a strong likelihood that the work is indeed inspired. To simplify matters, I refer exclusively to musical compositions, as I have studied this area the most extensively (Funk, 1982, 1989), but the observations are generalizable.

1. If the work is unanimously (or nearly so) regarded as being great, revolutionary, almost inexplicable, even when compared to other works by the same composer. Beethoven's *Eroica* is generally regarded as a quantum leap beyond anything that had come before, and is still regarded as one of the greatest of Beethoven's middle-period works (Funk, 1982).
2. If the composer reports divine guidance, or at least accessing an altered state (dream, vision, etc.) during some or all of the composing process. Handel reported seeing and hearing angels singing glorious praise to God. This vision was transcribed and eventually became the "Hallelujah Chorus." As a result of his "passive" role in the process, Handel believed he had not truly composed the piece, and dedicated all royalties to charity (Lingerman, 1982).
3. If the composition is composed incredibly quickly. Handel's *Messiah* was written in just over three weeks. Brahms and Mozart, as noted above, heard fully orchestrated compositions. One might wonder if this is hypomania or inspiration (Ludwig, 1995). Most hypomanics,

however, don't produce anything on the level of Handel, Mozart, or Brahms. Note that even some more slowly executed compositions, like many of Beethoven's works, can qualify if they meet the other criteria.

4. Perhaps the most crucial citerion: If the audience feels inspired, transported, even overwhelmed. The first time I heard Wagner's "Liebestod," from *Tristan and Isolde*, I was amazed and overwhelmed, and the effect has not lessened after many repeated hearings. The same reaction, although in a rather different way, can be induced by listening to the ethereal adagios of Beethoven's late string quartets (Funk, 1982). The anonymous response to hearing Iasos, cited above, is another instance. How is such music possible?

Surely, the most broadminded approach would acknowledge that the sources of creativity are multiple. There are the numerous familial, social, and environmental forces that have been explored by psychologists of creativity. There is ordinary egoic knowledge and the processes of ordinary cognition, as well as postformal integration and scope. From the transpersonal perspective, however, in many instances of genius or inspired creativity, *access to the numinous dimensions of consciousness is what makes the masterpiece realizable.* Without in any way minimizing the many valuable contributions to the psychology of creativity by mainstream researchers, the transpersonal perspective appears the more comprehensive. It includes the cognitive, social, and environmental realms, but adds the crucial transcendent dimension. In the future, researchers of creativity would do well to remember the subtle, and thus often overlooked, extraordinary source of inspired creativity.

NOTES

1. See Krippner (1981) for a fascinating account of the role of dreams in creativity. One illustration: The great Indian mathematician Ramanujan, who rediscovered centuries of work in number theory by himself and later made significant contributions to mathematics, claimed that many of his equations were given to him by an Indian Goddess who appeared in dreams.

2. The interested reader is invited to explore Iasos's website (http://www.iasos.com).

3. Iasos noted that he is speaking of a *universal* understanding of the Holy Spirit, and not specifically of a Judeo-Christian notion (Iasos, personal communication, November 17, 1998).

4. This report claims to be an instance of divine or angelic guidance. What one makes of such a letter, though, depends on one's underlying presuppositions. To one convinced of the reality of spiritual realms, the letter might well be

taken as a literally true account of a creative act, one in accord with accepted esoteric teachings (Leadbeater, 1912/1979). A psychiatrist, on the other hand, might diagnose the author as suffering from some form of psychopathology. A biologically oriented psychologist might admit that some eruption of right hemispheric sound imagery could very well have facilitated the creative work; the composer's *interpretation*, however, would be seen as prescientific or seriously misguided. The transpersonal psychologist walks a middle ground. While not necessarily accepting the story as literally narrated, the notion of holographic inspiration from a transcendent dimension of existence would nevertheless be considered plausible. The right hemisphere may well be involved, but it would be viewed as allowing, not causing the experience (Wilber, 1997). For another account of a composer supposedly guided by higher forces, see Tame's (1984) discussion of British composer Cyril Scott.

5. In addition, absence of severe psychopathology (Ludwig, 1995) seems, with some notable exceptions, an essential ingredient in a creative life. Although many creators have "benefitted" from hypomania (Ludwig, 1995), and occasionally pathological experiences can feed creativity—Kafka comes to mind—overall creativity works best unimpeded by serious pathology.

REFERENCES

Abra, J. (1988). *Assaulting Parnassus: Theoretical views of creativity.* Lanham, MD: University Press of America.

A. E. (1991). *Song and its fountains.* Burdett, NY: Larson Publications. (Original work published 1932).

Alexander, C. N., Heaton, D. P., & Chandler, H. M. (1994). Advanced human development in the Vedic psychology of Maharishi Mahesh Yogi: Theory and research. In M. E. Miller & S. R. Cook-Greuter (Eds.), *Transcendence and mature thought in adulthood: The further reaches of adult development* (pp. 39–70). Lanham, MD : Rowman and Littlefield.

Aron, E., & Aron, A. (1982). An introduction to Maharishi's theory of creativity: Its empirical base and description of the creative process. *Journal of Creative Behavior, 16,* 29–49.

Becker, E. (1973). *The denial of death.* New York: Free Press.

Berdyaev, N. (1965). The ethics of creativity. In J. M. Edie, J. P. Scanlan, and M-B. Zeldin (with G. L. Kline) (Eds.), *Russian philosophy* (Vol. 3, pp. 198–203). Chicago: Quadrangle.

Bohm, D. (1991). Creativity, natural philosophy, and science. In M. Toms (Ed.), *At the leading edge* (pp. 166–182). Burdett, NY: Larson Publications.

Briggs, J. (1988). *Fire in the crucible: The alchemy of creative genius.* New York: St. Martin's Press.

Cook-Greuter, S. R. (1990). Maps for living: Ego development stages from symbiosis to conscious universal embeddedness. In M. L. Commons, C. Armon, L. Kohlberg, F. A. Richards, T.A. Grotzer, & J. D. Sinnott (Eds.),

Adult development, models and methods in the study of adolescent and adult thought, 2 (pp. 79-104). New York: Praeger.

Csikszentmihalyi, M. (1996). *Creativity: Flow and the psychology of discovery and invention.* New York: Harper Collins.

Feldman, D. J. (1994). Creativity: Proof that development occurs. In D. H. Feldman, M., Csikszentmihalyi, & H. Gardner (Eds.), *Changing the world: A framework for the study of creativity* (pp. 85–101). Wesport, CT: Praeger.

Fingarette, H. (1963). *The self in transformation: Psychoanalysis, philosophy, and the life of the spirit.* New York: Harper.

Funk, J. D. (1982). Beethoven: A transpersonal analysis. *ReVision, 5*(1), 29–42.

Funk, J. D. (1989) Post-formal cognitive theory and developmental stages of musical composition. In M. L. Commons, J. D. Sinnott, F. A. Richards, & C. Armon (Eds.), *Adult development: Comparisons and applications of adolescent and adult developmental models* (Vol. 1, pp. 3–30). New York: Praeger.

Funk, J. D. (1991, July). *Music and the near-death experience.* Paper presented at the meeting of the International Association for Near-Death Studies, West Hartford, CT.

Funk, J. D. (1994). Unanimity and disagreement among transpersonal psychologists. In M. E. Miller & S. R. Cook-Greuter (Eds.), *Transcendence and mature thought in adulthood: The further reaches of adult development* (pp. 3–36). Lanham, MD : Rowman & Littlefield.

Gardner, H. (1993). *Creating minds.* New York: Basic Books.

Gebser, J. (1986). *The ever-present origin* (N. Barstad with A. Mickunas, Trans.). Athens, OH: Ohio University Press. (Original work published 1949)

Gemant, A. (1961). *The nature of genius.* Springfield, IL: Thomas.

Ghiselin, B. (Ed.). (1952). *The creative process.* New York: Mentor.

Godwin, J. (1979). Layers of meaning in The Magic Flute. *The Musical Quarterly, 65,* 471–492.

Godwin, J. (1987). *Harmonies of heaven and earth: The spiritual dimensions of music.* Rochester, VT: Inner Traditions International.

Gowan, J. C. (1975). *Trance, art, and creativity.* Buffalo, NY: Creative Education Foundation.

Greene, F. G. (1996). Homer's Odysseus as an ecstatic voyager. *Journal of Near-Death Studies, 14,* 225–250.

Grosso, M. (1985). *The final choice: Playing the survival game.* Walpole, NH: Stillpoint Publishing.

Krippner, S. (1981). Access to hidden reserves of the unconscious through dreams in creative problem solving. *Journal of Creative Behavior, 15,* 11–22.

Kubie, L. (1979). *Neurotic distortion of the creative process.* New York: Farrar, Strauss, & Giroux. (Original work published 1958)

Lauer, H. E. (1989). Mozart and Beethoven in the development of Western culture. In J. Godwin (Ed.), *Cosmic music: Musical keys to the interpretation of reality* (pp. 150–167). Rochester, VT: Inner Traditions.

Leadbeater, C. W. (1979). *The life after death.* Wheaton, IL: Theosophical Publishing House. (Original work published 1912)

Lingerman, H. (1982). *The healing energies in music.* Wheaton, IL: Theosophical Publishing House.

Ludwig, A. M. (1995). *The price of greatness: Resolving the creativity and madness controversy.* New York: Guilford Press.

Maslow, A. H. (1971). *The farther reaches of human nature.* New York: Penguin Books.

Melrose, L. (1989). *The creative personality and the creative process: A phenomenological perspective.* Lanham, MD: University Press of America.

Miller, M. E., & Cook-Greuter, S. R. (1994). From postconventional development to transcendence: Visions and theories. In M. E. Miller & S. R. Cook-Greuter (Eds.), *Transcendence and mature thought in adulthood: The further reaches of adult development* (pp. xv–xxxiv). Lanham, MD : Rowman & Littlefield.

Perkins, D. N. (1981). *The mind's best work.* Cambridge, MA: Harvard University Press.

Shear, J. (1982). The universal structures and dynamics of creativity: Maharishi, Plato, Jung and various creative geniuses on the creative process. *Journal of Creative Behavior, 16,* 155–175.

Simonton, D. K. (1994). *Greatness: Who makes history and why.* New York: Guilford Press.

Sternberg, R. J., & Lubart, T. I. (1995). *Defying the crowd: Cultivating creativity in a culture of conformity.* New York: Free Press.

Storr, A. (1992). *Music and the mind.* New York: Ballantine.

Tame, D. (1984). *The secret power of music.* Rochester, VT: Destiny Books.

Washburn, M. (1988). *The ego and the dynamic ground: A transpersonal theory of human development.* Albany, NY: SUNY Press.

Weisberg, R. W. (1986). *Creativity: Genius and other myths.* New York: W. H. Freeman.

Wilber, K. (1980). *The Atman project.* Wheaton, IL: Theosophical Publishing House.

Wilber, K. (1996). *A brief history of everything.* Boston: Shambhala.

Wilber, K. (1997). *The eye of spirit: An integral vision for a world gone slightly mad.* Boston: Shambhala.

Wilber, K. (1998). *The marriage of sense and soul: Integrating science and religion.* New York: Random House.

Part II

Personal Transformation and Integrity

chapter 5

Ethical Self, Spiritual Self: Wisdom and Integrity in the Writings of Erik H. Erikson

Carol H. Hoare
George Washington University

I ntegrity and wisdom, with a measure of despair and disgust, represent the final resolution of healthy adult identity development in Erik Erikson's concepts. To Erikson, these qualities were interwoven and active. They vie with one another to coexist in a dialectic, sometimes precarious, balance. Together, the attributes characterize the nuclear crisis of what Erikson saw as active, adaptive older adulthood in which ethical and spiritual elders, although soon to die, continue to affirm human life and stand in ongoing wonder and humility before the forces that created and govern them.

To Erikson, the wise person is also, by necessity, an informal leader who shows others "the way" to be and to live. Erikson himself was a sage, a wise and ethical force in his time. Yet, other than when describing the successful resolution of the eighth and last psychosocial stage of developmental life in his various books and articles (e.g., Erikson, 1950, 1963, 1968, 1976), Erikson wrote little, directly, about wisdom as that which emanates from insight and leads to both spirituality and ethical behavior far earlier in adulthood. In fact, it was not until late in his own life that Erikson wrote explicitly about insight, wisdom, and ethics as qualities that, along with care, define the best of adulthood throughout the range of years he had previously described as generativity/stagnation. Nonetheless, ideas

I thank Ray Hoare, my GWU colleague Eugene W. Kelly, Jr., Melvin Miller, and Susanne Cook-Greuter for suggestions that improved this chapter.

about this more generalized form of adult wisdom that are not limited to older adulthood alone are softly planted throughout the body of his work, an oeuvre of thought that, in his post-immigration U.S. period, extended from 1935 to 1985 and included 121 publications.

This chapter synthesizes Erikson's key ideas and concepts about wisdom. I first consider his developmental notion that wisdom, along with hope and faith, is the fruit of successful older adulthood, the accomplishment of a cumulative adult life that had been spent well in work roles, in close intimacy with loved others, and in caring deeply and actively about a few persons, issues, and ideas; such wisdom includes the elder's firsthand knowledge of rejection, the awareness that life and one's society are closing down and excluding the self. After exploring this dominant view of Erikson's on wisdom, I survey his various ideas about the qualities that characterize genuinely perceptive and wise persons in the middle and later years of adult life. For, late in his life, Erikson revised his earlier definition of wisdom and arrived at notions that were different from the early ones in important ways. In his revision, Erikson concluded that wisdom and ethical behavior can and must constitute the accomplishments of earlier adult life if the species is to survive its destructive nuclear inventions. This altered stance of Erikson's came to the fore in his mature years in, for example, his collected papers edited as *Insight and Responsibility* (1964b), in his 1968 address on "Insight and Freedom,"[1] and in his unpublished Harvard papers. Other lesser-known lectures and publications also show his implicit revision (e.g., 1964a).

WISDOM, THE FRUIT OF THE LAST SEASON

In 20th-century thought, particularly in the social sciences, major transformations are inseparable from the originator's belief system, adult stage, and work context at the creative moment. In 1950, when Erik Erikson revised and extended Freud's thought into the unified psychosocial and lifespan theory published as *Childhood and Society*, Erikson was middle-aged. He was culminating a period of study that had focused on children's play constructions and child psychoanalysis, and on the brink of beginning a decade of psychoanalytic work with troubled adolescents and young adults. He had not yet fully conceptualized ego identity and its extension throughout the adult years, nor had he yet experienced his own elder years. Thus, his concept about the ego crisis of older adulthood was based less on professional and personal experience than on established thought and on a projection forward in time of what he conjectured older adulthood would be like. This is important to understanding Erikson's ideas, for his concepts must not be amalgamated as one unified body of thought extending through a half century of writing.

Erikson's first edition of *Childhood and Society* in 1950 included his ideas about ego integrity and wisdom and the early rendition of his eight-stage model (p. 234). In that text, its second edition (1963), and in *Identity: Youth and Crisis* (1968), Erikson wrote that he did not have a "clear definition" of ego integrity (1950, p. 232; 1963, p. 268; 1968, p. 139). However, in *Childhood and Society* he established the position he adhered to, in principle, throughout his life. He wrote:

> Only he who in some way has taken care of things and people and has adapted himself to the triumphs and disappointments adherent to being, by necessity, the originator of others and the generator of things and ideas—only he may gradually grow the fruit of these seven stages. I know no better word for it than ego integrity. (1950, pp. 231–232)

In that statement and in related passages, he implied what he would later say: at his or her ego-consolidated and ego-integrated best, the older adult becomes contemplative and philosophical; such adults leave behind deep passions and old resentments to achieve perspective, acceptance, and a serenity born of their attainments, attainments that are inseparable from commitments born of knowing where one stands in ethical space. Freed from the full-tilt of productive work, elders can enjoy a "liberated wonder"; this includes a slower, deeper experience of time, and a period for new interests and fresh discoveries (Erikson & Erikson, 1978, pp. 7–8).

In his early period of writing, Erikson (1950) described the characteristics of ego integrity as:

> a post-narcissistic love of the human ego—not of the self—as an experience which conveys some world order and spiritual sense, no matter how dearly paid for. It is the acceptance of one's one and only life cycle as something that had to be and that, by necessity, permitted of no substitutions: it thus means a new, a different love of one's parents. It is a comradeship with the ordering ways of distant times and different pursuits, as expressed in the simple products and sayings of such times and pursuits. (p. 232)

In both editions of *Childhood and Society*, Erikson (1950, 1963) did not explicitly claim that wisdom was the exact strength or the best-case resolution of the old-age crisis. Rather, he described wisdom in terms of the leveling ground of older adulthood in which all wise elders hold and share certain understandings:

> Each individual, to become a mature adult, must to a sufficient degree develop all the ego qualities mentioned,[2] so that a wise Indian, a true gentleman, and a mature peasant share and recognize in one another the final stage of integrity. (1950, p. 232)

In that same source, Erikson defined the antithesis of ego integrity as the elder's fear of death, and as despair:

> the one and only life cycle is not accepted as the ultimate of life. Despair expresses the feeling that the time is short, too short for the attempt to start another life and to try out alternate roads to integrity. Disgust hides despair. (1950, p. 232)

Two points bear mentioning before we consider the range of ideas he included under the psychosocial rubric of integrity. First, it is clear that Erikson's developmental concepts were integral to his values (see, e.g., Erikson, 1976, p. 4; 1975, pp. 17–47). Particularly when it came to adults, he held strong convictions about what they *should* do. Erikson was a utopian thinker and a prescriptive theorist. Revising Freudian thought because he was troubled by its fixation on neuroses, its view "backward . . . downward . . . and inward" to controlling instincts and to pathology born of presumed childhood origins, Erikson eschewed the "implicit fatalism" it held (Erikson, 1968/1987, p. 598). He wrote: "I developed some of what I learned, asking: if we know what can go wrong in each stage, can we say what should have gone and can go right?" (Erikson, 1968/1987, p. 595). Thus, as a result of his various case, clinical, historical, and cultural studies, Erikson reasoned that adults can create a better world, one that would nourish and sustain the healthy development of many more humans. He was, of course, particularly interested in providing a better social, physical, and psychological environment for the sustenance and development of children. But he also believed that in creating such a world there are choices adults could and should make that would also improve their own developmental lot and its eventual trajectory. They could choose to love more and to engage more with others instead of isolating themselves; they could elect to care generously and responsibly for others instead of creeping deeply into their self-serving needs; they could choose acceptance of one life and its satisfactions over despair and fear of its end. Thus, he defined old age, in large measure, by the younger adult's own contributions to "self-perfectability" (Erikson & Erikson, 1978, p. 2).

The second point has to do with Erikson's own experiential knowledge as I noted earlier. As is true of every person, the context—of a life and of its needs, perspectives, and resolutions—can only be known in the epoch in which these are experienced. In his middle age, Erikson was much more positive about the stage of older adulthood than when he later experienced it firsthand. Early on, he also kept the "versus" intact in his ideas about each psychosocial crisis. For old age, integrity "versus" despair might well emanate in wisdom if the resolution held more of an ego integration and rather less of despair and of disgust. Later, Erikson quietly removed the "versus." He explained that he was omitting the word because it had confused some readers. To those readers it tended to turn his life stage model into an "'achievement' scale" instead of depicting the polar opposites and nonreductionistic tension he had meant to convey (1984, p. 157). However, especially for older adulthood, revising the resolution into "integrity/despair" (later "integrality/despair"; see Erikson, 1984, p. 163) without its "versus" also meant that Erikson could equilibrate the discrete poles of that stage to better represent the reality he came to know in his own old age. He could then show that integration and disintegration occur together and that there is much less personal control, even psychodynamically, than he had envisioned. Once bodily and mental decline become established, elders are ever less in charge of steering psychosocial resolution in a psychologically healthy, adaptive, direction. By his mid-70s, Erikson was writing about the "daily dread" all elders feel about the proximity of life's end (1976, p. 5). In his early 80s, he wrote that: "the demand to develop Integrity and Wisdom in old age seems to be somewhat unfair, especially when made by middle-aged theorists—as, indeed, we then were" (1984, p. 160).

Integrity and Wisdom through the Lenses of Erikson's Middle and Later Years

Considering the changes in Erikson's thoughts, his ideas about integrity and wisdom must be placed in the context of his age at the time of their publication. By plotting Erikson's observations according to his age and stage of life, both the substantial and subtle changes in his later iterations stand out. This section of the chapter shows Erikson's continuity and his changes in thought based on representative writings, selected because they contain his key ideas about the last stage of life and because they show a 35-year spectrum of thought.

Table 5.1 shows Erikson's various ideas about the final stage of life, its integrity, wisdom, and despair, and the various constituents as he defined them in the representative writings. In keeping with contemporary thought, it has become customary to divide older adulthood into "young-old" age and "old-old" age (see, e.g., Rowe & Kahn, 1998, p. 9) based on Neugarten's (e.g., 1974) distinctions.

Table 5.1   Concepts from Selected Erikson Writings About Ego Integrity, Wisdom, and Despair in Older Adulthood

Erikson's Concepts	Source/Date	His Age & Life Stage[a]
1. "Ego integrity is…the ego's accrued assurance of its proclivity for order. It is a post-narcissistic love of the human ego—not of the self—as an experience which conveys some world order and spiritual sense, no matter how dearly paid for. It is the acceptance of one's one and only life cycle as something that had to be and that, by necessity, permitted of no substitutions." [G & +][b]	1950, p. 232	48; Middle-age
2. "Ego integrity…thus means a new, a different love of one's parents." [G & +]	1950, p. 232	48; Middle-age
3. "Ego integrity…is a comradeship with the ordering ways of distant times and different pursuits, as expressed in the simple products and sayings of such times and pursuits." [G & +]	1950, p. 232	48; Middle-age
4. Ego integrity only "grows" in "he who in some way has taken care of things and people and has adapted himself to the triumphs and disappointments adherent to being, by necessity, the originator of others and the generator of things and ideas" [G & +]	1950, p. 231	48; Middle-age
5. "Despair:…the one and only life cycle is not accepted as the ultimate of life. Despair expresses the feeling that the time is short, too short for the attempt to start another life and to try out alternate roads to integrity. Disgust hides Despair." [G & −]	1950, p. 232	48; Middle-age
6. "Possesses a few principles which though gleaned from changing experience yet prove unchangeable in essence." [G & +]	1959/1964c; p. 95	55; Middle-age
7. "Recognizes" the "worthwhileness of his life"; therefore, can "*die actively*, as the agent of a living cause." [+]	1959/1964c; p. 95	55; Middle-age
8. "Can envisage human problems in their entirety." This is what "integrity means." [+]	1960/1964d, p. 134	56; Middle-age
9. Wisdom, along with Love and Care, are the "central virtues" of the adult years. [G & +]	1960/1964d, p. 115	56; Middle-age
10. Elders use the components of wisdom to "steer" themselves through the last years of life. Wisdom is also a rudder by which elders guide others. [+]	1960/1964d, p. 115	56; Middle-age
11. Wisdom: The "*detached concern with life itself in the face of death itself.*" [G]	1960/1964d, p. 133 & 1968, p. 140 & 1968/1987, p. 609	56; Middle-age

(*continued*)

Table 5.1   (Continued)

Erikson's Concepts	Source/Date	His Age & Life Stage[a]
12. Maintains a "childlikeness" seasoned with wisdom—or...a finite childishness." [G]	1960/1964d, p. 133	56; Middle-age
13. Wisdom: "ripened wits, accumulated knowledge and matured judgment." It is the essence of knowledge freed from temporal relativity." [+]	1960/1964d, p. 133	56; Middle-age
14. Understands the "relativity of all knowledge." [+]	1960/1964d, p. 133 & 1968/1987, p. 608	56; Middle-age
15. Can face the end of life and the transcedence of one life in his or her life in his or her own unique way, without neuroses "caused by emotional exploitation." [+]	1960/1964d, p. 133	56; Middle-age
16. Transcends the "petty disgust of feeling finished and passed by" and the fear of coming "helplessness." [G]	1960/1964d, p. 134	56; Middle-age
17. In this second edition of *Childhood and Society*, Erikson used the same wording as appears in items 1–4 above (*C&S,*1st edition), but changed one meaning in item #4, by substituting "or" for "and" as follows: "...the originator of others or the generator of products and ideas" [G & +]	1963, p. 268	59; Middle-age
18. "To be through having been and having made to be." To face not being." [G]	1968/1987, p. 597	64; Yng old-age
19. Adds "inclusive understanding" to #8 above. [+]	1968/1987, p. 608	64; Yng old-age
20. "Wisdom maintains and conveys the integrity of experience." [+]	1968/1987, p. 608	64; Yng old-age
21. Develops an extended "radius." "Mankind" is now "My Kind." [+]	1968/1987, p. 601	64; Yng old-age
22. "Integrity...implies an emotional integration faithful to the image bearers of the past and ready to take (and eventually to renounce) leadership in the present." [+]	1968/1987, p. 608 & 1968, p. 139	64; Yng old-age
23. "The lack or loss of...accrued integration is signified by a hidden fear of death: fate is not accepted as the frame of life, death not as its finite boundary. Despair indicates that time is too short for alternate roads to integrity: This is why the old try to 'doctor' their memories." [−]	1968/1987, pp. 608-609; Last 2 sentences also in 1976, p. 23	64; Yng old-age
24. "Bitterness and disgust mask...despair, which in severe psychopathology aggravates senile depression, hypochondria, and paranoic hate." [− & P]	1968/1987, p. 609 & in 1976, p. 23 with minor changes	64; Yng old-age
25. "the end of the (life) cycle...evokes 'ultimate concerns,' the paradoxes of which we must leave to philosophical and religious interpreters." [G]	1968/1987, p. 609	64; Yng old-age
26. "acceptance of the fact that one's life is one's own responsibility." [+]	1968, p. 139	64; Yng old-age

(continued)

Table 5.1   (Continued)

Erikson's Concepts	Source/Date	His Age & Life Stage[a]
27. "despair is often hidden behind a show of disgust, a misanthropy, or a chronic contemptuous displeasure with particular institutions and particular people—a disgust and a displeasure which, where not allied with the vision of a superior life, only signify the individual's contempt of himself." [− & P]	1968, p. 140	64: Yng old-age
28. Elders seek "transcendence by renunciation, yet they remain ethically concerned with the 'maintenance of the world.'" [+]	1968, p. 140	64; Yng old-age
29. The integrity crisis is a "new edition of an identity crisis." "I am what survives of me." [G]	1968 p. 141	64; Yng old-age
30. Old age can mean withdrawal from society and, sometimes, from intimacy with one's family. [−]	1976, p. 2	72; Mid old-age
31. Some older adults cling to an "overdefined" adulthood in a work role or profession. This leads one to forfeit intimacy, care of others, or both. [−]	1976, pp. 2 & 10	72; Mid old-age
32. An "inner" and "social discord" may be manifest. [− & P]	1976, p. 5	72; Mid old-age
33. Soon to die, the elder must continue, and sometimes re-learn, to "affirm life." [G]	1976, p. 7	72; Mid old-age
34. Life lived thus far has become deterministic. One's commitments have charted one's fate. There is an awareness that freedom and time to make fresh choices has elapsed. [G]	1976, p. 7	72; Mid old-age
35. The denial of death that characterized the middle years of work, care, and plans, wanes. [G]	1976, p. 7	72; Mid old-age
36. There is "an inner search for, and a wish to communicate with, that mysterious, that Ultimate Other." [G]	1976, p. 11	72; Mid old-age
37. The elder experiences "daily dread" about when life will "suddenly" end. [G]	1976, p. 5	72; Mid old-age
38. In old age, there is the "motivation…to affirm total Despair in order to gain some integrated sense of one's life: for is the life cycle, seen as a whole, perhaps a revelation?" [G & +]	1976, p. 12	72; Mid old-age
39. The elder experiences the "other" in the self; for each man, it is "his own female Self." [G & +]	1976, p. 13	72; Mid old-age
40. Older adults are no longer "defended against the absolute fact of death." [G]	1976, p. 16	72; Mid old-age

(continued)

Table 5.1   (Continued)

Erikson's Concepts	Source/Date	His Age & Life Stage[a]
41. Adults in old age reveal the various fates of "affluence," freedom, and "integration," as well as those of "poverty," "autocracy," "possessiveness," "ossification," and "misery." [G & S]	1976, pp. 16, 25	72; Mid old-age
42. "Wisdom…is the detached and yet active concern with life itself in the face of death itself, and…it maintains and conveys the integrity of experience, in spite of the decline of bodily and mental functions." [G & P]	1976, p. 23	72; Mid old-age
43. "All these (Integrity, Despair, and Wisdom) are ancient words, much too high sounding, it would seem for the experience of the unpretentious, not to speak of the powerless among us." [G & −]	Erikson & Erikson, 1978, p. 4	74; Mid old-age
44. This country "has put such a premium on newness (from the New Man to new products to new ideas, and from the New World to the New Deal and New Spirit) that to be young means to have the choice of always becoming new again and to be old is the loss of the choice." [S & −]	Erikson & Erikson, 1978, p. 3	74; Mid old-age
45. "old age 'Despair,' in some balance with the forces of 'Integrity,' is by no means a pathological or expendable state of mind, to be 'cured' or avoided at all cost: it is an essential component for the stage. For man develops through conflict." [G]	Erikson & Erikson, 1978, p. 4	74; Mid old-age
46. Old age can be a "time of discovery" and of "liberated wonder," a time for expanding the senses, and of "time 'to play with.'" [+]	Erikson & Erikson, 1978, pp. 5,7,8	74; Mid old-age
47. A "sense of Dread;…a sense of Evil;…a sense or lack of a sense, of "I" or existential identity." [−]	1984, pp. 162, 163	80; Old old-age
48. "may fulfill some of the promises of childhood like those which seem to be contained in such sayings as the biblical 'Unless you turn and become like children.'" [G]	1984, p. 156	80; Old old-age
49. "transmits some forms of faith to coming generations." [G & +]	1984, p. 159	80; Old old-age
50. Experiences a *"generalized sensuality"* in the face of declining sexuality. [G]	1984, p. 160	80; Old old-age
51. "Faith" is a syntonic (healthy, adaptive, positive) pole for the integrity stage of older adulthood. [G]	1984, p. 160	80; Old old-age
52. "By the end of life…faith…(is) deeply experienced (and) richly realized." [G & +]	1984, p. 161	80; Old old-age

(continued)

Table 5.1 (Continued)

Erikson's Concepts	Source/Date	His Age & Life Stage[a]
53. The sense of "I": "An individual's uniqueness gradually and often suddenly seems to have lost any leeway for further variations such as those which seemed to open themselves with each previous stage. Now non-being must be faced 'as is'." [G & –]	1984, p. 162	80; Old old-age
54. "time appear(s) forfeited and space depleted quite generally." [G & –]	1984, p. 162	80; Old old-age
55. "The power of Will is weakened; Initiative and Purpose become uncertain; meaningful work is rare; and Identity restricted to what one has been." [G & –]	1984, p. 162	80; Old old-age
56. "fate...can limit the chances...of continued intimacy and of generative (and even 'grand generative') relationships." [G & –]	1984, p. 162	80; Old old-age
57. "the sense of autonomy 'naturally' suffers grievously in old age, as the leeway of independence is constricted." [G & –]	1984, p. 163	80; Old old-age
58. One can "mature" through an "active acceptance of appropriate limitations and a 'wise' choice of involvements in vital engagements of a kind not possible earlier in life." [+]	1984, p. 163	80; Old old-age
59. "Integrity," a sense of coherence and wholeness...is at risk under such terminal conditions of a loss of...somatic, psychic, and social organization." [–]	1984, p. 163	80; Old old-age
60. "Integrality," a readiness to "keep things together." [+]	1984, pp. 163, 164	80; Old old-age
61. "the new and final sense of existential identity (frees one) from the despair associated with unlived or mislived...or overdone identity potentials. [G & –]	1984, p. 163	80; Old old-age
62. "Throughout life...[there is] the gradual maturation of a quality of being, for which integrity does seem to be the right word." [G]	1984, p. 164	80; Old old-age
63. Develops a historical and life-historical identity that mirrors the period in which one lived and the compatriots with whom one shared that era. [G]	1985, p. 7	81; Old old-age
64. Experiences a "sometimes desperate" need to have an "existential identity" that incorporates one's own unique life. [G]	1985, p. 7	81; Old old-age

Notes: [a] Middle-age = 48–59 yrs. of age; Young old-age = 60–64 yrs. of age; Middle old-age = 65–74 yrs. of age; Old old-age = 80+ yrs. of age.

[b] "G" denotes a general idea; "S," a social commentary, "+," a positive resolution, "–," a negative resolution; "P," pathology.

FIGURE 5.1.   Erik H. Erikson

Mobility, reasonably good health, and independent daily functioning characterize the "young-old," while frailty, limited mobility, and largely dependent, poor functional competence characterize the "old-old." Since Erikson enjoyed a longer life and more "successful aging" (see Rowe & Kahn, 1987) than most men of his generational cohort, I divide his elder years into the three periods of young old-age (when he was 60 to 64 years old), middle old-age (when he was 65 to 74 years old), and old old-age (when he was 80+ years old). This division acknowledges his middle old-age during which period he continued to write actively, to teach, and to travel, a period before he experienced society's exclusion of the old.

Some clear trends in Erikson's ideas about the integrity crisis emerge when one peruses Table 5.1 comparing his middle with his elder years. In the writings of his middle-years, when Erikson was 48 to 59 years old, he was more dichotomous about the respective poles of integrity and despair. He was also more prescriptive. He posed separate, discrete resolutions for the separate poles of integrity and of despair, and warned of either/or repercussions: If adults do not produce and care for children, products, or ideas earlier in their adult years, ego integrity could not "grow." In that period, Erikson's writing was far more psychoanalytic and theoretical than later. He wrote in a manner that shows his personal detachment from the realities of the older years of life. In his later years, Erikson softened his stance. He portrayed a more balanced perspective, writing that both integrity and despair are joint, everyday experiences. Together, he found, they result in a wisdom about life, its coherence, riches, and travails that are qualitatively much more than "terminal clarity" (1976, p. 26). His writing then showed his understanding that one can observe but should not prescribe for, or judge, seniors. They are likely doing the best they can in life's most difficult era of losses, a stage of life that one cannot know until one is immersed in it as a participant. Then, prior prescriptions about what the old "should" do disappear in the humility of knowing, firsthand, myriad deprivations and losses.

A second trend emerges when one compares the changing tone of Erikson's writings in his 48- to 64-year-old period (middle age through early old-age) with that of his later years of 72 to 81 (middle old-age through late old-age). His writings on the integrity crisis in his earlier period are much more positive; those in his later period are more negative. Excluding the concepts classified as "general," as "social commentary," or as "pathological" manifestations of aging, for his early and middle old-age (48 to 64 years old), there are 19 statements that portray a positive resolution, content, or tone, and 4 that convey negative content or affect. In his middle old- to old old-age (72 to 81 years old), this trend is reversed. There are 13 negative and 6 positive statements for that period. Again, I interpret this as a manifestation that the experience of aging took its toll on Erikson. As is true of all who live to experience advanced life and write honestly about it, Erikson had to give loss its due: Bodily deterioration, mental slowing, declining control, an increasingly peripheral social position, and daily thoughts about death became more important to his ideas. By his mid-70s, retired against his preferences and prohibited from traveling at will to freely participate in the intellectual exchanges he so cherished, he had abandoned both the balanced psychoanalytic thinking he had clung to earlier in life as well as many of the positives he had posed, in his prime, for the elder years.

We will now look to the facets of Erikson's ideas about integrity and wisdom that he held to over time and to those he added, expanded, softened, or deleted. Figure 5.2 shows a synopsis of the continuities and changes in Erikson's views at various points in his writing. Based on the content of his writing and his distance or experiential closeness to the realities of the integrity/despair crisis, I have separated Erikson's thoughts about wisdom, integrity, and despair into three periods. The first is his theoretical, developmentally optimistic period in which he indeed portrayed integrity versus despair as either/or poles of accomplishment. By the end of this highly theoretical period of his writing, Erikson was 59 years old. He was then barely on the brink of older adulthood and just about to begin his most prolific Harvard decade of writing, teaching, and presenting lectures and seminars throughout the United States and abroad.

For the second period of his writing, Erikson had become a more realistic theorist. This was the beginning portion of his older years (age 64) in which he stayed close to his theory. He refrained from incorporating into his psychosocial tenets the needs of elders for spirituality, belief in God, and faith in transcendence; he retained the "versus" for each of the eight psychosocial crises. Yet, his writing changed: Death became closer to the surface of his thought, not just as a concept but in words that expressed each elder's reality, that of looking at death face-to-face. In this later writing period, Erikson showed his concern for rejection, distress, and psychopathology among the old. And he juxtaposed the elder against the "Ultimate Other" (God).

The last period of his writing, when he was 72 to 81 years of age, shows the fullness of an experiential-existential thinker. In this period, Erikson radically altered his ideas. By that time, Erikson was, and felt, marginalized. He understood seniors' ongoing needs to be included; yet he also understood just how much the elder's choices are constricted and how society devalues and excludes seniors and their life experiences and values. As a result, the society and culture that the younger Erik Erikson had built carefully into his theory as anchoring points and fuel for child and adolescent development finally became central to his ideas about life's last stage as well. In this final of his writing periods, Erikson also gave faith and an existential, transcendent identity a paramount position. His writing shows an Erikson who was no longer constrained by either the quasi-objectivity of psychoanalytic theory or its phobic distance from faith and belief in God. He came as close as he would to abandoning the intellectual tradition of mainstream psychoanalysis which saw human belief in a deity as a projection of human need. God might just be real.

CHANGES

AGE 48

Is highly theoretical, detached, and psycho-analytically developmental: For old age, Wisdom and Integrity are couched in possibility: Adults can "grow" their later development.

Defines poles sharply —
• Integrity vs. Despair
• Either/Or thinking:
1. Either be Intimate and then Care for products, ideas, and children or suffer old age despair.
2. If can find one life meaningful and worthy, transcendence and Wisdom follow. If not, despair results.

AGE 55–60

Remains theoretical, psychoanalytical, and optimistically positive about the last stage and its resolutions.

Adds five constituents:
1. Wise elders possess a few principles that have held across time and changing experiences.
2. Wisdom is a guidance system for self and others.
3. Wisdom is a "ripening."
4. Integrity means seeing "human problems in their entirety."
5. Wise elders understand the "relativity of knowledge."

AGE 80

Revises Childhood and Society. *Holds to his original position at age 48 but indicates that:*

Adults need not procreate to achieve Care, Integrity, and Wisdom.

AGE 84

Is more reality- and less theory-based. Writes more about old age itself and less about Integrity and Wisdom. Beginning of change in tone. Softens denial of own death, writes about psycho-pathology in some elderly.

Adds six constituents:
1. Elderly look "not being" squarely in the eye.
2. Psycho-pathology aggravates bitterness, despair in some seniors.
3. Elders accept responsibility for own lives.
4. The old affirm life but renounce the world.
5. Disgust and rejection of others by some elders reflects self-rejection.
6. "Ultimate Concerns" are central to seniors; however, Erikson says he must leave this to philosophers and theologians.

A theoretical, developmentally optimistic period
about integrity, wisdom, and despair in old age

His realistic,
theoretical period

CONTINUITIES

1. Along with Love and Care, Wisdom is a central strength of the adult years.
2. Ego-integrated elders remain concerned about the maintenance and continuance of the world and the species. This carries an ethical position of affirming all life and, in particular, of affirming human life.
3. Integrity means an acceptance of life, a comradeship with others, and an expanded identification with mankind. Facing the dread of having to die and of death, it also means the desire to keep oneself psychologically together.
4. Integrity requires that elders transmit faith and hope to the young.

**FIGURE 5.2 Integrity, Wisdom, and Despair:
Erikson's Thought, 1950–1985**

AGE 80-81

Erikson is old. He shows Integrity and Wisdom through his own eyes of acceptance, transcendence, and the experience of disintegration and loss. He gives a sense of evil its due, notes that "sensuality" can replace sexuality, and, no longer at great psychoanalytic distance from belief, gives faith high berth.

He makes ten changes or emphasis points:
1. A sense of "I" or of its absence is now an existential "I." An existential identity is a deep need for transcendence, and it frees one from the despair of an imperfectly developed earthly identity.
2. He finds that the quality of being matures in the elder years.
3. Erikson writes that elders may sense evil.
4. The biblical sense of "turning back" to become like children assumes new importance to him.
5. He and Joan note that elders can experience a "generalized sensuality" that replaces genital sexuality.
6. "Faith" becomes an alternate term for Integrity; He notes that elders experience faith richly and deeply.
7. He notes the loss of "a sense of I," of individuality; He writes that elders feel depleted of time, space, and the strengths of many earlier stages of life as they face non-being.
8. Elders' transmission of faith to the young carries more weight in his writing.
9. "Integrality," replaces "integrity" in his work.
10. He writes of elders' historical identity, one that reflects the era in which they lived and an identification with those who shared that historical era.

AGE 74

Is marginalized. Sounds more authentic and less defensive. He notes that being old runs counter to U.S. "culture," builds in the joy of childlike discovery, and writes that despair is not expendable.

His four revisions:
1. "Ancient terms" such as Integrity, Wisdom, and Despair are too lofty for the "powerless" and "unpretentious" experience of elders.
2. "To be old means the loss of choice." He juxtaposes this against the U.S. valuation of newness, rejuvenation, re-invention, change, and choice.
3. There are playful, child-like possibilities of old-age wonder and discovery for those open to them.
4. Despair is essential in old age. It balances integrity.

AGE 72

Is newly marginalized and no longer integral to the institutions that foster identity. He alters thinking to build in God, Jungian thought, daily dread, fate, re-learning, U.S. society, and wonder.

Nine additions and changes:
1. "Inner discord" may reflect the peripheralizing of the old by U.S. society.
2. Some elderly withdraw from society and, sometimes, family.
3. Seniors may have to re-learn how to affirm life.
4. Elders are aware of no time left for fresh choices or paths to integrity.
5. Elders wish to communicate with the "Ultimate Other" (God).
6. There is "daily dread" about life's end. Many experience the desire to embrace total despair; this can rejuvenate elders to affirm life.
7. Elders experience the other gender in the self.
8. Fate has played a hand in life opportunities and current resources.
9. Elders' knowing firsthand their own integrity of experience and unity of principles edge out Erikson's earlier lofty ideas about ego-integrity as a "post-narcissistic love of the human ego" and meta understanding of human problems and knowledge relativity.

An existential-experiential era of writing

5. The wisdom of integrity implies a "cogwheeled" link with other generations and beings.
6. Integrity means the coherence of each life as a seamless tapestry. In this, there is an epigenetic and a memorial principle. Human life builds and unfolds in a narrative of meaning-making, of biopsychosocial potentials, of identifications and identity, of conscious and unconscious knowledge, and of memory.
7. Integrity invokes the acceptance of one's life as that which was, had to be, and could not be replaced by any other life.

8. Wisdom emanates from living each stage of adult life intelligently, lovingly, caringly, and fully.
9. The last stage of life is shaped in part by the legacy of assets and bankruptcies of earlier stages and by the assets and maladaptations that were passed along from the nuclear family (and progenitors) into which one was fatefully born.
10. At the far fringe of life, integrated elders give dread and death their due while continuing to live as vitally and actively as possible.

FIGURE 5.2   (Continued)

In this last period, Erikson departed both Freudian thought and his own earlier notions. He built the Jungian gender-other into the self of the elder years. He wrote of wonder, sensuality, and the joy of discovery as possibilities for elders' development. And, he gave fate a greater role: The accident of a person's birth into a particular family, his or her early and later social position and resources, and life in a particular historical period carried greater weight in his thought. He then showed his understanding that some elders might well have had opportunities that paved a road toward ego integrity and wisdom while, for others, their pathways had been seeded with such trauma and psychosocial deprivations that they eventually were led to a greater share of disgust and despair. Corresponding to this, he gave old adults latitude for being "childish" instead of "childlike" when fate had dealt them the blows of senility, forced isolation, psychopathology, or some mix of all three.

Looking across Figure 5.2 and its three eras, as he moved from middle-age to the most elderly of his writing years, one finds Erikson's writing to have become more elaborative about the elder years, less distanced and lofty, and more authentic. By the time he was 80 to 81 years old, not only was Erikson himself experienced about aging, but he was then conducting some of the interviews of elders whose resolutions led to *Vital Involvement in Old Age* (Erikson, Erikson, & Kivnick, 1984), the book that Joan Erikson would write for them. As his Harvard papers[3] show, many of those elders were home-bound and socially peripheral. They added another personal reality to that of his own experience.

In the last of his writing periods, Erikson abandoned his 1960 view that elders see "human problems in their entirety" (1964b, p. 134) and gave up his notion that wisdom includes understandings about the relativity of knowledge (1964b, p. 133).[4] Faith then becomes integrity's companion. A transcendent identity replaces adults' earlier vocationally based identity. This includes a freeing, self-accepting permission to forgive oneself for identity missteps earlier in life. And, writing about sensuality, Erikson framed for us a new view, one of psychosensual pleasure instead of psychosocial resolutions alone. Erikson loved the experience of nature. This led him eventually to show how touching, seeing, hearing, smelling, and tasting nature in a new and joyful way could become resources that might fill in some of the space that is otherwise depleted in the elder years. This, as Joan Erikson showed in her book, *Wisdom and the Senses* (1988), is a different form of wisdom.

Just as there are changes in his thoughts about wisdom and integrity over time, there is considerable consistency in ideas that Erikson held to resolutely in his various writings. Those continuities appear at the bottom of Figure 5.2. Briefly, Erikson had changed his mind about the meaning of integrity and wisdom among those who are old, but he did not abandon these strengths as essential adaptive virtues of the adult years. In the writings reviewed and in other works, he noted that elders need to remain ethically concerned about the maintenance and continuance of the species and of the world, that they need to accept one life, that they need to try to keep themselves together in the face of decline and the proximity of death, and that they need the experience of continuity with other humans. This continuity, and its ongoing ego investment, included an expanded sense of identification with humankind, a transmitting of faith to the young, and ongoing, active concerns for the welfare of family, friends, and the species. Erikson never abandoned his belief that all adults, varying according to their stages of life and social positions, should contribute their active care so as to maintain their own portion of the world and their "cogwheeled" link to persons in other generations. Throughout, he consistently depicted life as a seamless tapestry that led to an eventual wholeness, unity, and rounding-out. He continued to believe that many of each elder's resolutions were shaped by earlier adult work in intimate and generative encounters. Although he was more explicit in his later than in his earlier writing, Erikson did not dispute his earlier thinking about epigenesis or about each human life that unfolds according to a preexisting design and groundplan. Throughout his 121 publications, Erikson wrote about the needs of all adults, no matter what their life stages might be, to function actively, adaptively, and vitally. To him, taking up residence at the far end of life's continuum meant living in as engaged a way as one could, all the while giving death, dread, the "Ultimate Other," faith, hope, and the wisdom of perspective their respective places. To Erikson, this helped to keep the elder "integrally" together as she or he faced the otherwise tragic reality of life's ending.

INSIGHT, WISDOM, AND ETHICS IN GENERATIVE ADULTHOOD

In order to place Erikson in the overall context of his thinking about wisdom, several points bear mentioning. These have to do with Erikson's intentions and needs and with the way he worked and thought, for Erikson the man is inseparable from his concepts. First, I underscore the importance to Erikson of keeping his psychosocial view and thought intact. As Coles (1970) said, Erikson understood early in his creative life that "truth" is in constant flux, that no truth or "fact" will permanently resist revision, and that a point of view, a way of inquiring, and a manner of looking at things and seeing are far more enduring. Erikson's way of seeing was visual-spatial, psychoanalytic, and developmental. His mode of inquiry was psychoanalytic, scholarly, and inductive. His point of view was that healthy development can be nurtured, that adults can improve their own and others' development. Insofar as Erikson cared deeply about his viewpoint and way of seeing, he wished to ensure the continuity of his thought. His theory was the important product of his and Joan's middle years; therefore, he could not abandon it nor would he refrain from saying what it was that humans had to do to ensure the best for themselves in the last years of life. This necessarily meant caring deeply about others and about those ideas, products, and principles for which one stood. Erikson would have been nongenerative in his own eyes if he had failed to care for and nurture that which he had so carefully origi- nated and deeply meant. As a result, he largely held to and defended his original position, and his various psychosocial terms and meanings. He continued to permit words such as wisdom to describe only that which would lead the reader to rationally and pre-consciously agree with the messages and interpretations he planted. Thus, the word wisdom held its singular meaning throughout most of Erikson's writing life. Until his 80s, Erikson held that wisdom was the outcome of the last stage of life. Yet in studying Erikson carefully, one finds his notation that wisdom emanates from insight. As such, wisdom can be found throughout the adult years in those who are disposed to develop insight, to depend on insight as a form of knowing, and to permit insight to lead to responsible, ethical behavior. Erikson refrained from using the actual term "wisdom" throughout the bulk of his writing to describe the outcome of important qualities such as prudence, sustained reflection, sensitivity to the needs of others, sound judgment, and responsible action. These, among other attributes of the wise, are nonetheless found in his writings, primarily in his psychobiographies.

Exploring Erikson's view of wisdom as a quality that is found in some throughout their adulthood years, the student of Erikson must think somewhat as he had done and look to the major influences on his thought. First, Erikson was interested in etymology, in the meaning, ori- gin, and development of words. This interest emanated from his careful scholarship and from his forced transmigration through several languages in youth and early adulthood. His first language had been Danish. He then learned German and grew up, cognitively/linguistically, in that tongue. On immigration to the U.S. well into his adult years, he learned to write and to think in English. This is important, for through- out Erikson's work, we find him looking up words in both English and German dictionaries as he wrote.

Erikson's alignment of insight with wisdom came partially from his knowledge that *wis*, and its earlier *wys*, come from *vise*, the pluperfect stem of *videre* which means "to see" (*Compact Edition of the Oxford English Dictionary*, 1971, p. 3794). *Wis* also derives from "moral" and "certain."

It refers to those who show others the way by directing, guiding, leading, or by exemplifying prudent conduct (p. 3794). *Dom* is a "title of honor" (p. 785). In German, *Weise* means a wise person or sage; *Weisheit* is wisdom or prudence (*Cassell's German Dictionary*, 1996, p. 278). Thus "wisdom" is an honorific that is attributed to those who can see and who, in their behavior, show others a depth of discernment and a high road of conduct worth emulating. As Erikson knew, such wisdom becomes a preferential, consistent way of life. It is the embodiment of what he described as the ethical adult, he or she who cares responsibly for others and the world, a care exemplified to him in the Galilean Jesus and, in different ways, by Mahatma Gandhi, Martin Luther, and Martin Luther King, Jr.

A second point about Erikson and his choice of words is that he did not feel compelled to honor any standard term. When words seemed inadequate to his needs, Erikson might change a meaning or, at other times, make up his own words to replace inadequate terms. With respect to insight and to wisdom, Erikson was at odds with his dictionary. His thinking came through most clearly in his "Insight and Freedom" address at the University of Cape Town, South Africa, on August 6, 1968. It was the 23rd anniversary of the bombing of Hiroshima and not long after the Cuban Missile Crisis. In the United States, John and Robert Kennedy and Martin Luther King, Jr., had recently been assassinated; involvement in and protests of the Vietnam War were then escalating; and civil rights protests had peaked. Erikson was 66 years old. Increasingly, he feared that the human species might well destroy itself. To lend his own insight to the causes of peace, disarmament, and equality, he had conducted recently a psychohistorical study of Mahatma Gandhi and his militant, nonviolent strategies that wrought social change (see Erikson, 1969). All of these factors led him to reposition wisdom earlier in the adultspan.

In his "Insight and Freedom" speech Erikson (1975) brought three items to light. First, he defined insight, changing the dictionary's meaning to portray his own post-Freudian interpretation:

> when my Webster tells me that insight is the power or act of seeing into a situation *or* myself, I would unhesitatingly talk back to my Webster and say that true insight is the power or act of seeing into a situation *and* into myself *at the same time*: for the two are, in fact, one power, one act. (p. 173)

Thus, to Erikson, insight meant a way of knowing and both a habit and style of cognitive functioning. In that source and elsewhere, Erikson wrote of insight as the path to wisdom.

Second, Erikson wrote that wisdom can be acquired and, in fact, must be acquired earlier than the last stage of life if humanity is to survive its aggressiveness and ethnocentrism, and the diversion of these into nuclear weapons. In this and other works, Erikson wrote that knowledge, if that is all we have, inculcates slavery to the overly intellectualized methods by which it is acquired. Perceptions, insight, empathy, and integrity are then too easily obscured or compromised. Erikson's original placement of wisdom as occurring last among life's strengths had been partly based on Socrates' observations that insight is based on, but comes after, knowledge. However, by 1968 Erikson was compelled to reframe wisdom. By the time of his South African speech, Erikson placed the accomplishment of wisdom squarely in the center of both human affairs and the ethical, generative years of each person's life. In a way, he moved from Socrates to Kierkegaard and to the high ideology of his own identity construct. He argued that insight and wisdom develop after, but come from, ideological convictions in youth and from the passionate beliefs and interests of young adulthood. Although these changes were later edited out of Erikson's 1975 published version (see "Freedom and Nonviolence," pp. 169–189), in his Capetown lecture he said that one need not be advanced in years to possess either insight or wisdom. Drawing examples from Freud and Gandhi, Erikson wrote that the prodigious creations and leadership that come to fruition in the middle and later years truly emanate from the knowledge, insight, and deep fervor that had existed in young adulthood.

In his later years, Erikson searched for but did not find the origins and developmental antecedents of insight, wisdom, and ethics. But he did describe the wise person in many of his writings. To Erikson, wisdom was based on self- and other-reflective observations that emanate in insight and lead to responsibility (ethical action). He found that wise adults possess perceptual acuity that frequently permit them to see to the heart of a matter. Such persons are careful observers and listeners. They are temperate, refraining from quick responses, impulsive decisions, or immediate conclusions. They do not judge or stereotype others. They treat others as ends instead of as means to an end. They hold to principles and human values and keep these intact in a material world. They behave authentically, eschewing affectations born of pretense or of the defensive need to appear as other than they are. They care deeply about others in a manner that does not expect a quid pro quo exchange in like kind.

Wise adults are spiritual persons and moral leaders. Without necessarily choosing leadership roles, they tend to be those who others look to and emulate as role models, for their consistently principled behavior shows high ideals, courage, purpose, and unswerving conviction that is worth following. Among the wise, Erikson described adults who value knowledge and who sublimate other desires to attain it; yet they are aware of the limits of knowledge and understand, as well, that wisdom does not emanate from the accretion of knowledge, years of life, or educational credentials. He found that this awareness necessarily results in humility instead of self-aggrandizement.

To Erikson, the rare wise adult knows that adulthood, in its role and stability requirements, extracts the price of conformity and seriousness and the loss of some essential elements of the child within. Erikson admired those few adults who had maintained a childlike sense of wonder, a freshness of appreciation, and the ability to see things anew. He found the older-adult maintenance of childlike wisdom in the wide-eyed face of Albert Einstein and in the late-life paintings of Henri Matisse. He reminded readers of the wisdom of the trusting infant and the still-hopeful, childlike, faith-filled elder. This continuity through time was expressed to him by the name and teachings of Lao-Tse, the ancient Chinese sage whose name means "old child" (Erikson, 1982, pp. 78–79).

In the years following his Capetown address, Erikson did not explicitly reposition wisdom earlier in life, nor did he seem to believe that it could arrive as early as young adulthood within that stage's intimacy/isolation resolutions. It remained his Kierkegaard-based belief that young adults hold only the rudiments of wisdom and ethics. He remained convinced, it seems, that one must have some others, some products, and some prevailing ideas and principles about which to care deeply before the wisdom that is itself inherent in ethical generativity is possible. Yet, he wrote that passion about such cares must be maintained, for any one who lacks "intense convictions" is but a "robot with destructive techniques" (Erikson, 1958, p. 209).

The space of one chapter does not permit rounding out Erikson's views by showing how his thoughts about developmental insight, wisdom, ethics, and the experiencing of the "Ultimate" were influenced by various philosophers, mystics, religious thinkers, visionaries, and political activists. Beyond those mentioned (Freud, Socrates, Kierkegaard, Gandhi, Luther, King, Einstein, Jesus, biblical sources, the dictionary, and Joan Erikson), other thinkers who were of considerable influence on his ideas about wisdom and ethics were Aristotle, St. Augustine, Kant, Aquinas, and ancients from as early as the 6th century B.C. Erikson had one additional source for his thoughts about insight as that which must emanate in wisdom and ethical action. This was Erikson himself, the theorist who psychoanalyzed himself as the subject of his own insight, wisdom, and creativity.

Closing out this examination of Erikson's views about that interrelated set of attributes he linked together—insight, wisdom, ethics, and a sense of the Ultimate—two closing comments about his thoughts are in order. First, as is true about those whom we call adult, if the term wisdom is to hold any significance at all, its attribution must come from other than the "wise" person. No one who is truly wise will claim to be so. Rather, he or she is said by others to manifest such qualities. Erikson knew this. His work manifests the wisdom of ancient thought brought into contemporary times through the psychoanalytic lens, discoveries achieved through his use of that lens, and his developmental knowledge about humans.

Second, as Erikson himself said, he was a developmental psychoanalyst. He understood that insight into the unconscious self and its motivations, however incomplete, is essential to each human and to the entire species. As a visionary, he believed he saw evidence that humans as a species were becoming more consciously aware of themselves, their motivations and needs, their unconscious rages, and their need for a wider, collective human identity. Ethical growth requires that the species develop a view of one universal humankind. It is a view he pressed consistently. To Erikson, every qualitative leap in human awareness, individually or for the species, necessarily carries responsibility. Hence, the title of his book: *Insight and Responsibility* (1964b).

It seems clear that Erikson scripted a developmental trajectory of enhanced insight, wisdom, and ethics for the adult years but understood that these could come too late in life. He believed that "in office" one should function as a Confucian, and "in retirement" as a Taoist (1964b, p. 132). The Confucian is the "pole-star" (Waley, 1938, p. 88), an honorable guidance system for others. The Taoist is transcendent. In retirement it is too late to influence much of the world. Therefore, insight, wisdom, and ethics have to be subtly repositioned for they are essential in the central portion of adulthood when others can see and model the acts through which these are revealed.

NOTES

1. Erikson's "Insight and Freedom" lecture of 1968 was edited and later published as "Freedom and Nonviolence" in Erikson, 1975, pp. 169–189.

2. By saying "all the ego qualities mentioned," Erikson meant the resolutions of the seven prior stages.

3. In particular, see item 95M-2 of the Papers of Erik and Joan Erikson, Harvard University.

4. Erikson's belief in 1960 (published in 1964b) that elders see "human problems in their entirety" and that they understand the "relativity of knowledge" may have been due, respectively, to his meetings with Piaget in 1955 and to his own understanding of relativity and of the ways in which Einstein's concepts of physical relativity found their way into Freud's thought and his own.

REFERENCES

Cassell's German dictionary (Concise ed.). (1996). New York: Macmillan.

Coles, R. (1970, November 14). The measure of the man. *The New Yorker, 64.*

The compact edition of the Oxford English dictionary. (1971). New York: Oxford University Press.

Erikson, E. H. (1950). *Childhood and society.* New York: Norton.

Erikson, E. H. (1958). *Young man Luther.* New York: Norton.

Erikson, E. H. (1963). *Childhood and society* (2nd ed.). New York: Norton.

Erikson, E. H. (1964a). The golden rule and the cycle of life. In R.W. White (Ed.), *The study of lives* (pp. 412–428). New York: Atherton Press. (Originally the George W. Gay Lecture on Medical Ethics, Harvard University, 1963)

Erikson, E. H. (1964b). *Insight and responsibility.* New York: Norton.

Erikson, E. H. (1964c). Identity and uprootedness in our time. In E. H. Erikson, *Insight and responsibility* (pp. 83–107). New York: Norton. (Originally an address given as a plenary session at the World Federation of Mental Health, University of Vienna, 1959)

Erikson, E. H. (1964d). Human strength and the cycle of generations. In E. H. Erikson, *Insight and responsibility* (pp. 111–157). New York: Norton. (Originally a lecture given for the Psychoanalytic Institute and the Mt. Zion Medical Center, San Francisco, 1960)

Erikson, E. H. (1968). *Identity: Youth and crisis.* New York: Norton.

Erikson, E. H. (1969). *Gandhi's truth.* New York: Norton.

Erikson, E. H. (1975). *Life history and the historical moment.* New York: Norton.

Erikson, E. H. (1976). Reflections on Dr. Borg's life cycle. *Daedalus, 105,* 1–28.

Erikson, E. H. (1981). The Galilean sayings and a sense of "I." *The Yale Review, 70,* 361–362.

Erikson, E. H. (1982). *The life cycle completed.* New York: Norton.

Erikson, E. H. (1984). Reflections on the last stage—and the first. In *The Psychoanalytic study of the child, 39,* (pp. 155–165). New York: International Universities Press.

Erikson, E. H. (1985). Afterthoughts 1985. In E. H. Erikson, *Childhood and society* (35th anniversary edition of 2nd ed.) (pp. 7–11). New York: Norton.

Erikson, E. H. (1987). The human life cycle. In S. Schlein (Ed.), *A way of looking at things* (pp. 595–610). New York: Norton. (Original work published 1968).

Erikson, J. M. (1988). *Wisdom and the senses: The way of creativity.* New York: Norton.

Erikson, E. H., & Erikson, J. M. (1978). Introduction: Reflections on aging. In S. Spicker, K. Woodward, & D. Van Tassel (Eds.), *Aging and the elderly, humanistic perspectives in gerontology*, (pp. 1–8). New Jersey: Humanities Press.

Erikson, E. H., & Erikson, J. (1987). Papers. Harvard University.

Erikson, E. H., Erikson, J. M., & Kivnick, H. Q. (1986). *Vital involvement in old age*. New York: Norton.

Neugarten, B. L. (1974). Age groups in American society and the rise of the young-old. *The Annals of the American Academy of Political and Social Science, 415*, 187–198.

Rowe, J. W., & Kahn, R. L. (1987). Human aging: Usual and successful. *Science, 237*, 143–149.

Rowe, J. W., & Kahn, R.L. (1998). *Successful aging*. New York: Pantheon Books.

Waley, A. (1938). *The analects of Confucius*. London: George Allen & Unwin.

chapter 6

Edith Kramer—Artist and Art Therapist: A Search for Integrity and Truth

Melvin E. Miller
Norwich University

Susanne R. Cook-Greuter

> Art is my destiny; Art therapy is my beloved profession.
> —Edith Kramer

Edith Kramer at 82 is gracious, articulate, poised, and self-assured. It is a rare and awesome pleasure to meet an artist, therapist, writer, teacher, innovator, and explorer of such caliber. Kramer's activities have bridged continents, integrated disciplines, and crossed domains of expression,[1] yet meeting her casually one might not be able to distinguish her from other people of advanced years.

We met with Edith Kramer because we wanted to learn what influenced her and brought her to art, and what has engaged her for a lifetime. We hope to sketch the expanse of Kramer's theoretical and creative explorations and to document how she pursued her inspirations and followed a path of integrity in both her art and in her scholarly work. We wonder how any person of her complexity and brilliance man-

We thank Gladys Agell, Edith Kramer, and Loren Miller for their helpful comments and suggestions on earlier versions of this chapter. In addition, we also express our appreciation for the many hours of transcription work contributed by Sharon Dickinson, Administrative Assistant for Counseling and Psychological Services at Norwich University, and many thanks to Alan Stubbs from the University of Maine, for his generous, professional assistance with the photographs of Edith and her work.

FIGURE 6.1.   Edith Kramer in her studio, December 1997

ages to develop a good life. In this context, we hope to illuminate parts of her background and her personality that made her who she is and allowed her to live such a singular, exemplary life. Moreover, the positive energy and indomitable spirit that Edith Kramer embodies can be an inspiration for all of us who wish to find a path to wisdom and integrity as we age.

Edith Kramer, according to her own account, is an artist by destiny and by temperament. From the earliest years of her life, she was convinced that she would become an artist. "Art is my destiny; there was no question as to what I would become." She has dedicated her life to the study and practice of her art with "precision, diligence, and honesty" (Halevi, Waymire, & Conners, 1994). From childhood through the current stage of her life, Ms. Kramer has kept to her vision of the artist with single-minded dedication. Today we marvel at her many sculptures and paintings, and at her seminal contributions to the field of art therapy.

But Edith Kramer is still evolving as an artist. At 82 she works daily in her lower West Side Manhattan studio, usually walking there from her apartment 30 minutes away. It was in that studio on a bright, early winter day in December of 1997 that we had the pleasure to meet with Kramer, conduct an interview, and attempt to take in and assimilate the numerous paintings, etchings, sculptures, mosaics, and works-in-progress that were on hand. Most of the information in this essay comes from that interview;[2] other details derived from subsequent contacts with the artist.

Interviewing Edith Kramer was a challenging and, at times, baffling experience. Although she was most gracious, cooperative, and frank, it was also clear that she was fully in control of the interview and intended to remain so. She seemed to know exactly what she wanted to say—what she wanted us to know about her and her history. At times it appeared as though she wanted to dictate the precise slant on the information revealed in the interview process. When she did not want to answer a question we posed, she skillfully put it aside and we did not press, respecting her cues. As a result, several potentially important events in her life remain in the shadows.

Kramer talked to us and fed us that afternoon. In fact, as we write this, we are reminded of the luncheon she served. On the way to her studio earlier that morning, she had bought some cheeses and European bread. After she spread these offerings before us, she picked up a large, round loaf, clutched it to her chest, and began to saw off slices for us. As she did it, Susanne recognized this as the way women in the old country have cut bread for generations. Kramer instructed us in many different ways that afternoon as she led us artfully on a tour through her studio and her life. We quickly developed a great appreciation and fondness for this marvelously complex woman—a fondness that deepened through each subsequent contact with her. We imagine, and we hope, that some measure of our admiration for Kramer as a vital person is reflected in this chapter.

In this chapter we explore how Ms. Kramer became such a rare and exceptional individual. We start out by touching on the primary periods and influences that shaped her before she came to the United States and then examine what has enabled her to create, consistently and exquisitely, throughout her adulthood.

The following are some of the questions we attempt to address: What circumstances and personal traits allowed her to pursue success and fulfillment as an artist? What people, conditions, and ideas supported and challenged her? In the end, we plan to show how Kramer is a living model of what it means to be an inspired, mature creator—a topic that other chapters in this book explore theoretically. Thus, we hope to contribute a qualitative study to current knowledge of the factors that inform creativity and the beliefs and feelings about art and life espoused by a creative person.

THE BACKDROP OF AN ARTIST'S LIFE

Kramer was born in Vienna, Austria, on August 29, 1916—in the midst of the chaos and turmoil of the First World War. She was the daughter of Josefine Kramer-Neumann and Richard Kramer. Due to family disruptions related to the war, Kramer spent her early years living with her grandparents in Vienna where she attended a Volksschule. Kramer describes being raised in a Bohemian environment, an environment in which "doing things like painting or acting was the norm." Her childhood friend, Maria Feder, however, remarked that Kramer had a certain kind of "inventiveness" that went beyond the norm and that she couldn't be without "doing something with her hands" (Halevi, Waymire, & Conners, 1994).

Her energetic and creative mother was involved with the arts in general, and was especially supportive of Edith's artistic involvement. Kramer noted that "art was very important between us—as if art were a kind of language or currency mother and daughter could share and understand. Kramer described her mother as an "interesting, witty, fragile, and seductive woman." Information gathered from the interview and other sources suggests that Kramer's relationship with her mother was very complex. She seemed to both love and admire her mother greatly, and, at the same time, be troubled by her seductiveness. Her mother's suicide in 1937, when Kramer was 20 years old, likely compounded further the ambivalent feelings she held toward her mother and motherhood.

Her father, a "communist and an intellectual," worked steadfastly for the party in its early years, sharing with Kramer a spirit of political activism and a keen social awareness. Her father parted ways with the communist party around 1930. Another central figure in Kramer's childhood was her mother's sister Elisabeth. "Aunt Liesel" was a professional character actress, playing roles in both theater and film. It was Liesel who stimulated Kramer's interest in the arts early on, and remained an active presence in her personal and emotional life by offering support and encouragement throughout Liesel's life, until her death in 1994.

Thus, Kramer describes herself as having had an "interesting, stimulating, not simple, complicated childhood" (Halevi, Waymire, & Conners, 1994). She mentioned that "it just wasn't anything outlandish for me to do painting—or anything else, for that matter." Kramer readily views herself as having been "lucky" in life, given her rich, artistic background and exposure to challenging intellectual and political influences. In fact, she cannot remember a time "when art was not the center of my life." She conjectures that she began her artistic career when she was around two years old. In her own words,

> It all started as soon as I could take something in my hand and draw with it. I always knew I wanted to be an artist. There was never any doubt in my mind. I was always interested in making things. I always knew that I was gifted in art. There was never any question as to what I would become . . . never any doubt.

Kramer may have felt a natural sense of entitlement to the life of the mind and the arts. This may have spared her many of the self-doubts people from less privileged backgrounds often experience.

The Berlin Years (1924–1929)

When Kramer was around eight years old, she and her mother moved to Berlin, where they stayed with Aunt Liesel for about three years. Living with Aunt Liesel was important because she modeled an artistic way of life for young Kramer through her theatrical activities. Kramer would later claim that it was Aunt Liesel's influence and example that made it possible for her to speak in front of groups (to teach and conduct workshops) with alacrity and ease.

During this period, she became friends with Hans Bellmer, a surrealist painter and her mother's then friend and lover. He provided Edith with brushes, paints, and other art materials. Kramer remembers Bellmer fondly, and remains appreciative of his benevolence and generosity to this day.

Aunt Liesel also brought Kramer closer to the psychoanalytic life as a result of her partnership with Siegfried Bernfeld, a prominent Viennese psychoanalyst and scholar. Aunt Liesel and Bernfeld lived together from 1925 to 1932; they were married for the last two years of this period. Childhood conversations with Bernfeld filled Kramer with ideas about the unconscious and its motivations, and whetted her intellectual appetite for this fascinating, emerging field of knowledge. In addition to his psychoanalytic contributions to Kramer's background, Bernfeld was also the one who advised Edith's mother to send her to a progressive residential school for children in Germany. Kramer attended this school between the ages of 9 and 12 years. She remembers that she positioned herself as "the artist" among both faculty and students without delay:

> I think I became famous immediately, because I drew in the sand. At that time there wasn't much paper around, just like when I was a child and had to draw on slate. Then, you couldn't have endless paper. I made carica-

tures of some of the teachers in the sand. So, from the moment I arrived there, I became known as the artist—as the "one who can draw."

During our interview, Kramer enthusiastically exclaimed that Bernfeld had been "an important influence on me during these years—he taught me to think. . . . I learned about the unconscious—its influence and its power—from this man." She mentioned with a chuckle that she read his books even "before I could understand them."

The Return to Vienna (1929–1934)

After returning to Vienna from Berlin, around the age of 12, Kramer continued with her education. When she was 15, she enrolled in evening classes in life drawing at the Kunstgewerbeschule. She continued with these challenging classes until she was 17. Kramer's childhood friend Maria Feder, in a 1993 interview, described Kramer as: "a very serious, self-contained, and inventive person, . . . someone with an eye for what things look like" (Halevi, Waymire, & Conners, 1994). She remembered marveling at her predilection for creating and making things and realizing early on that there was something very special, very gifted about her friend Edith—her shyness and aloofness notwithstanding.

Back in Vienna, Kramer first met Friedl Dickers-Brandeis, a friend from her mother's youth and a fellow student at the Bauhaus with Franz Singer. It was at Singer's house in Vienna that Friedl initially discovered Kramer's artistic talent. Realizing her creative potential, Friedl became her friend and mentor.

On the psychoanalytic side of things, more growth and exposure were forthcoming during these years. When Kramer was 17 and in the midst of final exams, her mother gave her Sigmund Freud's *Introductory Lectures on Psycho-Analysis*. As Kramer tells it, this was perhaps an imprudent thing for her mother to do. Did she not want me to study for my exams? Kramer remembers sequestering herself for hours, and reading the text from cover to cover because it captured her mind and nourished and challenged it in ways that art had not. As she told us:

> I was always interested in psychic processes. You see, the visual arts don't make much of a demand upon the intellect—upon conceptual thinking. The visual arts may have done so during the Renaissance period when one was also an architect. Then an artist had to know mathematics and all of that. If one just paints and sculpts, you don't exercise those faculties. And, I have them. I need to exercise that part of me. Psychoanalysis somehow provided this exercise of the intellect.

It is from remarks like these that one realizes that Kramer was not only a consummate artist, but was equally interested in analyzing and writing about the creative process. Thus began her longstanding interest in art, art theory, and psychoanalysis during late adolescence. It culminated when she became one of the pioneers of art therapy, a new field of research and intervention.

From Vienna to Prague (1934–1938)

After graduation from high school at 18 in 1934, she moved to Prague, Czechoslovakia, with the intent to study art and painting with Friedl Dicker-Brandeis, who had preceded her there from Vienna. Because Friedl had so ably encouraged Kramer to pursue her artistic passions, she became *the one* with whom she wanted to study professionally. "I went there because of her, because she was a magnificent teacher—an inspired teacher, and I knew I could learn more from her than anybody else." Kramer placed herself in what essentially amounts to an apprenticeship with Friedl. Friedl did not charge Kramer for instruction, but demanded serious and rigorous devotion to art practice in return for her time. According to Kramer, she would coax, cajole, or brow beat her students into challenging themselves to do their best work. Standing over Kramer, Friedl might say:

> I know you can draw; I know you can see; I know that you can do more than that. I know you can do something that looks like that. . . . The "trick" involves what you do with what you see. You have to create the essence of the eye, and not just something that looks like an eye.

Friedl's requirement for precision and truthful expression, it appears, cultivated Kramer's own desire for truth, honesty, and exactness in artistic expression. Under Friedl's tutelage, Kramer became an arch enemy of all kitsch, imitation, and intellectual and artistic dishonesty.

In addition to being a student, Kramer helped Friedl with various projects during this period. Many communist intellectuals and political refugees from Nazi Germany had fled to Czechoslovakia in search of safe haven at a refugee camp near Prague. There they waited for admission to other countries. As a fervent communist herself, Friedl was determined to help the children of these families deal with these difficult and traumatic times. She taught them to express their experiences through the visual arts. Friedl achieved impressive results with these youngsters who had been living under such duress. After the Nazi occupation of Czechoslovakia, Friedl and her husband (both Jews) were interned in the Nazi ghetto at Terezin. Friedl devoted herself to teaching art to the children of Terezin as well. Although Friedl and most of the children were killed at Auschwitz, their surviving artwork has been widely exhibited in Europe and Israel. Kramer acknowledged that she learned numerous concepts and teaching techniques from observing Friedl at work with the refugee children, pedagogical approaches that later launched her own explorations into the world of art therapy.

Immigration to America

In 1937 to 1938, the worsening European situation and the increasing power of the Nazi movement were becoming a threat to Jews and communists everywhere. Many decided to flee Europe, looking for asylum in places like South America and the United States. Kramer herself made plans to emigrate. In 1938, she found her way from Prague to Poland from where she sailed to the New World just before the Polish countryside was overrun by invading Germans.

Upon arriving in New York City, Kramer was met by her old friend and ally, Aunt Liesel. Liesel got her settled in her first apartment on the Lower East Side of Manhattan. With connections she had made in the psychoanalytic and art worlds of Europe, Kramer was able to land her first job. She became a shop teacher at the Little Red School House, a famous, progressive school in Greenwich Village. During her three years there, Kramer learned much about teaching young children art and carpentry.

> Later [during this period] I worked in various neighborhood houses and other after-school programs. Thus I became acquainted with the art of children whose lives are rich in cultural and intellectual stimulation as well as of those who are deprived of it. (1971, pp. xiv–xv)

Beginning in 1943, Kramer worked as part of the war effort in a machine shop on Grand Street. She was eager to contribute directly to thwarting the Nazi movement. Although the only woman in the shop, Kramer quickly became a highly skilled machinist. After her daily shift was over, Kramer would spend hours creating pen and ink drawings of the machinery and the men who operated them (Figure 6.2 and 6.3). She produced more than 50 of these drawings during her two-year machine-shop period. Thus began her unusual fascination with the world of laborers, craft people, tools, and machines. Very recently she produced a series of large, intricate oil paintings of a subway train repair station (Figure 6.4).

After the war, Kramer decided to return to Europe for a while, spending most of her time in France. This sojourn to the old country afforded her the opportunity to explore how she was going to live her life as an

FIGURE 6.2.   Portrait of a Lathe, 1947. Oil on canvas, 22 x 29 inches.

artist. Kramer eventually decided that New York City was to be her home. She returned there, and began to look for work in the world of art and art education.

Around the same period (1939), Kramer entered psychoanalytic treatment with a Viennese analyst, Dr. Annie Reich. This segment of her analysis was terminated in 1942, when Kramer was 25 years old. Her

**FIGURE 6.3.   Machinist at Pentagraph, ca. 1944. Pen and
ink on paper, 11 x 12 inches.**

analysis was resumed for two additional years beginning in 1950. This
was an important transition period for her. Her last two years of psychoanalysis coincided with her first two years as an art therapist at the
Wiltwyck School for Boys. The understanding of psychic processes,
transference, and countertransference, gained through her personal
analysis, became essential background for her work as an art therapist.
Her double interest in psychoanalysis and the arts made her a natural
choice for a new staff position at the Wiltwyck School. On recommenda-
tion from a New York psychoanalyst and Columbia University professor,
Dr. Viola Bernard, Kramer interviewed for the job with Wiltwyck (ca.
1950) and was accepted. Thus began a seven-year period as art teacher
and art therapist working with emotionally troubled boys.

During our interview, Kramer reminisced about the good times at
Wiltwyck. She kept a diary of her experiences at Wiltwyck, making
entries every night after work. After five years or so, she had a hunch
that "there was a book in it" and proposed writing about her Wiltwyck

FIGURE 6.4.   New York Subway Repair Station, 1996. Oil on canvas, 50 x 42 inches.

experiences to the school's Board of Directors. Not only did the board accommodate her, they offered "some very small help, some paid vacation, and assistance" so she could write her book. In 1958, *Art Therapy in a Children's Community* was published with a foreword by Dr. Viola Bernard. In her first book, Kramer emerged as a gifted writer and scholar. She intellectually grounded the field of art therapy and expanded it with her own ideas, and she did so with great clarity of thought and style. By now Kramer was recognized as a pioneer in the emerging field of art therapy and as a formidable writer in a second language.

After Wiltwyck, Kramer worked at many sites on a number of pioneering art therapy projects. From 1960 to 1963 Edith Kramer was instrumental in bringing art therapy to the Leake and Watts Children's Home in Yonkers, New York. She then worked as art therapist at the Jacobi Hospital (child psychiatric ward) from 1963 to 1974, and at the Jewish Guild School for the Blind from 1964 to 1974. In addition, she helped develop a psychiatric pilot program for severely disturbed youngsters at the Albert Einstein Medical College in the Bronx (1974–1975).

In addition to her clinically oriented positions, Kramer has held a variety of postsecondary academic appointments. She taught a course entitled Art and Art Therapy in Children's Groups at the New School for Social Research (1959–1974), and she taught the Arts-in-Therapy class for the Turtle Bay Music School (1951–1971). She taught art therapy at the Hahnemann Medical College (1968–1971), and together with her friend and colleague, Elinor Ulman, initiated an Art Therapy Training Program at George Washington University in 1972. She began lecturing in the New York University graduate art therapy training program in 1974; she continues to teach in the NYU art therapy program to this date in the capacity of Adjunct Professor of Art Therapy.

Over the years she has lectured on art and art therapy at colleges, universities, hospitals, and clinics in Sweden, the Netherlands, Iceland, Italy, Australia and throughout the United States. Moreover, she has authored numerous articles on art therapy (many of which have been translated into foreign languages), and has written two additional books: *Childhood and Art Therapy: Notes on Theory and Application* (1979) and *Art as Therapy with Children* (1971). In short, Kramer has been a high profile participant in the inner circle of art therapy from its inception.

Edith Kramer has been the recipient of numerous awards and honors over the years. She was a founding member of the American Art Therapy Association (AATA), and founding member of—and catalyst for the formation of—the New York Art Therapy Association. Kramer has been the recipient of the AATA's highest award, the Honorary Life Membership Award. In addition, she was awarded the Honorary Degree of Doctor of Art Therapy by Vermont College of Norwich University in 1996 for her many contributions and years of service to the discipline.

Yet all the while, Kramer had been careful to make room and time for her ongoing studio work. In this respect, as in others, Edith Kramer is an exemplar of the integration of theory and practice—living out the truths and insights that established the foundation for her work.

ESSENTIAL THEORETICAL FORMULATIONS

Through varied academic and clinical experiences, Kramer developed a strong sense of her own theoretical orientation along with a practical approach to art therapy. She has never shied away from writing or lecturing about her views—often taking a controversial stance. Kramer is unabashedly Freudian in her perspective, never straying too far from positions taken by some of her earliest teachers. We must assume that their theories, in Kramer's mind, explain various psychopathologies more cogently than newer approaches. Two others who have influenced Kramer include the philosopher Susanne Langer and the educator Victor Lowenfeld. Langer's notion of the irreducibility of certain experiences to discursive thought supports Kramer's defense of art therapy as fundamentally different from talk therapy or psychotherapy. From Victor Lowenfeld she learned many felicitous pedagogical practices, especially those designed to help handicapped, disadvantaged, and blind children (Kramer, 1979).

A few months after the interview, we had the opportunity to observe Kramer conduct a case presentation to a group of art therapy students. Her superb ability as a teacher, her uncanny clinical acumen, and her infinite compassion and care for disadvantaged and traumatized children were moving. Kramer seemed intent on giving life and "wings" to those who are handicapped and fighting to survive against great odds (Figure 6.5).

I think we must reflect on the degree of identification Kramer may experience with these disadvantaged patients—a possible identification that may enhance her empathic stance and her ability to perform liberating therapeutic work. In addition to Freud's own writings, Kramer acknowledges the foundational influence of psychoanalysts such as Anna Freud, Heinz Hartmann, and Margaret Mahler. These theorists contributed to the understanding of the ego's function within the individual's psychic life, and, in turn, influenced Kramer's conception of art therapy:

> Art therapy is conceived of primarily as a means of supporting the ego, fostering the development of a sense of identity, and promoting maturation in general. Its main function is seen in the power of art to contribute to the development of psychic organization that is able to function under pressure without breakdown or the need to resort to stultifying defensive measures. (Kramer, 1971, p. xiii)

The ego-supporting and identity-forming objectives of art therapy are succinctly postulated by Kramer in the above quote. According to Kramer, art therapy contributes to the development of psychic organiza-

A disturbed young man draws a bird on the top half of a piece of paper. The bird can't fly, imprisoned by the edge. The art therapist, Vera Zilzer, places a larger sheet of paper behind the original drawing. No words are exchanged. The young man extends the wings. Through this simple act, a soul is released—even if just for a moment.[3]

FIGURE 6.5. Patient Drawings. Pastels on paper.

112

tion and helps bring to pass what might be called reparative, developmental objectives. Kramer came to her definition of art therapy—and this explanation of the healing power of art therapy—from working with both highly disturbed children and normal children. Kramer first witnessed the value of art therapy for children under stress in her work with Friedl Dickers in the late 1930s. She writes:

> It was among those traumatized children that I first observed the different responses to stress as they manifested themselves in children's art, responses that later would become so familiar to me. I saw regression; repetition that told of unresolved conflict; I first observed identification with the aggressor in children who identified with Hitler, who had proved his power by the very damage he had done to them; I saw withdrawal into frozen rigidity, and, finally, the capacity for creative expression surviving under difficulties. (Kramer, 1971, p. xiv)

In the Wiltwyck School, Kramer garnered additional firsthand experience of the healing dynamics that arise when a process such as art therapy is implemented—a process that enables children to express their inner conflicts and struggles visually. Through this expression, by way of the artistic creations and manual activities, children regain their emotional health and an attendant sense of self (Katz-Stone, 1997, p. 5). Art therapy enables children to develop a sense of mastery, a sense of "can do," as well as pride in their accomplishments. Furthermore, such activities support and foster their ego development and identity formation. Her new approach to therapy showed consistent beneficial results. Although these successes arguably may appear the same as those achieved through play or talking psychotherapy, Kramer insisted that in art therapy, the emphasis must be placed on "the idea of art as therapy rather than on psychotherapy that uses art as a tool" (Kramer, 1971, p. xiii). Particularly in light of the ego-strengthening and maturational properties, art therapy can stand on its own while it can also be used to complement psychotherapy.

KRAMER'S COMMITMENT TO HER OWN
ART AND CREATIVITY

Throughout her years as a practicing art therapist, Kramer has been very clear about keeping art therapy as a profession *separate* from her passion for art. Just as she was emphatic about preventing art therapy from becoming psychotherapy, she assiduously worked to keep art therapy from replacing the role of art in her life. In this vein, Kramer was determined to keep patients out of her studio, and to keep her art therapy work in the clinic, school, or hospital. From Kramer: "If you get your studio filled with patients, then that's the end, you know."

Kramer considers her studio time inviolate and protects it vigorously. At the end of the long interview we invited her to supper, but she encouraged us to leave so she could get some work done. Kramer's stance here serves as a reminder of just how dedicated she has been to her own artwork and how able she is at defending her territory. Although she contributed to the development of a new field, she remained determined to persist with her art. Remember Kramer's words from the epigraph: "Art is my destiny; Art therapy my beloved profession." Her art comes first; it matters above and beyond anything else. In Kramer's words, "The most important thing to me at any time is the art that I am currently working on." Kramer's long-time friend Maria Feder understood this dimension of Kramer: "Art is the breath of life for Kramer; she lives by it; art *is life* for her" (Halevi, Waymire, & Conners, 1994). Making art was more important than relationships, even romantic relationships. Likewise, Kramer made a very deliberate decision to not have children. From Kramer:

**FIGURE 6.6.   Christina, 1989. Ceramic clay,
8.5H x 12L x 6.5W inches.**

Children need love and care. I don't have any extra of that to give to children of my own, and at the same time keep up with my art. I have offered a lot of love and care in the art therapy arena. That is enough. The same is true for intimate friends and lovers. If they would get too close or involved, they would soon find that my passion was for my art—my projects— for what I was going to make next. I am always thinking ahead that way. That style or personality type doesn't make a good candidate for a long-term committed relationship.

In thinking about Kramer's decision to not have children, one wonders if there were other factors that contributed to her *unwavering* position on this matter. Did her own childhood, her relationship with her mother, her awareness of the Holocaust and the devastation of Europe's Jewry, all collectively contribute to her firm stance?

Perhaps the most remarkable aspect of Kramer's commitment to her art is found in the singularity of purpose (the "precision and diligence") that she brings to her craft. She knew from very early on in life that she was to be an artist. She had a sense of mission in respect to both her art and her life. As a young adult, she set out to find ways to take care of herself financially, so her practice of art could become her vocation. She worked diligently. She kept her nose to the grindstone and never wavered from her chosen path. Thus, not only did Kramer develop into an exceptional artist, she also created the kind of life—the kind of artistically exciting and engaged life—that she had dreamed for herself.

Despite Kramer's hard work and single-minded focus, and the impact this effort has had upon her success, she stressed during the interview that she felt "lucky" or "fortunate" to have the life she has had. "I was very lucky in knowing exactly what I wanted to do in life. I was fortunate in many ways, and this (knowing exactly what I wanted) was one way I was fortunate."

Things kept working out well for Kramer. She had good mentors and teachers; she often seemed to be in the right place at the right time. In her modesty, she speaks of luck and good fortune, but one wonders what else played a role. Was the certainty with which she embraced her destiny one of the factors that put her in the right place at the right time? She developed her "gifts" or "genius" as she envisioned them. She fought to maintain personal integrity—with herself, with her art, and with her creative gifts—regardless of whether this effort made her appear ornery, eccentric, or even selfish.

Kramer's overall humility and modesty must be juxtaposed against her unflinching declaration of superior attributes and qualities in relationship to her artistic sense of self. She is not shy about acknowledging them. "I was good. I was gifted at art. I always knew I was gifted—from very early on." In spite of Kramer's awareness of her artistic gifts and intellectual abilities, and in spite of seemingly having achieved her life goals, she asserts that she always had a difficult time promoting herself. She dismissed this tendency as a neurotic conflict that she could not get rid of. She half-jokingly expressed disappointment that this was so and claimed that nothing short of an additional ten years of psychoanalysis would possibly change the situation. At this point in her life, Kramer has decided to leave the "promotion of Kramer" up to other people. Again we notice how much in charge Kramer remains even when she seemingly admits to a "problem."

THOUGHTS ON ETHICS AND INTEGRITY

A profound concern with ethics and integrity was evident throughout our interview with Kramer. Sometimes she spoke about these matters in terms of her own choices and convictions. At other times, Kramer seemed to demand a universal, social integrity from everybody, but her primary focus was on artists in relation to their art. She believes that "*all* artists must be truthful and honest in their art." She plays down the degree to which an artist's personal life and professional life must coincide. In fact, she believes that life and art must be kept distinct on many fronts. Nonetheless, an artist must be true to herself, her perceptions, and her sense of the aesthetic. In Kramer's own words:

> I don't take certain things lightly or easily. For example, . . . the artistic morality is that you cannot be a fake. It is a cardinal sin to lie in art—to be a fake. You have to be genuine. That means to work, you have to be free to work. You have to be free to shout and scream—to rant and rave.

Kramer wanted, even demanded, permission to rant and rave throughout her life—in her artwork, in her writing, and in her teaching. She believed that if one did not feel the freedom to express oneself freely and openly, one might begin to compromise with oneself and one's vision of truth.

Critical aspects of Kramer's opinions on ethics and integrity are concisely summarized in one of her favorite phrases: "You can't have your cake and eat it too." By this, Kramer seems to mean that an artist cannot have it both ways. Kramer requires that the authentic artist be true to his/her creative vision and produce only the highest quality work. To remain authentic as an artist, one cannot create art to be popular, to mass produce or mainly to make money. According to Kramer, "[artists] might become fakes; they might become something cheap; they

FIGURE 6.7.   Karin Machover, 1989. Oil on canvas.

might do something cheap," if they do not take such a pure stance on
these matters.

Kramer believes artists must do the very best they can in their work.
That requires tough choices. "For me the question arises when I find
that I did something that is less than the best I can do. What does one
do? Do you keep it? Do you destroy it? What do you do with it?" She
believes that the artist must discard it; "throw it out." Otherwise, "You
will be punished for it." It seems that part of that punishment is the

resulting dependence on other's approval and a loss of creativity. Kramer continues: "Producing bad art—something that is not up to your own standards, is the worst thing you can do. You might as well have stayed in bed." One wonders here by what criteria she judges her own work. Is it a matter of her knowing she did the best she could even if the result is less than what she had hoped for? How does an artist account for the natural fluctuations in her output if she holds herself to such rigorous standards? With a large studio filled to the brim with artwork, sketches, and sculptures, one wonders how much Kramer actually discards. Given her lifelong work with disturbed and disadvantaged children, how does she split her consciousness when it comes to judging perfection in her work? The tension between her own espoused absolute artistic standards and a more relative, tolerant, context-dependent attitude are evident and not easily reconciled. When asked how she combines the kind of tolerance she demonstrates toward the art of patients with the severe demands she makes upon her own art (and that of other artists), Kramer responded by quoting a dictum often used by her friend Elinor Ulman: "Tell the patient the truth, nothing but the truth, but not the whole truth." Kramer went on to say that "Patients have the right to sanctuary, but artists have no such right. Artists must face the whole truth."

Likewise, she believes that artists must not "play to an audience," or create to flatter a patron, or produce kitsch. If they do any of these "deplorable" acts and break the artist's implicit ethical code, Kramer believes that the price to be paid by the artist is high in terms of her inner self and the quality of her work. It is clear from the above, that for Kramer, personal and artistic integrity are inextricably intertwined. She holds herself, all artists, and the world of art to the highest of standards. What is more, she is willing to remind the world of its duty and "to rant and rave" to promote her position.

Even at the risk of alienating some gatekeepers in the art scene, Kramer has chosen to play the role of the prophet in the wilderness and to hold up a mirror to society, demanding that artists adhere to a stringent code of ethics, an unpopular yet essential and courageous position to take in human affairs. For remaining true to her convictions, Kramer is consciously and willingly paying a price.

We believe that it is her quest for quality and truth—coupled with her integrity and courage, her determination and single-minded focus—that make Edith Kramer the exceptional individual she is. In addition, these vital concerns and personal attributes will likely give her the buoyancy and stamina essential for continuing to be an artist well into old age.

SOCIAL CONSCIOUSNESS AND SOCIAL COMMENTARY:
THE RULE OF INTEGRITY APPLIED

Kramer not only holds herself, her art, and all artists to a high standard of integrity, she also applies the same critical index to culture at large. She has been a stern but fair and discerning commentator on the American

FIGURE 6.8.   Man Talking, 1981. Oil on canvas, 40 x 32 inches.

social context. We speculate that her perspective derived in part from exposure to her father's keen social consciousness, and, in part, from her familiarity with psychoanalytic theory. Furthermore, we can only imagine how spending formative years in the midst of the Holocaust must have strengthened her critical social stance.

Perhaps the early and intense exposure to radical ideology made Kramer aware that sociocultural and political dynamics were the kinds of events to which one must pay attention. According to this ideology, we are the keepers of our sisters and brothers. Both psychoanalysis and the Holocaust enhanced Kramer's naturally keen observation of human motivation. She learned to attend to both the pressures from within and from without that lead people to act in certain ways. It looks as though she assimilated psychoanalysis and radical political theory into a world-view that informs her social perspective, her writing, and her art. Kramer has remained critical of herself, the world of art, and the contemporary social and cultural milieu throughout her years.

For example, Kramer laments the absence of symbolic life in the United States and blames this loss for much of the personal and social malaise that seem epidemic in our culture:

> Symbolic life is really missing in America these days—in the industrial culture. It is a very important element that artists and art therapists bring to people's lives. I think we are meant as a species to make art. It can be very important for the feeling of self—for the individual to be able to mature and grow.

Kramer argued a similar point concerning the loss of the symbolic and the innate human need to create in her 1971 text. Here she laments the psychological and emotional losses that have accompanied extensive industrialization in our culture.

> When things are produced by machine, the average person misses the sense of well-being that comes about when the pattern of life is reflected and confirmed by the physical appearance of the environment. It is no longer possible to contribute to these forms simply by working with one's hands on tasks that are a part of everyday life.
>
> I believe this deficiency has created a hidden hunger, a feeling of emptiness, and a fear of a loss of identity that drives people to seek out art experiences where they can still be found. (Kramer, 1971, pp. 1–2)

Kramer's social commentary includes compelling reflections on the American superego. She contends that the American superego is constructed in such a way that it can "only make demands; . . . it doesn't give rewards" (p. 15). According to Kramer, this leads to fragmentation and inner emptiness.

[To most Americans] . . . the award must come from the outside. The pat on the shoulder must come from the outside. But if the awards are not there, culturally not there, there is going to be trouble. I was brought up in a way that afforded me inner rewards. . . . it is the inside of you that pats you on the back, and says: All right, now you have done well. O.K., I'm pleased with you. Or, it says: I am angry with you if you don't do this or that.

This leads to a situation in which most people become externally driven, extrinsically motivated, and alienated from their neighbors. It also contributes to inner emptiness. The absence of this internal gyroscope or monitor keeps people always looking outside of themselves. It keeps them from championing big ideas; it keeps them from being creative.

Kramer criticizes contemporary politics, social sciences, and the helping professions as contributing to the malaise. A lack of differentiation in thought and expression has become pervasive in the general modern populace. She compares these modern-day language aberrations to Orwell's 1984 Newspeak, a language that was "created with the aim of reducing the number of available words, eliminating ambiguities, multiple meanings, and subtle differentiations, so that the tools for independent thinking would be eliminated" (Kramer,1996, p. 41).

In the social sciences, Kramer is especially critical of words such as *reinforce, clients, adaptive,* and *maladaptive.* How dare we insist on helping people adapt to wrong and sometimes evil systems, even as we water down our language and concepts? "[There] are indeed individuals who need to be helped to come to terms with a world they must live in. We should help them—not to adapt if it kills them—but to find ways of adjusting without sacrificing their integrity" (Kramer, 1996, p. 41).

Kramer's comments here seems like a reflection of a personal battle that she has fought with the demands of conformity throughout her years. All her life she has resisted pressures to conform, to follow ordinary role scripts, to be in only one profession, or to settle down with one person. She suffered the loss of her mother and the horrors of the Holocaust. She faced the challenges of immigration and being a woman artist, but refused to give in to demands of conventionality.

In addition to the chaos, emptiness, and the Newspeak-induced malaise from which people suffer, Kramer suggests that contemporary individuals have also lost touch with the beautiful, the aesthetic. No one can see these days; we are all "blind in the eye" (Halevi, Waymire, & Conners, 1994). We can't seem to see our way down a moral, ethical path.

Yet in the midst of all this darkness, Kramer seems to have kept a deeper vision despite her age. Again, in the words of her childhood friend Maria Feder, "Kramer is one who has an eye for what things really look like" (Halevi, Waymire, & Conners, 1994)—whether it be in the arts, academia, or society at large. We found indeed that this is so. She also has shown herself to be a person with great integrity, determination, strength of conviction, and lively spirit. In an age of moral relativism and apathy, Kramer emerges as a true educator, one who can lead the way out of darkness.

CONCLUSION

Kramer has fought for artistic license and personal integrity her entire life. She found encouragement and support in the early years; she has had the good fortune of gifted teachers and mentors who recognized her talent and fostered it. She was influenced by powerful historical events, and by critical, poignant family events. She has shown herself to be flexible and open; she also has exhibited a kind of stubbornness and toughness. She is determined to fulfill her destiny with zest and hope. She has created and invented in both art and art therapy. Kramer combines in one person many rare and extraordinary gifts. She is intellectually sharp and highly educated; she has superb artistic talent that she expresses in many media; and she has a way with words. Her most unusual feat has been to bridge these different dimensions of herself and integrate them for her own and our benefit. She has contributed a distinct opus of artwork and beautifully crafted, scholarly books on art therapy, as well as articles on the impoverishment of modern culture and the contemporary worldview.

Kramer is full of individual strengths and contradictions. She is both harsh and warm, unforgiving and compassionate, cantankerous and gracious, self-protective and generous, methodical and playful, but always seemingly in control. She embodies the kind of qualities, paradoxes, and complexities that Csikszentmihalyi (1996) characterizes as symptomatic of the creative personality.

Kramer prefers to live alone; yet she likes and enjoys people. She plays down the role of the spiritual, yet she leads a very spirited life. She inspires others with her indefatigable spirit. She is a fervent advocate for the disadvantaged, but does not like to promote herself. She wanted no children of her own, yet she has dedicated much of her life to the healing of children. Kramer is equally at home in crafting scholarly works and in crafting beautiful things with her hands. As researchers of creativity, we appreciate the very contradictions and multiple layers of meaning that encompass Kramer's life and work.

Edith Kramer is a maverick—a creator, an integrator of Old World and New, a pioneer in crossing disciplines. She has made tremendous personal and theoretical contributions to the worlds of art, art therapy, and the rehabilitation community. Who better than the artist herself to summarize a life well lived?

> *When I was young, I had the courage of innocence. In middle life I became a little too cautious. Now at my old age, I have the courage of experience. I have arrived at this final stage; long may it last.*

POSTSCRIPT

Edith Kramer's advice to the next generation of art therapists:

> I advise you to maintain yourself maladapted to all in our society that would stifle independent thought and action. You have before you an old lady who has been comfortably maladapted all her life, and yet, because she has been so maladapted, is now being honored with a doctorate. (Kramer, 1996, p. 41)

NOTES

1. See the recent book on Edith Kramer entitled: *Edith Kramer: Malerin und Kunsttherapeutin zwischen den Welten* by Charlotte Zwiauer (1997).

2. The interview took approximately four hours. All direct quotes in this essay that do not cite specific books are taken from the transcript of that interview.

3. In addition to witnessing Kramer discuss this strategic art therapy interaction, it is also described in Zwaiuer (1997, p. 117). Vera Zilzer is the art therapist credited with this intervention, although Edith Kramer enjoyed using it as an example of a particularly creative therapeutic action.

REFERENCES

Csikszentmihalyi, M. (1996). *Creativity: Flow and the psychology of discovery and invention*. New York: Harper and Row.

Halevi, M. (Producer), Waymire, K. (Director), & Conners, C. (Director). (1994). *A portrait of Edith Kramer: Artist/art therapist* [videotape]. (Available from Edith Kramer, 95 Vandam Street - 3 F, New York, NY 10013)

Katz-Stone, A. (1997). The quiet invasion continues: Edith Kramer finds understanding through art. *Austrian Information, 50,* 5–6.

Kramer, E. (1958). *Art therapy in a children's community.* Springfield, IL: Charles C. Thomas.

Kramer, E. (1971). *Art as therapy with children.* New York: Schocken Books.

Kramer, E. (1979). *Childhood and art therapy.* New York: Schocken Books.

Kramer, E. (1996). Commencement address to the August, 1996, graduates of the master's of arts in art therapy program, Vermont College of Norwich University. *American Journal of Art Therapy, 35,* 39–41.

Zwiauer, C. (1997). *Edith Kramer: Malerin und Kunsttherapeutin zwischen den Welten.* Vienna: Picus Verlag.

chapter 7

Healing Images: Art and Meditation in Recovery from Cancer

John J. McKenna
Trinity College of Vermont

That one experiences a diagnosis of cancer as traumatic is expected. What is less expected is that treatment will also be traumatic. Living through such an experience tests one's stamina and courage to the limit, and surviving the illness and the "cure" may very well etch lasting lessons for living wisely. At the time of wrestling with the illness, however, one's energy is consumed with merely getting through each day, and the thought of drawing lessons for the future is furthest from one's mind. As years pass after the experience, the realization deepens that one has gleaned important learning about the journey through illness, the encounter with death, and living. In these pages, I want to share reflections on my own experience of such a process.

A few personal remarks may help the reader better understand the perspective that I bring to this experience. The eldest of seven children, I was raised in an Irish Catholic family. For 12 years of my early adulthood I was a Cistercian (Trappist) monk and I learned the centuries-old practice of meditation and prayer associated with the Western religious tradition. For all of my middle adult years I have been married and a teacher at a small Catholic liberal arts college in the Northeast. For ten years I have conducted a small practice as a licensed clinical psychologist. Death has been no stranger to me; I had witnessed the deaths of relatives, my father among them, as well as of colleagues from the monastic, academic, and clinical practice communities—not a few of them from cancer.

DIAGNOSIS: DESCENT

The day my cancer was first diagnosed is as sharp and vivid as today is in my memory. One week before, February 28, 1991, I awakened to find a lump in my neck just under the left side of my jaw. The lump had appeared overnight; it was the size of half an egg and initially an object of curiosity. It was only slightly tender, and caused no real discomfort. I could not associate any injury with the lump. Maybe it was a cold symptom, although I noticed no other symptoms; it might be related to an occasional generalized ache in my lower jaw, or perhaps an indication of a tooth or gum infection, although there were no other signs of an infection (e.g., fever). A few days later, since the lump had grown slightly larger, I called my doctor's office and was encouraged to schedule an appointment with the dentist. Within the previous month I had passed my semi-annual physical with flying colors.

By 9:00 A.M. on Wednesday, March 6, the dentist had taken X rays and examined my lower left jaw thoroughly. After a consult with his son, an associate in the practice, he advised me that there was no evidence of cavity or gum problem and referred me to an oral surgeon. I began to surmise that something out of the ordinary was occurring.

At 2:30 P.M., the oral surgeon examined me and studied the panoramic X ray of my entire jaw. He appeared to be very concerned with what he saw in the X ray but was reluctant to reveal his diagnosis. He referred me in turn to an ear, nose, and throat specialist at the University Health Center and arranged for an immediate appointment. With each referral my concerns multiplied but I had nothing substantive on which to ground my suspicions.

Within the hour the otolaryngologist, attended by a cadre of interns and medical students, examined me. Sitting on the side of the gurney, I felt that I was a demonstration subject. While he examined me, the physician never spoke directly to me except to give orders, such as, "open wider," and "stick out your tongue." After checking my throat externally and internally he proceeded to draw a needle biopsy. By this point I could not dismiss the horrors that raced through my imagination. After a few minutes he had obtained the specimen and the cadre of interns disappeared. Then he announced that I should be admitted to the hospital within 48 hours, "the sooner the better." He would perform a "radical neck dissection," and I should expect to be out of work for at least four to six weeks or more. In the surgery he would remove the "node" and lymph glands and possibly also a "node" on my lower tongue. Listening to him, I was in a state of shock, and felt the floor and earth reeling beneath me. As we walked from the examination room, the physician's adamant insistence that surgery was required immediately overwhelmed the effect of his efforts to be reassuring. At the secretary's office, he ordered that a room be booked for surgery within 48 hours, while I meekly protested the immediacy of the admission and mumbled doubts that I could arrange to cover my responsibilities within such a short time.

I drove home in a daze and shared my shock, confusion, and terror with my wife. We both agreed that first thing next morning I would call my own doctor, an internist who specialized in hematology. I slept fitfully that night, praying with an earnestness that I had not felt in a long time. Fragmentary and frightening images about the future blended with condensed memories from the past. What would life be like without being able to speak? How would I teach without a voice? Perhaps I might learn sign language, or carry out pantomimes with puppets, or amplify my voice with a computer. I felt as though I was being sucked down into, and swallowed up by, a spiraling vortex of water.

The threat of losing my tongue and voice to cancer was eminently real to me. A colleague from graduate school, whose wife is a member in my practice group, had died of cancer only 15 months earlier. His cancer had first appeared about 10 years previously when, as a senior graduate student, he supervised school consultations in my final year of internship. He underwent surgery that removed a large part of his tongue, and his rehabilitation required extensive speech therapy. He had been in remission for 8 years when the cancer reappeared, and he lived only several months more, much of it in great pain. His wife, friends, and family, I among them, were still grieving his death.

The next morning's telephone conversation with my physician offered some comfort. She assured me that there would be no immediate surgery, advised me that the "node" was possibly "benign," and if not, surgery would be used only for a biopsy. A final diagnosis would await further tests and consultations. Within 48 hours, my doctor reported to my wife and me that the results of the needle biopsy indicated a malignant growth. She scheduled me for the tissue biopsy.

Over the course of the following week, the results of X rays, CAT scans, and the tissue biopsy pointed to an aggressive form of lymphoma. However, I also learned that this form of lymphoma was very responsive to chemotherapy and radiation. Tests indicated no evidence of other nodes or metastases or that the spinal fluid was affected. Prognosis was excellent, overall. Nonetheless, the regimen of chemotherapy would be intensive for the first month, with four less rigorous maintenance cycles to ensue during the next year. Radiation would follow and complement the chemotherapy.

My memory of this period of diagnosis and testing is as of a whirlwind or tornado. The metaphor of a vortex of water spiraling down into darkness applied to the first several days of shock on learning that I was likely to have cancer. While the whirlwind raged on the surface, the earth beneath me and on which I had stood yawned open crevasses and trembled in its depths.

One episode is quite revealing of my state of mind at this time. It concerns my misinterpretation of the study that evaluated the chemotherapy regimen that I was to undergo (Eastern Cooperative Oncology Group, 1984–1988). Following the first phase of treatment, only one-third of the patients attained complete remission while another third attained partial remission. Two years after the beginning of treatment, more than half of the patients who received chemotherapy had died, and average survival was marginally more than one year. I did not find these results at all encouraging and wondered seriously if enduring a year of intensive chemotherapy and the accompanying side effects was worth one more year of life. Several weeks later, however, a closer reading of the report revealed that 60 percent of the patients accepted into the study had been diagnosed at stage 4 disease, a fact that had eluded my attention completely on the initial reading. I had also minimized the significance of an additional outcome statistic, namely, that 80 percent of those who attained complete remission after the initial phase of treatment were disease free two years later.

Although being diagnosed with cancer is extremely distressing at any time, several factors made the diagnosis of cancer especially difficult for me. As I noted above, I was still grieving the death of a colleague from throat cancer. I also remembered clearly my father's agonizing death from lung cancer over 20 years ago. In addition, this illness came at what seemed to be the peak of my professional career. Recently, I had realized several milestones in my teaching, research, and practice and was actively pursuing several challenging initiatives. All of this fell into new perspective as a result of the illness.

I recall vividly confronting the prospect of death and one period in particular, lasting perhaps a few days, when I was engaged in an intense inner debate about whether to undergo treatment. I wrestled with questions such as: What would I gain from living a year or two more, particularly when I would be totally debilitated from the effects of the chemotherapy? What unfinished business did I need to attend to? Was this an opportunity for me to prepare for imminent death? Although I had been assured by the doctors that my chances of complete remission and long-term survival were excellent, I don't recall that being a major factor in my ultimate decision. At the time I felt that I was faced with a choice to live or to resign myself to die. Finally, there came a point when I chose consciously and deliberately to engage wholeheartedly the mystery of life, death, and rebirth present in this crisis. For me this meant living fully in the present moment and being an active agent in my treatment and healing. From that point on I never questioned my resolve to pursue the course of treatment that would ensue.

My wife, family, friends, and colleagues provided abundant support throughout the ordeal of testing and treatment. My colleagues and department chair, along with the academic dean, graciously adjusted my workload at college. Numerous cards and letters brought encouragement and well wishes from colleagues, friends, and former students. At the end of testing I drafted a letter that I later sent to family, friends, and colleagues to thank them and to update them on the status of my treatment. I wrote that this experience had summoned me to "reaffirm my desire to live and to reclaim my reasons for being. That I would not choose to do other than what I [was] doing at this point in my life, though I would wish to do it more lovingly and with greater sensitivity to what really matters—persons and community—where heart speaks to heart, love binds all wounds, and hope holds fast to what we know to be real in the loving commitment of faith."

CHEMOTHERAPY: ENGULFMENT

Chemotherapy started on April 1, and, on awakening that day, I wished that someone might tell me that the events of the previous weeks were only part of an elaborate April Fool's joke. However, no such luck! The attending physician outlined the course of treatment to me, and left the details to the resident to explain. Together we worked out a schedule for chemotherapy for the next five weeks. The treatment called for four powerful drugs (referred to by the acronym COMP) in varying amounts during the first month. Approximately four weeks after the initial outpatient cycle, there was a briefer outpatient cycle, followed by three days of in-hospital intravenous administration of a fifth drug, which required continual monitoring. To offset the effects of these powerful drugs, additional drugs were administered.

Before starting chemotherapy, I read several booklets about the various drugs (e.g., National Cancer Institute, 1985), and adjusted my diet to include a better balance of fruit, grains, and vegetables. When I inquired about the value of exercise, I was advised that serious exercise would best wait until the entire regimen was completed; each cycle of chemotherapy would destroy any muscle buildup. My reading and conversations with the doctors led me to anticipate a major assault on my physical constitution. Despite my discomfort with the imagery of war, of assault and counterassault, I was readying myself to wage as vigorous a resistance as possible both to the illness and to the ravages of the chemotherapy and radiation.

In preparing for chemotherapy, I reviewed recent articles and books on mind-body medicine (e.g., Borysenko, 1988; *Advances*, 1991–) and some additional works that focused on coping with the emotional aspects of cancer (Fiore, 1984; LeShan, 1980). I reread the Simonton's report (Simonton, Matthews-Simonton, & Creighton, 1978) concerning the power of imagery in overcoming cancer, and I studied particularly the role of relaxation, meditation, and imagery in the healing process (Achterberg, 1985; Jaffe, 1980; Rossman, 1989). As a result of these readings, I was convinced that the best resistance to the destructive aspects of the illness and the treatment consisted of some combination of these activities.

During my visits to the oncology department, I had opportunity to examine the large room where patients received chemotherapy. It was furnished with several hospital beds and a television, with doors opening to a lavatory and an adjacent office to and from which the nurses entered and exited. It was a very sterile environment in which to spend four to six hours of chemotherapy several times each month. I wanted to nurture both my body and soul during these times and so I prepared a survival kit to bring to each of the chemotherapy sessions. The kit included a portable tape player, several tapes of soothing music, some light reading, a liter of iced tea or lemonade or spring water, a cup of chicken broth, and a light snack.

Within the first two weeks of treatment, prednisone disrupted my sleep cycle; at best I slept only two hours per night. But it also gave me a feeling of boundless energy, a novel experience for me. By the third week, the effects had changed; unusually vivid dreams disturbed my brief episodes of sleep, and even waking hours were interrupted by hallucinatory images, and marked difficulty in concentration, attention, and memory. Only with great effort could I attend to my academic chores. Late in the cycle, I missed several meetings that I had scheduled myself only weeks previously.

From mid to late April, I often spent the early hours sorting nuts and bolts on my workbench in the garage, or rearranging the contents of the drawers and cupboards in the kitchen or bathroom. Although sparked with bursts of energy, I could not sustain or direct that energy to fulfill any challenging goals. My handwriting, already poor, deteriorated to such an extent that it was barely more than a scribble.

The latter weeks of April brought other side effects that were unpleasant in addition to the disruption of sleep and cognitive functions. My fingertips had developed deep cracks, which required that I coat them with lotion and wear rubber gloves to bed at night. My fingers and toes were often completely and painfully numb. My gait had degenerated into a shuffle and my joints felt frail and mechanical. I became short-tempered and quick to erupt in anger or hurt feelings.

On the other hand, counterbalancing these side effects of the chemotherapy, my tumor had entirely disappeared after the first week of treatment. Tests indicated no evidence of the cancer, and I was classified as being in complete remission.

In late May and early June, after prednisone was withdrawn, I endured the most hellish phase of the entire treatment. I experienced persistent and incapacitating headaches, and severe muscle spasms in both arms and legs. Several times a day I stood in an alternately warm and cold shower for relief from the spasms. Relief from the headaches came only by "wearing" a bag of ice on my head day and night. In the morning, my wife would tell me how during the night I had wakened her to report dreams that were incoherent and bizarre—I rarely remembered them. I had also developed a persistent hacking and wrenching cough, excruciating neuropathy in hands and feet, difficulties with coordination and balance, feverishness, swollen and light-sensitive eyes, a sense of total exhaustion, profound weakness, and absence of energy and strength.

That period of three to four weeks was by far the most distressing of the entire ordeal. Although, during the next ten months, I would spend three days in hospital for intensive chemotherapy approximately every other month, I experienced nausea only twice in reaction to the drugs, and these episodes were mild and short-lived. The physical and psychological depletion that I experienced in the first cycle of chemotherapy was beyond my wildest imagining. I cannot fathom how anyone might anticipate the degree of debilitation and discouragement that attend such treatment.

During the chemotherapy I often visualized the process of cell destruction that the drugs were affecting. Frankly I felt overwhelmed by the technical wizardry that was being accomplished in my body. Observing my skin become like that of a child—soft, pink, covered with peach fuzz—helped me to give concrete meaning to the mystery of death and rebirth that was being enacted.

RELAXATION/MEDITATION: ACCEPTANCE

Before starting chemotherapy, I scheduled a visit with a psychologist at the behavioral medicine unit of the University Health Center, to help me prepare for the effects of chemotherapy and the lifestyle adjustments that treatment would require. I was looking for practical steps that I could implement immediately in order to sustain a sense of efficacy in the face of the onslaught of treatment. At our first session, which fell during the first week of chemotherapy, the psychologist showed me a relaxation exercise and gave me a tape with instructions to practice daily. I continued this practice every day for the duration of my treatment and beyond.

For the next 15 months, part of my early morning ritual was to sit comfortably, insert the tape into the tape deck, adjust my earphones, and follow the simple instructions for relaxation. Guided relaxation was not new to me, nor was the practice of meditation. What was different in this instance for me was using the same tape every day. Looking back, I believe that having a tape made the practice so simple, so nontaxing that, even when my physical and mental energies were utterly depleted, minimal effort was required to comply and to experience the benefits.

The tape contains a self-guided relaxation induction (Hadley & Staudacher, 1985) that concludes with a brief visualization, inviting one to imagine oneself in a "special place . . . the most peaceful place in the whole world for you" (p. 35). My "special place" was a secluded forest grove in the coastal area of northern California. There enormous redwoods created a cathedralesque canopy through which flecks of sunlight filtered to the forest floor. More than 20 years earlier I had been awed by the majesty of this place and had often visualized myself there in moments of deep relaxation and reflection. Within weeks of daily relaxation, I could imagine myself in that sheltered forest grove almost immediately on hearing the tape, and realize profound peace. Even in my most difficult hours during the first months of chemotherapy, this image was a potent stimulus for very deep relaxation, and a haven of peace and surrender.

The practice of relaxation reawakened my experience of meditation as a monk, a practice that I found richly rewarding and continued for many years after leaving the monastery. I was able to recall and reinstitute mantra-like phrases and imagery to deepen the meditative state. One of my favorites comes from the tradition of the Eastern Church and calls for an attitude of prayer in which one "stands with the mind in the heart before God."

Mindfulness meditation (Kornfield, 1993; Nhat Hanh, 1976) cultivates an attitude of acceptance and surrender to balance the extroverted, instrumental orientation of so much of conscious living. In this case, meditation disposed me to deeper engagement with the experience of "diminishment" which the illness and the treatment wreaked on my body and soul. I had a deep appreciation for death as an integral part of life, and for the "diminishments," particularly "passive" ones such as a serious illnesses, that life offers us as unique opportunities to affirm our faith in the transforming power of wholehearted acceptance (de Chardin, 1968).

My faith perspective encouraged me to embrace the darkness and engage humbly but hopefully the mystery of death-and-rebirth, and the unknown in my life. I often recalled the metaphor that God is present in the mystery that enters one's life, the unknown that accompanies us along our life journey, and is revealed to us in our relationships with others (Dunne, 1975). From the time I first wrestled with the reality of death as a young monk, more than 30 years earlier, this perspective had sustained me in finding meaning and purpose in life. Faith yielded an even deeper appreciation of this mystery when I came to terms with my father's death 10 years later. Now, a younger man than my father when he died, I confronted the prospect of my own death.

A major outcome of my daily practice of meditation was that I became more accepting of the cyclic course of healing and more committed to doing with care and attentiveness whatever I was engaged in at each moment. My entire experience with being ill deepened the realization of how important it is to live in the present moment, and to be open to the fullness of experience. This notion was not new to me, and, in fact, was an ideal I had long aspired to realize. Looking back from the vantage point of several years, I see that various elements of my experience of illness and the healing process, including the practice of relaxation, therapy, and art, all converged to help me appreciate the sacredness of the present moment.

PSYCHOTHERAPY: HOPE

By early summer, I had mapped out a schedule of the remaining phases of chemotherapy over the next eight months and finalized arrangements for a lighter teaching load for the coming year. As summer waned, the intensive phase of chemotherapy and one maintenance cycle were complete but still I faced three more cycles of chemotherapy that would run into late February. School was to start in a matter of weeks and I was quite discouraged that I had so little energy. So, in late August, I scheduled a visit with another psychologist who specialized in behavioral medicine and who was experienced in working with cancer patients.

Over the next seven months I met more than 30 times with this therapist, more frequently at first and less so the last two months. By the time we started our work together, I had been using the relaxation tape daily for nearly five months, and finding the practice very beneficial. I began psychotherapy with the desire to reconnect with my creative energies, to enter more fully into the process of healing, and to deepen my commitment to a healthful and creative life. Together with my therapist, I reviewed my life history at the outset, and within a few sessions we decided to focus on my current situation. I recall feeling quite anxious when we started, and concerned about how well I could manage my responsibilities with the low energy level that I experienced.

My therapist and I worked as partners in the therapy. In the early stages, she shared with me very helpful perspectives on cancer, on dealing with medical specialists, and on the experience of being in hospital. She recommended a recent work of LeShan (1989), which confirmed my own experience with some of the doctors and of being in hospital. I had certainly experienced both the infantilization and depersonalization that unfortunately accompanies too much of the practice of modern medicine. I also concurred with LeShan's emphasis on the importance of psychological and emotional factors in healing from cancer.

With the help of therapy, I learned to anticipate the ebb and flow of energy and stamina that accompanied each cycle of chemotherapy. During each new cycle of prednisone, I would experience a burst of new energy, only to have it disappear as the drug was withdrawn. As my energy level declined, I would become discouraged and depressed. With my therapist's guidance and support, I learned to accommodate my expectations for work productivity to the level of energy that I could reasonably assume to draw from.

Never before had I experienced such rapid cycling of phases of energy and exhaustion, of elation and depression, of hope and discouragement. I had always considered myself resourceful, but this experience was testing the limits of that resourcefulness. Coping with the psychological consequences of the treatment was clearly as daunting a challenge as was coping with the physical effects of the drugs.

Reflecting on this period of therapy and the process of healing that therapy fostered, I see it as a time of confronting discouragement and reawakening hope. I had often read this Dickinson poem [c. 1861] (Johnson 1960, p. 116), but it spoke to me with new meaning:

Hope is the thing with feathers
That perches in the soul,
And sings the tune without the words
And never stops at all.

PSYCHOTHERAPY AND ART: TRANSFORMATION

Several months into therapy, early into one session, my therapist presented me with a blank sheet of paper and a packet of colored markers and asked me to draw a circle on the page. She then invited me to draw something inside the circle that portrayed "where I was and how I felt at the time." I used about seven or eight colors and partially filled in the circle. I also described associations to the various colors I used and penciled in those associations outside of the circle. I do not recall any dramatic response to this drawing nor do I recollect any instruction to create other drawings. For some time I had talked about taking up watercolor painting, but had never made the time.

The next morning, immediately after my relaxation exercise, I sat down at a table and used my own colored markers to complete the drawing I had started in the office. I later described this initial drawing as representing "my tumor," though when I first created the drawing I did not make that association. Then I cut a cardboard template of a circle about eight inches in diameter and used it to trace a circle on a blank page. For my second drawing, I sketched the dappled redwood grove in which I located myself during meditation (Figure 7.1).

For the next 2½ months I followed a similar ritual almost each morning. Following 15 minutes of meditation, I sat for another 15 minutes and completed a drawing using colored markers. I began each drawing with a pencil tracing of the circle and within it an outline of the composition of the drawing. I completed each drawing with a limited number of colored markers. From mid-November, 1991, when I created the first one, until early February, 1992, I made 70 mandalas. One month later, at the beginning of March, I added the final 2, bringing the total to 72.

Only occasionally did I start drawing with a specific image in mind. Sometimes I intended to produce a definite image, as for example, the sunset framed by redwoods (see Figure 7.1). In some instances a specific memory or image prompted a sketch, such as a house that was on the street corner opposite the hospital room I occupied, or a scene from a National Geographic TV show. More often, however, I began to draw with a feeling, a mood that I hoped to convey. At times, the mood was joyful, and at other times more somber.

On several occasions, I deliberately experimented with a particular technique in executing the drawing, for example, making all the strokes of the marker go in one direction (Figure 7.2), or separating edges of forms by narrow white borders (Figure 7.3). In doing so, I sought to enhance creative expression by working within more challenging constraints. In a brief series of drawings, I playfully attempted to emulate

FIGURE 7.1.

FIGURE 7.2.

Van Gogh's expressionistic use of color and patterns. At these times as at all other times, I worked without an image to copy from and drew only on my memory or sense of the original image. Finally, in the latter part of the entire series, I experimented with drawing using my non-dominant hand in order to give freer rein to the unconscious.

Each week I brought the new drawings I had made to my therapy sessions and laid them out on the floor in a sequence, occasionally with earlier drawings also. I discussed with my therapist the themes or associations reflected in the drawings; most often these associations surfaced only during therapy. However, to my best recollection, during the course of therapy we never attempted any detailed analysis of composition, or color, or even of content.

FIGURE 7.3.

At different times over the years since completing the drawings, I have briefly entertained a desire to interpret them from a more systematic perspective. For example, one might approach such an interpretation from a psychodynamic or object relations point of view or from a more cognitive viewpoint that would assess the properties of the drawings, that is, form, color, shading, as well as the content (similar to a Rorschach interpretation). In the end, however, I have resisted adopting any of these approaches to interpreting my drawings. One reason may well be that such an approach is not consistent with how the drawings were used in the course of my therapy. Although my therapist and I discussed my associations to the images, and identified themes associated with a series of images, our focus was *the experience of creating the drawings* and how the process of drawing was reviving my hopefulness

FIGURE 7.4.

and providing access to inner wellsprings of creativity. I continue to believe that an overly analytic approach to interpreting the drawings would devalue the existential dimension and significance of my experience.

An approach to working with the images in the drawings that appeals much more to me is that of dialogue with the images. Allen (1995), McNiff (1992), and Kast (1993) describe a process of working with art and imagery that draws on principles of depth psychology and that recognizes the role of the image and symbol in expressing the unconscious. In many respects, this approach to working with imagery parallels the depth exercises of Progoff's (1975) intensive journal. The goal of such work is to deepen the connection of conscious living to the unconscious sources of life energy. A detailed discussion of my drawings from this perspective, however, is beyond the scope of this chapter.

Despite reservations about interpreting the drawings too analytically, I want to share several observations concerning the drawings. First, many images appeared in the drawings without conscious intent or design; it is as if they arose from the unconscious and invited representation. These images took form only as I was sketching. Moreover, the symbolic meaning of the images often was not immediately evident to me. One instance is the lotus and butterfly (Figure 7.4). Only when I talked about these images with my therapist did I make a connection with themes of transformation, enlightenment, and wholeness. Other examples are the several drawings that include a crab; I made no conscious association of the crab with cancer until I discussed the images in therapy. The later sketches produced with my left hand are more primitive both in terms of style and also in their symbolic character; several of them might be described as totemic or chthonic (Figure 7.5). In fact, it was only when I began to draw with my left hand that human figures appeared in the drawings. I am inclined to think that all of these phenomena point to the power of art to tap into the unconscious.

Evidently, the drawings reflect a variety of moods; some reveal light-heartedness, serenity, or joy, while others convey soberness, turbulence, or sadness. Yet, what strikes me most forcefully now just as at the time I showed them to my therapist, is the variety and stark contrast of scenes (and moods) as well as of styles within the series. Despite the constraints of having used color markers, and of drawing within the confines of a circle, the series contains a panoply of images executed in a variety of techniques. Some portray Eden-like settings of natural bliss and contentment and others ominous sea catastrophes. There are tropical paradises, sea vistas, and pastoral landscapes, parched deserts and lush rainforests, verdant summer scenes, ripe fall harvests, and cold snowy woodlands or mountainous crevasses. Some are highly symbolic drawings while others

FIGURE 7.5.

are more representational. The variety in imagery and variability in mood is what remains most striking to me seven years later. I was then and am still surprised by the richness and variability in these images. A torrent of life-affirming imagery emerged from the throes of a life-threatening illness.

A second observation recognizes that, as a whole, the drawings have a cartoon-like quality. This assessment is not intended to denigrate the quality of the drawings; rather it acknowledges the fact that the drawings have the character of quickly executed sketches, where elements are represented in only two dimensions, at times only by outline, and without significant use of shading or texture. The brilliant colors resulting from use of the markers reinforce the cartoon-like impression of the sketches. Furthermore, some drawings could qualify as cartoons because they seem to be caricatures, and some appear to convey a whimsical or ironic outlook (e.g., the dragon; the clowns).

Although the drawings are merely sketches and have a cartoon-like quality, some show definite technical skills. In this connection, I might note that from childhood I had often copied cartoons, and occasionally more detailed photographs or illustrations, and in the process learned about composition and perspective. My skills were honed in a high school senior art class, and years of practice with calligraphy and graphic design while I was a monk.

A third observation concerns my experience of drawing within the boundary of a circle. Surprisingly, I found this aspect of the exercise extremely liberating. By contrast, just before beginning this series of drawings, I had been working on a pencil sketch of a fish for several weeks, and I recall my frustration in trying to fill the page with underwater foliage of different shapes. Having a circle on the page allowed me to work without any concern about filling the page. In fact, in 17 of the drawings I did not fill the circle with content or with color. I suppose that I learned to value the border as a guide, rather than as a master, with strict expectations of being filled up. Curiously, however, in no case does any element of the drawings cross the border of the circle; even though I did not always fill the circle, I nonetheless kept each drawing within the confines of the circle.

As I noted earlier, because of the circular form of the drawings, I have referred to the series as my "mandala" drawings (Fincher, 1991). Besides being contained within a circle, other features of the drawings that are commonly observed in mandalas include symmetry, opposites, and triads and quartets of figures. Most appropriately, however, I think of the mandala properties of the drawings as applying to the series as whole. In various combinations, the drawings form composite mandalas that portray the seasons of the year, landscapes of life's journey, or archetypal characters that symbolize aspects of the psyche.

REFLECTIONS ON ART AND MEDITATION AS AGENTS OF HEALING

In this section I comment briefly on the role of meditation and more fully on the role of art in my therapy and healing. The daily practice of relaxation/meditation was initiated with the onset of the chemotherapy. The practice encouraged and reinforced a commitment to living in the present moment, and to a nonjudgmental open acceptance of conscious and unconscious experience. I believe that this practice played a central role in deepening openness to the range of feelings I would experience, as well as acceptance of the diminishment that the illness wrought, and appreciation and reverence for the mystery of life. Elsewhere I have written of the importance of the practice of a spiritual discipline in order to bring mind, body, and spirit into harmony (McKenna, 1999).

Art was introduced at about the midpoint of therapy and I continued to create sketches until therapy ended. Looking back, I believe that the timing of the introduction of art was critical not only in shaping the images that emerged but more importantly for accessing the inner well-springs of the creative process itself. Although the act of drawing was not taxing, I doubt seriously that I would have persisted at this activity had I tried it earlier in the course of my treatment. I am skeptical because I know how physically and emotionally drained I was when I began therapy. By the time I began drawing, I had regained both some physical energy and hope.

A second issue concerns how the drawings were integrated with the work of therapy. As I noted earlier, the drawings served as a point of conversation in therapy, but more as tokens of the healing process itself than of the specific meaning attached to the imagery in any one sketch. This approach is fully congruent with my view of the role that art played in my healing.

I believe that the process of drawing served as a medium for expression in imagery and color of profound feelings that were not always accessible to consciousness or to language. The drawings served several functions. They expressed, contained, and helped to transform my feelings about the meaning of my journey through the final phases of formal treatment. In fact, completing these drawings was an extension of the meditative process that was initiated in the relaxation exercise each day. In a very real way, the images in these sketches served to elaborate and amplify feelings that were often only subliminally perceived during the period of relaxation and meditation.

Langer (1957) observes that the truth of art rests in its power to symbolize feeling.

> Art . . . gives form to something that is simply there [i.e., feeling], as the intuitive organizing functions of sense give form to objects and spaces, color and sound. It gives . . . "knowledge by acquaintance" of affective experience, below the level of belief, on the deeper level of insight and attitude. (p. 263)

From the vantage point of several years after the experience, I am able to see the process of drawing the entire series as an extended meditation on the cycle of life, death, and rebirth—for which a "circle" is an appropriate frame—a meditation whose intensity was occasioned by my illness. I recall that when I reviewed photos of the drawings with a close colleague shortly after completing therapy, she was deeply moved by the entire series and remarked on the richness of feeling and images which were represented in the drawings. At the time I was still too close to the whole experience to appreciate what these drawings represented.

In retrospect, I recognize that the series of drawings as a whole represents an extended reflection on the seasons of life. The drawings are "landscapes of life and death," and are a celebration of the process of transformation through life and death into new life. Transformation through death into new life is evident in several sequences of drawings in the series, but perhaps most strikingly recapitulated in the final drawings in the series, the scarecrow, the dark moonscape, and the shaman between two stylized griffins (Figure 7.6).

FIGURE 7.6.

My experience offered confirmation of the power of art, indeed of creativity itself, to transform raw experience, even physically and psychologically devastating experience. Through imagery (whether in paint, sculpture, architecture, movement, or music), art can give symbolic expression to realms of experience that rational or discursive thought finds inaccessible and everyday language often fails to convey. Art can elevate the most banal and ordinary aspects of the everyday as well as give form to unimaginable horrors and engulfing feelings. In poetry and story, as in prayer and song, words also achieve this transformative power.

I suppose that the power of art to affect healing might also be related to the fact that art is bred of the same forces that promote healing in the psyche. Among these are a gentle attention, an openness to the totality of experience, full acceptance of feelings and inner conflicts, an active and playful imagination, and an appreciation of paradox and the interplay of opposites. Similar forces appear to be at the heart of meditative practice and can be facilitated through relaxation (Kornfield, 1993). They are also recognized as healing dynamics in humanistic and Jungian psychotherapy (Gendlin, 1981; Jung, 1966; Kast, 1993; Rogers, 1961).

CONCLUSION

Finally, I want to comment briefly on the enduring influence of my encounter with death in illness, and of the engagement with healing forces through relaxation, meditation, and art. Of course, it is difficult to estimate how profound an effect that one year, and within that year, several months of therapy and the few months of art, have had. Regardless, it seems appropriate to include some reflections on this dimension of the experience.

First of all, let me address the impact of this experience on my personal life. As one instance, after years of talking about it, my wife and I first traveled out of the country during the year I underwent chemotherapy, and we have done so regularly since. We have enjoyed especially visiting Mayan ruins in Mexico, studying Native American art and lifestyles in British Columbia, and tracing ancient burial and ceremonial sites as well as abbeys and castles in Ireland and Scotland. We also have enjoyed the natural beauty of these countries, particularly the coastal and mountain regions. My drawings include many land- and seascapes, and totemic images that our travels have made real for us.

Furthermore, I was challenged by this experience to reevaluate my relationships with family and friends. While I may not always succeed in showing my deepened appreciation for these connections, I am aware of a profound change in how I value the persons who make up the fabric of my life. I also know that with each new day I strive to reaffirm how much I cherish those whose lives are so deeply intertwined with mine.

The experience of my illness and healing has influenced my professional work as a teacher, scholar, and therapist in many ways. Through new courses, presentations at professional conferences, community workshops, and articles I have found opportunity to explore the meaning of the experience of illness and confronting death at midlife. I have deepened my appreciation of the heart-work of therapy and my ability to listen and sit with my clients' moods of anxiety, discouragement, and sadness. I attend better to the voice of intuition and of the unconscious both in myself and in others. I am more playful in my use of metaphors and storytelling, and I value the contribution of relaxation and meditation as adjuncts to therapy.

Perhaps most difficult to describe briefly is the effect of this experience on my spiritual life. I believe that I have been enriched immeasurably through the experience of confronting death and befriending what was previously terrifying. Through the process of sitting attentively and reflectively with fear and loss and hope and desire, it seems that one may establish a standpoint from which to construct a meaning for one's life. At the same time, the withdrawal from immersion in the activities of daily life that is necessitated by the illness and rigors of treatment provides opportunity to explore the heritage of ancient wisdom traditions. I have written elsewhere of the complementarity of these processes (McKenna, 1999).

In summary, being diagnosed with cancer and enhancing the healing process through relaxation/meditation, therapy, and art has been a rich and transformative experience for me. I strongly believe that each of us in some way encounters such an opportunity in our journey through life. It is a summons to choose life, and to enter more fully into the dance of life/death, and to reawaken to the mystery and exquisite grandeur of being.

Often during my healing journey, I read meditatively from T. S. Eliot's (1943/1971) *The Four Quartets*. I close with a brief selection from East Coker, which captures the themes of embracing darkness and celebrating the dance of death and life:

> I said to my soul, be still, and wait without hope
> For hope would be hope of the wrong thing; wait without love
> For love would be love of the wrong thing; there is yet faith
> But the faith and love and the hope are all in the waiting.
> Wait without thought, for you are not ready for thought:
> So the darkness shall be the light, and the stillness the dancing.
> Whisper of running streams, and winter lightning.

The wild thyme unseen and the wild strawberry,
The laughter in the garden, echoed ecstasy
Not lost, but requiring, pointing to the agony
Of death and birth. (p. 28)

REFERENCES

Achterberg, J. (1985). *Imagery in healing: Shamanism and modern medicine*. Boston: Shambhala.

Advances: The Journal for Mind-Body Health (1991–) Vol.7–. (Fetzer Institute; Vols. 1-6 published by The Institute for the Advancement of Health).

Allen, P. B. (1995). *Art is a way of knowing: A guide to self-knowledge and spiritual fulfillment through creativity*. Boston: Shambhala.

Borysenko, J. (1988). *Minding the body, mending the mind*. New York: Bantam.

de Chardin, T. (1968). *The divine milieu*. New York: Harper & Row.

Dunne, J. (1975). *Time and myth: A meditation on storytelling as an exploration of life and death*. Notre Dame: University of Notre Dame Press.

Eastern Cooperative Oncology Group. (1984–1988). Treatment of Burkitt's Lymphoma and Undifferentiated Non-Burkitt's Lymphoma with alternating cycles of COMP and high-dose Ara-C, (1984). Addendum #1, (1985); Addendum #2, (1986); Protocol Termination, (1988). Unpublished manuscript, University of Wisconsin, Madison.

Eliot, T. S. (1971). *The Four Quartets*. New York: Harcourt, Brace, Jovanovich. (Original work published 1943)

Fincher, S. (1991). *Creating mandalas for insight. healing. and self-expression*. Boston: Shambhala.

Fiore, N. A. (1984). *The road back to health: Coping with the emotional aspects of cancer*. New York: Bantam.

Gendlin, E. T. (1981). *Focusing* (2nd ed.). New York: Bantam.

Hadley, J., & Staudacher, C. (1985). *Hypnosis for change*. Oakland, CA: New Harbinger.

Jaffe, D. T. (1980). *Healing from within: Psychological techniques to help the mind heal the body*. New York: Simon & Schuster.

Johnson, T. H. (Ed.). (1960). *The complete poems of Emily Dickinson*. Boston: Little, Brown & Company.

Jung, C. (1966). *The practice of psychotherapy: General problems of psychotherapy* (2nd ed.). Princeton, NJ: Princeton University Press.

Kast, V. (1993). *Imagination as space of freedom: Dialogue between the ego and the unconscious*. New York: Fromm International.

Kornfield, J. (1993). *A path with heart: A guide through the perils and promises of spiritual life*. New York: Bantam.

Langer, S. (1957) *Philosophy in a new key: A study in the symbolism of reason, rite, and art*. Cambridge: Harvard University Press.

LeShan, L. (1980). You can fight for your life: Emotional factors in the treatment of cancer. New York: M. Evans.

LeShan, L. (1989). *Cancer as a turning point*. New York: Dutton.

McKenna, J. (2000). On being at both center and circumference: The role of personal discipline and collective wisdom in the recovery of soul. In M. Miller & A. West (Eds.), *Spirituality, ethics, and relationship in adulthood: Clinical and theoretical explorations*. (pp. 257–282). Madison, CT: Psychosocial Press.

McNiff, S. (1992). *Art as medicine: Creating a therapy of the imagination*. Boston: Shambhala.

National Cancer Institute. (1985). *Chemotherapy and you: A guide to self-help during treatment*. Bethesda, MD: Author.

Nhat Hanh, T. (1976). *The miracle of mindfulness*. Berkeley, CA: Parallax Press.

Progoff, I. (1975). *At a journal workshop: The basic text and guide for using the intensive journal*. New York: Dialogue House.

Rogers, C. (1961). *On becoming a person: A therapist's view of psychotherapy*. Boston: Houghton Mifflin.

Rossman, M. L. (1989). *Healing yourself: A step-by-step program for better health through imagery*. New York: Pocket Books.

Simonton, O. C., Matthews-Simonton, S., & Creighton, J. (1978). *Getting well again: A step-by-step self-help guide to overcoming cancer for patients and their families*. Los Angeles: Tarcher.

Part III

Theoretical Approaches and Reflections

chapter 8

Scientist and Artist within the Mature Self: The Integration of Two Worlds

Ernest Zebrowski, Jr.
Southern University, Baton Rouge, Louisiana

B y "scientist," I mean someone who goes about teasing Mother Nature into giving up her secrets. Science is a process rather than a collection of facts or nomenclature, and it is inductive, proceeding from specific observations to the discovery of general principles. Scientists are attracted by pockets of ignorance, for they know that only where questions continue to confound us does the scientific mind flourish. In fields where everything is already known and chiseled in stone, there can be no science.

"Art" is usually viewed as standing quite apart. The artist interprets and/or manipulates some aspect of nature, and usually expects the viewers or listeners to draw their own conclusions on what the art is all about. Auto-exegesis by artists is rare, and indeed most recipients find it disappointing when the artist does provide it. Science builds on an edifice of prior science (no neophyte, for instance, ever gazes into the night sky and immediately ponders whether neutrinos have mass); art, in contrast, embodies its intellectual products in concrete works that are accessible, to some degree, by virtually everyone. Stereotypically, the scientist is introverted, structured, and specialized; the artist is extroverted and free-spirited. From an Aristotelian perspective, science and art stand at the diagonal corners of a square of opposition: the scientist grinding from the specific toward the universal; the artist leaping from his/her personal but holistic worldview to the creation of a specific work of art.

Yet in practice, art and science are intimately symbiotic. This is true not only for professional artists and scientists, but, more relevant to the theme of this chapter, for the millions of more ordinary folk who seek to enhance their sense of self amidst the bewildering complexity of the universe around them. One does not need to exhibit in the Louvre to be an artist, nor conquer cancer to be a scientist. The development of the self, and the growth of wisdom, always reflect an intensely personal integration of artistic and scientific worldviews, regardless of whether or not the individual ever makes *Who's Who*.

I don't claim to have made any earthshaking scientific advances in my own career, and I admit that the best I've been able to do with my paintings is to give them away to my dearest friends. I write this chapter as an expert nonetheless. One does not teach science without planning the theatrics of presentation, and to write science I've learned that I must reduce a universe of possibilities to a single work, with a sense of the reader peering over my shoulder. Yet I have observed that what the reader or listener gets is not necessarily what I intend, and occasionally, to my delight, I play a role in getting someone to arrive at an idea that I had never thought of myself. Indeed, finding that a student has transcended one's pedagogy is the deepest reward of teaching.

Meanwhile, to indulge in even the simplest creative tasks, for example, cooking a meal or painting a room, none of us can afford to ignore what we know about the laws of nature. Yet even on this level our efforts often produce surprises. So it goes in art, so it goes in science, and so it goes in life. In what follows, I modestly suggest that any purely scientific or purely artistic worldview is necessarily incomplete, and that only through their integration do we grow in wisdom and maturity.

THE AESTHETIC SENSE

The concept of the aesthetic, fuzzy though it may be, plays a major role in both art and science. I won't attempt a comprehensive discussion of aesthetic development here. It is relevant, however, that we humans *do* recognize beauty, that some aspects of this recognition are crosscultural, and that the antithesis of the aesthetic can also exert dramatic influences on how we view the world.

Artistically, what we usually find most beautiful are those human creations that reflect the tranquility of Mother Nature's more benevolent moments. We are comfortable with the natural color schemes of sunsets, seascapes, and landscapes, but are jarred by unnatural contrasts and discordant colors. We are drawn to symmetries, convergences, and natural intervals in both visual art and music, but cringe when a B-flat is played with a C, or when the new building on campus looks like a collapsed mausoleum. We relish stage plays in which the characters' personalities unfold linearly, but if the personalities flip unexpectedly, as in Samuel Beckett's *Waiting for Godot*, we fidget in intellectual discomfort.

Scientists too seek the aesthetic (Tyson, 1997), and the criteria are pretty much the same as in art. Professional scientists are drawn to symmetries, recurring intervals, and general orderliness. This orderliness is often expressed in the symbolic formalisms of mathematical equations, and such equations have indeed proven to be successful guides to discovering new asteroids, new subatomic particles, and the invention of lasers and other imaginative devices. Scientists have learned, over the centuries, that truth often lurks in the aesthetic.

Yet good art, as well as good science, can also be unaesthetic. Pablo Picasso's painting *Guernica* is hardly beautiful; it is full of distorted and unnatural forms, sharp angles, and fear and terror in the eyes of both humans and horses; it is discordantly larger than life, lacks geometrical perspective, and is painted solely in black and white. Why is this a masterpiece? For the very reason that it is ugly. We look at *Guernica*, and we immediately react that something is wrong. We cannot shrug off the image without thinking more deeply about the subject: an air attack on a town of civilians during the Spanish Civil War, a precursor to the carnage that was to follow in other parts of Europe during World War II.

Similarly, when a scientific inquiry serves up an ugly equation, or an unaesthetic theory, scientists are jarred into looking beyond that equation or theory for a new source of truth. Ptolemy's geocentric theory of the universe collapsed on the basis of Copernicus's appeal to aesthetics, and not because Copernicus's heliocentric theory yielded better predictions (in fact, at that time it didn't). We view the aesthetic as an ideal, but we flock to the unaesthetic as a call to action. Ugliness screams out at us to do something about it.

THE SCIENTIFIC WORLDVIEW

Order and Chaos

The fundamental working assumption of all scientists is that the universe is at some level orderly. Indeed, the law of gravity is not likely to be repealed overnight or from place to place, Lavoisier's discovery of hydrogen remains valid after two centuries, and carbon-14 dating can be used to establish chronologies of organic materials that have been dead for millennia. If natural events sometimes appear to be disconnected and disorderly, the scientist assumes that this is only because no one has yet thought deeply enough about that class of events to discover the general governing principle.

The extreme version of this view of an orderly universe was the New-tonian determinism that dominated scientific thinking in the 18th and 19th centuries. With the discovery of radioactivity and other indeterminate quantum phenomena circa 1900, the concept of statistical determinism was embraced by the physicists (Glashow, 1994), and this in turn lent an external validation to the use of statistics by the life and social scientists. In the statistically deterministic view, some natural events may have intrinsically variable outcomes, yet the statistical measures of large numbers of such events remain predictable. More recently, scientists at the frontier have been struggling with events that do not yield to even statistical description; the result has been the development of theories of chaos and nonlinear dynamics (Gleick, 1987; Horgan, 1995). Even in chaos, however, scientists still seek evidence of a different level of order, in terms of "strange attractors," frequency bifurcations, self-similarity over scale changes, and so on.

Ultimately, when science has reached the stage at which it has answered every answerable question, we may find that the entire universe is chaotic over the long term, and that statistical determinism is but a short-term illusion, with classical Newtonian determinism applying only to those small classes of events in which a specific short-term outcome occurs with nearly 100 percent probability. But "short-term" in a universal context is, of course, quite long for a human. And science, as I am treating it here, is done by humans.

There is, in other words, no irrefutable reason to believe that the universe is orderly in all places and across all time scales. Yet in our short, personal lifetimes, we embrace those snippets of orderliness our environments serve up, while struggling in bewilderment to see through the nonsense of chaotic events. Our working assumption throughout life is that our universe does indeed "make sense" at some personal level, and that on this basis it lies within our human abilities to negotiate a mutually respectful relationship with Mother Nature. In approaching life in this manner, we are all scientists.

All scientific inquiry, whether formal or informal, is built on the assumption of orderliness extrinsic to the self. One does not expect the finding of today to be different tomorrow, unless the parameters have somehow changed. When a scientist fails to replicate a prior finding, one does not jump to the conclusion that the laws of nature are in flux. The conclusion, rather, is that someone has simply screwed up, perhaps failing to notice that new unidentified variables have snuck in and confounded the outcome. Lacking such confidence in the immutability of natural law, scientists would never have emerged intellectually from the mysticism and superstition of the dark ages. Lacking confidence that nature is not capricious, most of us common folk would have little incentive to even climb out of bed each morning.

The Knowable and the Unknowable

In the scientific worldview, the assumption of an orderly external universe does not stand alone. Equally fundamental is the assumption that it is possible for the human mind to *understand* the universe. Today we have some 6,000 years of circumstantial evidence that this is the case, punctuated by the truly great scientific insights that have arisen at an accelerated pace in the last few centuries. Yet once again, there is no compelling reason to believe that the universe *must* organize itself in a way that is lucid to *Homo sapiens*. Perhaps we are humanly capable of understanding only those elements of the universe that are physically homologous with the human senses and mind, and perhaps most of what happens around us will never yield to a completely satisfactory level of understanding, simply because such events are influenced by what we are incapable of seeing and processing intellectually.

This is a very curious issue, and one I can touch on only briefly within the scope and theme of this chapter. Let me say just a few words about it. In the physical sciences, for example, it's clear that most major advances have risen from structures of mathematical logic. Write down the law of gravity in mathematical form, combine it with the laboratory-verifiable laws of motion, solve the resulting differential equations, and we can predict mathematically that planet-like objects must travel in elliptical orbits with the sun at a focus, as indeed they are observed to do. But *why* does this work? Why should mathematical logic, a creation of the human mind, uncover physical truths? No one knows. It's just the way our universe is, it seems, and scientists take this as axiomatic.

Meanwhile, the same kind of mathematical logic suggests that as much as 90 percent of the mass of the universe is "missing," in the sense that we cannot observe it other than through its gravity. Some of this missing mass may be sitting right in the middle of Three Rivers Stadium in Pittsburgh, but no one sees it, no one feels it, and it does not affect Sunday's Steeler game. Or does it? For if it does, what experiment could we possibly perform to verify this? This type of dilemma recasts itself in some form at virtually every frontier of modern scientific investigation. Increasingly, modern science seems to be setting its own limits on what is knowable scientifically (Horgan, 1996; Zebrowski, 1999).

Yet the most compelling scientific questions are those posed not by the physical scientists or life scientists, but rather by ordinary people seeking to develop conceptual frameworks to guide them in their personal decision making. Such questions fall mostly in the social, psychological, or economic arenas, the very fields in which classical determinism fails miserably, and even statistical determinism is suspect. Here the variables are many, the observations limited, the uncertainties overwhelming, the "truths" elusive. Yet, in spite of these challenges, most of us remain committed to organizing our personal history of life experiences in frameworks that will illuminate our futures. We do this inductively, and we do it with the faith that the future follows a continuum with the present and the past. We do so with the belief that we are capable of gaining some level of understanding about external realities. Although our personal intellectual journeys may be less formal than those of the professional research scientist, they are scientific nonetheless. We are all, to some degree, scientists.

THE ART OF DOING SCIENCE

Hypothesizing

There is no such thing as *the* scientific method, textbook expositions notwithstanding. Certainly there are specialized techniques (lots of them, only a small fraction of which any individual scientist is familiar with), and there are strategies for conducting empirical studies (e.g., control of variables, sampling protocols, error analysis, propagation of uncertainty analysis, etc.). The good scientist also keeps in mind a string of caveats about observer bias, systematic errors, and synergistic effects. But there is no actual scientific method, in the sense of a single, ordered procedure for developing predictive theories from empirical observations.

As a simple example (Zebrowski, 1997), consider the following scenario: A team of archaeologists unearths a section of a centuries-old stone wall in England, on which are chiseled the sequence of letters O, T, T, F, F, S, S, E, N. Beyond this point, the rest of the wall is missing, the stones carried off by villagers in times past to become parts of other structures. The question is: what were the next three letters? Is there is a "scientific method" that tells us how to develop a hypothesis? Hardly. Although there are methods for evaluating a hypothesis once it is proposed, no textbook or manual can tell us how to develop one in the first place. Hypothesizing is an act of creativity, and each hypothesis is a work of art.

One archaeologist suggests E, S, S as the next three letters, while another argues for T, E, T. The first explains that he's hypothesized that the pattern reverses. The second hypothesizes that the letters stand for the cardinal numbers: One, Two, Three, Four, and so on, up to Nine, so the next three would be expected to be Ten, Eleven, Twelve, or T, E, T.

Aha! We surely *like* this second hypothesis better than the first, if for no other reason than it is the more aesthetic of the two. It certainly appeals to our sense of order and connection with the broader cultural environment. Of course, we still have no validation, until we find the next few lettered stones. Still, we are comfortable with accepting the T, E, T hypothesis pending any new information that might undermine it.

But now we ask the originator of this hypothesis to explain how she arrived at the idea that the letters represent the cardinal numbers. What "scientific method" did she use? At best, she is at a loss to explain. She says she pondered the wall, puzzled over various interpretations that didn't make much sense, stopped at a pub to have a beer with some friends, went home, and watched the news; then when she wasn't even consciously thinking about the problem, the answer came in a flash. Left brain, right brain.

Albert Einstein described such an explosion of creative scientific insight as a "leap of faith"; others have referred to an "Aha!" phenomenon (de Bono, 1970). Whatever it is, this leap does not result from the application of a methodology. It *is*, however, something that feeds upon itself. Those who experience it tend to get hooked on the experience, and begin to relish puzzling over other such problems (sometimes to the neglect of more mundane matters). In fact, as scientists mature in their careers, they tend to spend less time on detailed empirical investigations and more time on holistic modeling and theory building.

Validation and Falsification

Science never does lead to absolute truths. Scientific hypotheses, regardless of how compelling, are always doomed to remain forever unproven. Our earlier archaeologists, for instance, on searching the village, may be successful in finding the next few missing stones. They diligently assure that these stones mate with the wall, and they confirm that the next three letters are indeed T, E, T. This certainly supports the cardinal number hypothesis, but it does not prove it, because the following stones could still break the pattern, and in any case the whole sequence of letters might still have represented nothing but gibberish from the beginning. As Karl Popper pointed out long ago (Popper, 1934/1959), a scientific hypothesis or theory can never be proven; all one can do definitively is to *disprove* it, by finding that its predictions are *not* verified by subsequent observations (by finding a stone with a Q on it, for instance). It is impossible for any scientist to bulletproof a theory (or even most hypotheses, for that matter), because it is impossible to observe the entire universe for all time. We observe just an infinitesimal slice of reality, then we make a leap of faith to grand speculations.

The scientist who proposes a hypothesis or a theory sets him/herself up as a turkey at a turkey shoot. S/he sticks out his neck, and attracts a volley of bullets that can dispatch him/her. Although the turkey occasionally wins in the short run, in the long run, better guns and better marksmen are sure to come along. No theory stands for all time (although certainly the germ of a theory may survive in its offspring).

Given that all theories are incomplete and therefore vulnerable to being invalidated, by what criteria do we ever accept a theory? We do so through a social consensus that (a) the theory adequately explains a class of phenomena in a manner consistent with the current body of observational records, and (b) the theory embodies within itself the means by which it can be disproven empirically. Failing these criteria, a theory will not be taken seriously by the scientific community. "Creation science," for instance, fails the second test, for no creation theorist has ever explained how special creation might be disproven; "natural selection," on the other hand, can easily be falsified: all one needs to do is find a single organism whose DNA molecules spiral counter-clockwise rather than clockwise. Bingo! Down tumbles one of the fundamental paradigms of natural selection—the one that says that all organisms are cousins. And lacking this paradigm, the rest of the current theory of natural selection would likewise collapse.

The Aesthetic in Science

Formal criteria cannot be the whole answer, however, for why some theories seem "better" than others. The first person to write on this issue was probably William of Occam (ca. 1285–1349), a Franciscan philosopher who taught at Oxford for 14 years, and who proposed a principle of parsimony usually referred to today as "Occam's Razor" (Moody, 1976). In its original form, the principle was apparently stated as "What can be done with fewer [assumptions] is done in vain with more." Today's scientists usually apply the principle in the following spirit: When choosing among competing explanations for the same observations, the explanation that is "best" relies on the fewest independent assumptions.

On November 1, 1755, for instance, the grand city of Lisbon was, in one terrible day, struck by a devastating earthquake at 9:40 A.M., a series of seismic sea waves (a tsunami) starting around 11:00 A.M., and sometime that afternoon a fire that proceeded to burn out of control for the next three days to complete the destruction of the city. Some 30,000 to 40,000 perished in the immediate disaster, and perhaps another 20,000 in the winter famine that followed. Thinkers of the time assumed that the events were independent, and struggled to come to grips with why a single city should have been singled out as the target of so many calamities in such a short time interval. Theologians answered as only they could: God wished to punish the city, and when the earthquake didn't complete the job, He unleashed the tsunamis, and when this fell short of destroying everything, He started the fires. Officers of the Inquisition, their court reduced to rubble, accordingly began hanging heretics as their own decisive action to prevent future earthquakes, tsunamis, and fires.

By a century later, scientists reconsidered this event and concluded that all aspects of the disaster could be attributed to a single, major, undersea earthquake off the coast of Portugal (Kendrick, 1956; Reid, 1914). The earthquake tremors presumably traveled quickly through the sea floor and shook down the buildings in Lisbon. The tsunami triggered by the same earthquake traveled more slowly, and arrived in Lisbon some 80 minutes later to wash away everything within a 40-foot elevation of the wharves. The fire was a collateral effect, probably originating with overturned stoves in homes that had already been reduced to splinters. The famine was also a collateral effect, considering that the food warehouses were naturally situated near the harbor, where they were most vulnerable to the tsunami. Occam's Razor suggests that, lacking evidence to the contrary, the "best" explanation is that all the terrible things that happened in Lisbon that day were the result of a single primary event: an undersea earthquake.

But in what sense is this explanation "best"? Certainly not in any objective sense, given that all the direct evidence is long gone, and cannot be replicated. There is no formal reason to endorse Occam's Razor with regard to the Lisbon disaster of 1755, or to any other event. Yet our intrinsic sensibilities tell us that a scientific explanation that invokes a multitude of converging but independent variables is messy at best, and if one can find an alternative explanation that calls for fewer assumptions, it is certainly the more appealing aesthetically. Occam's Razor, in other words, is primarily an *aesthetic* criterion.

The Cultural Baggage of Science

Implicit in Occam's Razor, however, is another assumption: that scientists intend to communicate their theories to others. Science is seldom done in a social vacuum. Scientific progress is intimately dependent on communication, for no human has time to observe firsthand everything that may be relevant to his/her interests, nor to replicate all past studies that have so far stood the test of time. In this context, Occam's Razor may be viewed as a caveat to the scientist who wishes to provide a convincing scientific explanation to others: ignore preceding traditions of scientific thought, introduce a plethora of new assumptions instead, and you can be assured that the scientific community will view you as a quack.

Aristotle, of course, believed that humans could arrive at the fundamental truths of the universe through pure logic and rhetoric. To validate conclusions through empirical hypothesis testing and predictive validation was beneath the station of the Athenian thinker-elite. The highest-order truths, once established through formal intellectual inquiry, were forever immune from further dispute, and that was that.

Two millennia later, this remains far from an obsolete perspective; indeed, some very good scientists have found it more expedient to challenge and argue than to do the harder work of empirical validation. A few incidents from the history of science are worth pondering. Around 1680, for instance, Isaac Newton invited Christian Huygens from Holland to deliver a presentation before the Royal Society on his wave theory of light, which stood at odds with Newton's own corpuscular theory. In front of the assembly, Newton then proceeded to unmercifully attack Huygens, who was less than proficient in the English language. Newton won of course, and Huygens abandoned his work in optics and moved on to other scientific questions. As a result, the science of optics was set back a hundred years, until c. 1805, when Thomas Young discovered the phenomenon of interference and unambiguously demonstrated that light is a wave just as Huygens had claimed. Newton's corpuscular theory had been accepted on the weight of Newton's rhetoric, rather than on any objective measure of his science.

A similar incident took place around 1928, when the young Indian physicist S. I. Chandrasekhar traveled to England to propose that the laws of general relativity predicted the existence of massive singularities in space which are now known as "black holes." This time it was Sir Thomas Eddington who ridiculed the young visiting scientist, and so devastated him that he left the field of astrophysics. In 1983, Chandrasekhar won the Nobel Prize in physics for work unrelated to his initial discovery. By then, however, he had been vindicated, for the "black hole" had indeed been accepted as a legitimate scientific theoretical concept.

The art of doing science, then, involves creative insights, deference to tradition, an appeal to aesthetic sensibilities, but also effective communication. Science cannot be done by a cookbook, nor communicated by merely following a style manual. Science is the antithesis of "common sense" (which Mark Twain defined as the sum total of the prejudices one acquires before the age of 18). Successful scientists realize that they must transcend their preconceived notions to embark on the adventure of teasing Mother Nature into giving up her own secrets. They also realize that Mother Nature alone remains the final arbiter of whether their scientific findings reflect objective reality.

Science and the Self

No science, as noted above, is devoid of subjectivity. In fact, our personal quests for making sense of our place in the universe are essentially scientific investigations, built on a worldview that (a) there exists an external reality, (b) this reality exhibits some degree of order, and (c) that it is within our power to understand this order and act upon this understanding for our personal fulfillment. We do not blindly cast ourselves on turbulent seas, to be carried where Mother Nature chooses. Instead, we observe those metaphorical seas, develop hypotheses to predict their future behaviors, then act in ways that meld these hypotheses with our own preferred futures. If things don't work out as planned, as in a new job or a new marriage, this may falsify our current hypothesis. We then reevaluate and try again, hopefully now a little wiser.

Yet our task is not straightforward. At one extreme, there are always those discontinuities in life, those glitches that seemingly invade from outer space and trigger major personal upheavals: accidents, natural disasters, and crimes, to name a few. There is no way to integrate such discontinuous events with the concept of an orderly universe. In formal science, the investigator can simply throw out a few bad data points, but in life, one does not easily dismiss losing a foot to a landmine. At the other extreme is an event-sequence that few modern humans ever experience: each day is like the day before, life unfolds in perfect order, and no surprises ever disturb anyone's regimens. Boring at best, and a perfect recipe for turning one's brain to mush.

Between these two extremes, in a continuum where order and chaos overlap, most of us seek to organize our lives. We never fully discard our childlike belief in classical determinism (which is why magic acts entrance even adults), yet we grow increasingly wary of even the simplest statements of absolute truth ("The sky is blue? No, son, at least half the time it's black."). We begin to think in terms of probabilities, the language of statistical determinism, and we couch our personal hypotheses in such schema, for example, from "this new job will be great," to "this new job has better than an even chance of working out." We seek feedback more diligently and with greater sensitivity, the better to reevaluate our working hypotheses. We grow more cautious in some endeavors, and perhaps come to be viewed by others as more conservative than we view ourselves. Time, after all, is running out, and mistakes get more costly.

Yet if this is all we do, we fail to grow in wisdom. The dilemma of our informal science grows from the observation that our environment is at best statistically determinate, and that we simply don't live long enough to establish the validity of any personal working hypothesis of life to any statistically significant degree of confidence. We can experience only so much in so much time. In life, we are forced to create premature hypotheses and to act on them prematurely.

So when the external world responds with a negative reception, what is our appropriate response? To immediately back off and try something else, assuming that our statistical hypothesis is invalid, based on a single event? Or do we get headstrong, and plow forward time and again using the same old patterns? Clearly, no purely scientific algorithm can resolve this dilemma. To leap this roadblock to wisdom, we need to draw upon something else: an artistic spirit.

THE ARTISTIC WORLDVIEW

The fundamental working assumption of all artists is that the world can be enhanced through creative reorderings of physical materials or processes. This enhancement may be visual (as in painting, sculpture, or architecture), behavioral (stage plays and ballets), auditory (symphonies and rock music), or written works. As noted earlier, the art need not be pretty. Even visual ugliness, discordant sounds, and morbid stories can sometimes enhance the world, if they stimulate us to develop deeper insights into the human condition.

Art is proactive rather than reactive; the universe is always a bit different after the artistic act. Extrinsic and intrinsic realities are merged during the execution of the art, and the end work stands as concrete evidence that the self is not irrelevant in the future course of the world. We delight in contemplating the fruits of our creative labors, whether it be in remodeling a room or cooking a gourmet meal, for these are our personal imprints on external reality. We are at home in the universe, and the universe would be different without us.

Yet, unless we happen to be marooned alone on a desert island, our artistic spirit is driven by an additional factor: a desire for social validation. In science, ultimate validation comes from Mother Nature herself; in art, it comes only through human communication and feedback. Every work of art reaches out in an attempt to challenge some recipient's preconceived notions, and effective art induces the recipient to accept this challenge. All of us have viewed art that we quickly walked away from with a shrug, or began novels that we quickly laid aside as too obscure, banal, or bizarre. Clearly, such art was not effective (for us, at least). The artist whose solutions fail to communicate is an artist whose efforts have failed. Artistic communication is a considerable challenge, for it must be based on presumptions about the collective mind of the audience. Van Gogh is the archetype of the artist who failed to communicate with the audience of his time and died frustrated at an early age, his art still unvalidated.

The perceptive artist can approach the problem of community validation through several avenues. On the one hand, the artist can actively seek new recipients that will provide a supportive forum for the extant work: if an exhibition fails in Soho, try Boca Raton; if a marriage fails, seek a different type of partner. Alternatively, the artist might change the presentation or the medium: if velvet Elvis paintings fail to convey the essence of 1960s culture, move on to clay sculptures; if one's last class lecture put everyone to sleep, next time try a group discussion. Both of these strategies recognize that art cannot be all things to all people at all times, yet both have their obvious pitfalls. The choice of an appropriate strategy to draw validation is itself an artistic choice that offers no guarantees.

Meanwhile, the strategy with the least chance of success is this: doing more of the same, just a little bit louder. Culture changes, and so does the audience. Theater of the absurd is an idea whose time has come and gone, pop art is passé, and the partner one divorces is never the same person one originally married. To develop in wisdom and maturity, the artist must seek a basis for deciding how to change either him/herself or the medium that carries his/her message. S/he must, in other words, develop an organic working hypothesis of life.

THE SCIENCE OF ART

Every morning when we wake, we are more ignorant than the morning before. Each 24 hours, a great deal more knowledge is added to the collective human information base than we as individuals can possibly assimilate. We learn arithmetically in time: if it takes a day to come to grips with a new idea, we are limited to only about 300 new ideas in a year. Meanwhile, collective knowledge increases geometrically in time (witness the explosion of data on the Internet) with thousands or millions of new ideas generated daily, each breeding several other new ideas in a geometrically branching chain.

The scientist confronts the challenge of this information explosion by specializing in a particular scientific discipline, then further in a subdiscipline, then probably even further to the paradigms of a particular class of phenomena (e.g., physics to fluid dynamics to turbulent flow to supersonic turbulent flow). Such increasing scientific specialization walls scientists off from many of their colleagues, and reduces the population of peers who can legitimately evaluate any given scientific work.

The artist takes a different approach. The universe of available information is not a big concern. Instead, the artist represents himself as but one person who offers interpretations of what he has experienced and learned as an individual. The burden of generalization is transferred to the recipient of the art.

Yet the artist does not, and cannot, function in a vacuum of ignorance. The artist develops a sensitivity to sensory inputs and his personal emotional reactions, then seeks to extrapolate. S/he does this at a continuum of levels. At the most basic level (often characterized as "skill"), the artist experiments with the medium, learning that certain oil paints dry and contract at different rates, or that the shadows thrown by stage lighting can be controlled to enhance or detract from a choreographed score. As with the scientist, the artist is guided by the earlier discoveries of others. Yet he cannot simply mimic old solutions in an attempt to solve new problems. The development of artistic skill is tantamount to the scientific quest of teasing Mother Nature into giving up her secrets. The result is the ability to manipulate physical and concrete entities to yield desired outcomes.

Although the artist develops his own skill empirically, he also defers to more formal theory about his medium: the musician must understand the physics of sound; the chef, chemistry and bacteriology; the dancer, biomechanics; the photographer, optics and chemistry (and increasingly, electronics); and so on. Scientific theory not only opens vistas for new art forms, but it also helps the artist channel his energy in directions where it will be most productive, avoiding the physically impossible. There is no sense, for instance, in designing a large sculpture to be cast in solid lead, since beyond a height of a few feet this metal is too weak to support its own weight. Similarly, one does not expect a 200-pound actor to do a stage-jump into the arms of a 110-pound ballerina, nor does one position a microphone in front of a speaker (try this, and you'll quickly hear why).

Yet the successful artist also embraces scientific induction at a higher level. Given that a work of art is a concrete embodiment of an abstract concept, the artist must somehow generate that concept, that hypothesis of life, from which the specific work flows. If the hypothesis is nonexistent, or lacks communicative generality or appeal, the final art will be received poorly by others. The recipient of the art legitimately assumes that the artist has something relevant to say, and that he did some deep thinking about this message before he put a brush to canvas. To the artist, then, the challenge is this: How do I personally make sense of the complexity of worldly events? How do I organize what I have seen and experienced into a conceptual framework that illuminates the broader human condition? This is informal science, but it is science nonetheless.

The artist accepts this scientific challenge with zest. S/he actively seeks out new ways of looking at the universe—making new friends, doing new things, possibly exploring a variety of religions and cults, maybe even experimenting with mind-altering drugs. The successful artist grows wiser as the phenomenological scope of his or her own experiential base expands. The personal working hypothesis of life grows more sophisticated, and the artistic message, hopefully, matures as a result.

THE INTEGRATION OF SCIENCE AND ART IN THE MATURE SELF

We are all simultaneously scientists and artists. We assume that there is order in extrinsic reality, yet we accept and often embrace deviations from that order. We assume we are capable of understanding the objective world we live in, yet we also strive to reorder that world. We embark on quests for truth, even as we create our own truth. We seek validations by Mother Nature, even as we solicit feedback from other humans who are just as confused as we are. We communicate. We laugh, we cry, and we share our mirth and tears.

The conduct of science is not purely objective, nor is art purely subjective. The two activities, and the two worldviews, are intimately symbiotic. Their integration encourages and enhances that ephemeral quality we call "wisdom." To ignore either our artistic or scientific facets is to deny ourselves the fullness of insight we are capable of developing in our personal lives.

Yet I do not state this position dogmatically, for the scientific side of me keeps whispering that there must be a plausible reason for every truth. In fact, science does offer reasons for an essential connection between art and science within the human psyche. Our "modern" view of ourselves notwithstanding, most of us are less than 100 generations removed from the stone age. The slow grind of natural selection does not accomplish major biological changes in such a short time. We still operate with stone-age genes, our internal biochemistry programmed to support our survival in a prior environment much different than today's modern global society. That our stone-age ancestors had artistic sensibilities is well established by the archaeologists. That they also were scientific, or at least proto-scientific, has also been argued persuasively (Bronowski, 1976). That *we* are here today because our ancestors were well adapted to cope with the risks of their stone-age environmental pressures is axiomatic.

To survive in spite of their obvious physiological handicaps, early members of our species needed to be both scientists and artists. As scientists, they sought to understand and predict; as artists they sought to create and communicate. Only in more recent centuries has any distinction or specialization arisen, where formalized subcultures have valued right or left brain thinking over the other. Our remote ancestors, survivors every one, were both artists and scientists. Our present successes and confusion are their biochemical and cultural legacy. Recognizing and embracing this intrinsic aspect of our humanity is an essential step to wisdom and maturity.

REFERENCES

Bronowski, J. (1976). *The ascent of man.* Boston: Little, Brown.

de Bono, E. (1970). *Lateral thinking.* New York: Harper & Row.

Glashow, S. L. (1994). *From alchemy to quarks.* Pacific Grove, CA: Brooks/Cole.

Gleick, J. (1987). *Chaos.* New York: Viking.

Horgan, J. (1995, June). From complexity to perplexity. *Scientific American, 272,* 104–109.

Horgan, J. (1996). *The end of science.* New York: Addison-Wesley.

Kendrick, T. D. (1956). *The Lisbon earthquake.* Philadelphia: Lippincott.

Moody, E. A. (1976). *Truth and consquences in medieval logic.* Greenwood Press.

Popper, K. (1959). *The logic of scientific discovery.* New York: Basic Books. (Original work published 1934)

Reid, H. F. (1914, June). The Lisbon earthquake of November 1, 1755. *Bulletin of the Seismological Society of America, 4*(2), 53–80.

Tyson, N. (1997, November). Romancing the equations. *Natural History, 106*(10), 80–82.

Zebrowski, E., Jr. (1997). *Perils of a restless planet: Scientific perspectives on natural disasters.* Cambridge: Cambridge University Press.

Zebrowski, E., Jr. (1999). *A history of the circle: Mathematical reasoning and the physical universe.* New Brunswick: Rutgers University Press.

chapter 9

Major Creative Innovators as Viewed Through the Lens of the Model of Hierarchical Complexity and Evolution

Michael Lamport Commons
Harvard Medical School

Linda Marie Bresette
Salem State College

Charles Darwin (1855) noted that finches had diverged into a wide variety of birds. If they had not been isolated in the closed environment of the Galápagos Islands, these finches would have represented a wide number of species, as was the case of mainland species of birds. Many people had been exposed to just such novel situations but made nothing of them. Although Darwin discovered this phenomenon in the early 1800s, it was not until many years later that he himself made any sense of it when he devised his theory of evolution. Darwin saw that evolutionary forces had transformed the birds differently. But while Darwin's specific observations of finches did not have much impact on the direction of science, his evolutionary theory did.

Darwin's theory constituted a radical innovation in the science of his time for three reasons:

Some of the material in this chapter comes from Commons & Goodheart (1999). Dare Institute staff members have edited the manuscript and made major suggestions for change.

167

1. he presented evolutionary evidence establishing the fact that human thought and action are continuous with animal thought and action;
2. he proposed an explanation for human evolution that was not teleological, that is, one that did not claim an ultimate purpose; and
3. finally, Darwin's theory brought together four distinct prior paradigms: biology, ecology, animal behavior, and geology.

Darwin created much of three new interrelated paradigms out of them: paleontology, evolutionary biology, and ethology. It is this achievement that has made it possible for studies of animal behavior to illuminate human behavior.

The survival of a society and its culture depends on major scientific innovations. Societies that have higher rates of major innovation have better economies, and the society with the largest number of innovations tends to dominate the world's economic scene. Yet it is an extremely small number of people who make such innovations. This chapter offers at least four cardinal reasons for why this is so. The major reasons posited for the shortage of scientific innovators are a lack of development of: extremely complex thinking, necessary personalities, sufficient education, and appropriate cultural conditions that support innovation. Charles Darwin stands out in this context as a positive example of someone who does not suffer from the aforementioned deficits—an exemplar of a major creative innovator.

CREATIVELY INNOVATIVE CULTURAL CONTRIBUTIONS

Minimally, creativity must be original action. The methods, theories, and so on, do not have to be original; only the manner in which they are used has to be original. In addition, creative acts become social memes of long standing (Dawkins, 1976, 1981; Feldman, 1980; Feldman, Csikszentmihalyi, & Gardner, 1994). *Memes* are to cultural evolution what genes are to evolutionary biology. Genes are the basic biological units of information that are transmitted from one individual to another in the form of DNA. Memes are the basic cultural units of information that are transmitted to other people in the form of behavioral patterns. In the course of positive adult development, major innovations are new memes that are extreme examples of generativity (Erikson, 1959, 1978). Generative acts are not only important to ourselves, but are useful to society. Innovative generative acts can lead to something new in society.

We approach this matter of creativity—of creative innovation—from the perspective of the Model of Hierarchical Complexity (MHC). The

MHC of Commons and Richards (1984a, 1984b; Commons, Trudeau, Stein, Richards, & Krause, 1998) is a system that classifies development in terms of a task-required hierarchical organization of required response. The model was derived in part from Piaget's (Inhelder & Piaget, 1955/1958) notion that the higher-stage actions coordinate lower-stage actions by organizing them into a new, more hierarchically complex pattern. The stage of an action is found by answering the following two questions: a) What are the organizing actions? b) What are the stages of the elements being organized?

THE MODEL OF HIERARCHICAL COMPLEXITY

As stated, the MHC is a universal system that classifies the task-required hierarchical organization of responses. Every task contains a multitude of subtasks (Overton, 1990). When the subtasks are completed in a required order, they complete the task in question. Tasks vary in complexity in two ways: *horizontal* (classical information) and *vertical* (hierarchical information), which are defined next.

Horizontal (Classical Information) Complexity

Classical information describes the number of "yes/no" questions it takes to do a task. For example, if you ask a person across the room, did a penny come up heads when they flipped it, saying "heads" would transmit 1 bit of "horizontal" information. If there were 2 pennies, you would have to ask two questions, one about each penny. Hence, each additional 1-bit question adds another bit. Let us say they had a four-faced top with the faces numbered 1, 2, 3, and 4. Instead of spinning it, they tossed it against a backboard like dice. Again, there would be 2 bits. You could ask them if the face had an even number. If it did, you could ask if it were a 2. *Horizontal complexity* is the sum of bits required by the task.

Vertical (Hierarchical) Complexity

Specifically, hierarchical complexity refers to the number of recursions that the coordinating actions must perform on a set of primary elements. Actions at a higher order of hierarchical complexity: a) are defined in terms of actions at the next lower order of hierarchical complexity; b) organize and transform the lower-order actions; and c) produce organizations of lower-order actions that are new and not arbitrary, and cannot be accomplished by those lower-order actions alone. After meeting these conditions, we say the higher-order action *coordinates* the actions of the next lower order. *Stage of performance* is defined as the highest-order hierarchical complexity of the task solved. Commons, Richards, Trudeau, Goodheart, and Dawson (1997; cited in Commons & Miller, 1998) found that hierarchical complexity of a task predicts stage of a performance, the correlation was .92 (hierarchical complexity of the task that is completed).

The MHC (Commons, Trudeau, Stein, Richards, & Krause, 1998) posits that an individual's perceptions of the world and its stimuli are influenced and constrained by frameworks. These frameworks embody an individual's conditioning history as well as his or her cultural, educational, religious, political, and social background. Such a framework is referred to as one's perspective. Perspectives differ in terms of hierarchical complexity. In addition, as the hierarchical complexity of an individual's response to task demands increases (i.e., as stage of development goes up), the individual becomes increasingly likely to take many perspectives into account (Commons & Rodriguez, 1990; Rodriguez, 1989).

POSTFORMAL ORDERS OF COMPLEXITY

We assert that coming up with innovations requires postformal thought. Four postformal orders of hierarchical complexity have been proposed (Commons & Richards, 1984a, 1984b), beginning with systematic thinking and developing through metasystematic thought to paradigmatic thinking and cross-paradigmatic thinking. The four postformal orders, according to the GMHC, are shown in Table 9.1. Innovators functioning at each of the four stages perform tasks of different hierarchical complexity that do not overlap with one another. They perform the different tasks using skills that are increasingly rare. The end results are entirely different for society. People have been known to buy the expertise of people functioning at the systematic and metasystematic stage. The results of innovation become much more expensive at the paradigmatic and cross-paradigmatic stages. In fact, at the cross-paradigmatic stage, so few people exist that societies have no mechanisms to encourage such activity, as far as we know. Yet it is the cross-paradigmatic skills that change the course of civilization.

Systematic Order

At the systematic order, ideal task completers discriminate the frameworks for relationships between variables for an integrated system of tendencies and relationships. The objects of the systematic actions are formal-operational relationships between variables. The actions include

TABLE 9.1.   Postformal Stages

	What They Do	How They Do It	End Result
Systematic operations	Constructs multi-variate systems and matrices	Coordinates more than one variable as input	Events and ideas can be situated in a larger context. Systems are formed out of formal operational relations.
Metasystematic operations	Construct multi-systems and metasystems out of disparate systems	Compares systems and perspectives occur in a systematic way. Reflects on systems, and creates supersystems of systems.	Supersystems and metasystems are formed out of multiple systems
Paradigmatic	Fits metasystems together to form new paradigms	Synthesis	Paradigms are formed out of multiple metasystems
Cross-paradigmatic	Fits paradigms together to form new fields	Forms new fields by crossing paradigms	Fields are formed out of multiple paradigms

determining possible multivariate causes: outcomes that may be determined by many causes; the building of matrix representations of information in the form of tables or matrices; the multidimensional ordering of possibilities, including the acts of preference and prioritization. The actions generate systems. Views of systems generated have a single "true" unifying structure. Other systems of explanation or even other sets of data collected by adherents of other explanatory systems tend to be rejected. At this order, science is seen as an interlocking set of relationships, with the truth of each in interaction with embedded, testable relationships. Behavior of events is seen as governed by multivariate causality. Most standard science operates at this order. Researchers carry out variations of previous experiments. Yet our estimates are that only 20 percent of the U.S. population can now function at the systematic stage.

Metasystematic Order

At the metasystematic order, ideal task completers act on systems. The objects of metasystematic actions are systems. The systems are made up of formal-operational relationships. Metasystematic actions compare, contrast, transform, and synthesize systems. The product of metasystematic actions are metasystems also known as supersystems. For example, consider treating systems of causal relations as the objects. This allows one to compare and contrast systems in terms of their properties. The focus is placed on the similarities and differences in each system's form, as well as constituent causal relations and the actors within them. Philosophers, scientists, and others examine the logical consistency of sets of rules in their respective disciplines. Doctrinal lines are replaced by a more formal understanding of assumptions and methods used by investigators. As an example, we suggest that almost all professors at top research universities function at this stage in their line of work.

We posit that a person must function in the area of innovation at least at the metasystematic order of hierarchal complexity to produce truly creative innovations. That means that at least two multivariate systems must be coordinated. We find that true adult creativity depends on an adequate performance on other related tasks. The solution to tasks the society deems creative quite often requires a new synthesis of systems of thought (the metasystematic order) or even a new paradigm (the paradigmatic order) or a field (the cross-paradigmatic order).

Paradigmatic Order

At the paradigmatic order, people create new fields out of multiple metasystems. The objects of paradigmatic acts are metasystems. When there are metasystems that are incomplete, and adding to them would create inconsistencies, quite often a new paradigm is developed. Usually, the paradigm develops out of a recognition of a poorly understood phenomenon. The actions in paradigmatic thought form new paradigms from supersystems (metasystems).

Paradigmatic actions often affect fields of knowledge that appear unrelated to the original field of the thinkers. They have to see the relationship between very large and often disparate bodies of knowledge and coordinate supersystems. Paradigmatic action requires a tremendous degree of decentration. One has to transcend tradition and recognize one's actions as distinct and probably troubling to those in one's environment. But at the same time one has to understand that the laws of nature operate both on oneself and one's environment—a unity. This suggests that learning in one realm can be generalized to the other.

Innovative scientists must function at least at the paradigmatic order

There are numerous paradigmatic-order scientists. For example, the 19th-century physicist, Clark Maxwell, constructed a fields paradigm from the existing metasystems of electricity and magnetism created by

Faraday, Ohm, Volta, Ampere, and Oersted with the mathematics of fields and waves. Maxwell's equations formed a new paradigm. This paradigm made it possible for Einstein to use space-time curved space to replace Euclidean geometry. Wave fields can easily be seen as the rings that form when a rock is dropped in water or when a magnet is placed under a piece of paper holding iron filings. Maxwell's equations showed that electricity and magnetism are united. Modern particle theory has been able to add still two more forces to the electromagnetic forces.

Cross-Paradigmatic Order

The fourth postformal order is the cross-paradigmatic. This order has not been examined because there are very few people who function at this stage. All that can be done at this time is to identify and analyze historical examples. The objects of cross-paradigmatic actions are paradigms. Cross-paradigmatic action integrates paradigms into a new field or profoundly transforms an old one. One might ask whether all interdisciplinary studies are therefore cross-paradigmatic? Is psychobiology cross-paradigmatic? The answer to both is no. Such interdisciplinary studies might create new paradigms, such as psychophysics, but not new fields.

Let us consider some examples of cross-paradigmatic stage attainment. Copernicus coordinated geometry of ellipses that represented the geometric paradigm and the sun-centered perspectives. This coordination formed the new field of celestial mechanics. The creation of this field transformed society—a scientific revolution that spread throughout our understanding of people's place in the cosmos. It directly led to what many would now call true empirical science with its mathematical exposition. This in turn paved the way for Isaac Newton to coordinate mathematics and physics forming the new field of classic mathematical physics. The field was formed out of the new mathematical paradigm of calculus (independently of Leibnitz) and the paradigm of physics, which consisted of disjointed physical laws.

René Descartes first created the paradigm of analysis and used it to coordinate the paradigms of geometry, proof theory, algebra, and teleology. He thereby created the field of analytical geometry and analytic proofs. Charles Darwin coordinated paleontology, geology, biology, and ecology to form the field of evolution, which paved the way for chaos theory, evolutionary biology, and evolutionary psychology (Darwin, 1897). Albert Einstein coordinated the paradigm of non-Euclidian geometry with the paradigms of classical physics to form the field of relativity. This gave rise to modern cosmology. He also coinvented quantum mechanics. Max Planck coordinated the paradigm of wave theory, energy with probability, forming the field of quantum mechanics. This has led to modern particle physics. Lastly, Kurt Gödel coordinated epistemology and mathematics in the field of limits on knowing. Along with Darwin, Einstein, and Planck, he founded modern science and epistemology.

HIERARCHICAL COMPLEXITY IN HUMAN SOCIETIES

The development of complexity in human societies depends on innovations by single individuals. The innovator has the tendency to discern and discriminate relationships among elements that are extremely complicated. Making an innovation is much more difficult than learning about it after it is made. Major cultural innovations require paradigmatic complexity (Commons & Richards, 1995) because there is no support whatever from within the cultures themselves. The difficulty of an action depends on the level of support in addition to the horizontal information demanded in bits, and the order of hierarchical complexity. The *level of support* represents the degree of independence of the person's action and thinking from environmental control provided by others in the situation.

There is little support for major innovations in culture because the history of the necessary hierarchical complexity surrounding the task is absent. Nor is there a history of reinforcement that would induce the subject to detect new phenomena. "Finding" a given question increases complexity demand by one order of complexity over solving a posed problem with no assistance. Finding the question allows for finding a problem to address that question, which increases the complexity demanded by one further order (Arlin, 1975, 1977, 1984). Finding and identifying the underlying phenomenon requires still a third additional order of complexity.

Therefore, even if understanding—or using the innovation, once it is created—requires only formal operations, to be the individual who creates the advance requires two more levels of support and therefore roughly paradigmatic complexity. In order for an innovation to be absorbed by/assimilated into the culture, the culture must perform at the formal order with respect to the innovation.

The Stage of an Inventor of Culture and the Stage of a Culture Differ

Individual and cultural development have a straightforward relationship to one another. The stage of cultural development is limited by the highest stage of performance of a member. From the Cro-Magnon *Homo sapiens* on, we argue that there were members who behaved at the paradigmatic stage. The requirement is for only one such member. Only one member at a time invents, even though the invention might be a joint enterprise in other regards. Even in cooperative behavior, one person exhibits the behavior first, even if only a millisecond before the other. Yet that inventing behavior is totally dependent on others' past inventions. Inventions can only build on the last inventions and are limited by the stage of those inventions. That is why the stage we assign to cultures can be so much lower than the stage attained by the most developed individuals.

Even though individuals might act at the highest stages, for example, paradigmatic, societal development tends to lag behind individual development because at each stage of cultural development the cultural innovators outpace their contemporaries, at least within their domain of innovation. In order for a culture to progress, there must be a supply of these innovators who work with minimal support from their culture. And it is the size of this supply that seems to be the largest bottleneck in cultural development.

Truly Creative Acts Change Culture

To be "truly creative," an act has to reach and influence a public. Otherwise, no memes are created. Sometimes potential creative acts are not communicated, either because the society is not proficient enough to receive them, or simply the acts themselves are inefficiently transmitted. For successful transmission and dissemination of innovation to take place, the culture must be able to absorb the discovery. A discovery may be regarded as a new pattern of behavior performed by an individual or individuals in various situations. Formal and informal education is the means by which memes are acquired (Cavalli-Sforza, Feldman, Chen, & Dornbusch, 1982). Most people cannot possibly understand an innovation on their own because they do not reason at a high enough stage. Increasing support through teaching and training ensures that they come to understand and possibly utilize a higher-stage behavior (Fischer, Hand, & Russell, 1984), including a discovery. Thus, it follows that the innovator must be some form of teacher in order for the new memes to be acquired by others.

Discoveries and findings need to be spread by *infection of memes* (Commons, Krause, Fayer, & Meaney, 1993; Trivers, 1985). This dramatically slows the process of discovery. People have to engage in activities that require the new cultural information. The transmission of memes usually requires that the uninitiated individuals receive some degree of support in order to learn the new memes. In learning the new actions required by the innovation, an individual is thereby infected with the memes of the innovation. In carrying out the activities associated with the innovation, as well as teaching others to do likewise, the individual is further infected. The more thoroughly an innovation is learned and taught, the greater degree of infection by memes. Learning innovations increases employability in the present culture. To learn one innovation, such as computer programming, puts one into an educational system that transmits other memes as well. The infecting memes become part of the participants' resulting behavior. All effective educating, training, and communicating result in a transmission of memes. The rate depends on increasing contagion so that the potential innovators come into contact with the most advanced forms of the present culture. A demand for the innovation also has to exist so that innovation pays off.

NOVELTY AND MORE HIERARCHICALLY COMPLEX BEHAVIORS

Novelty has two aspects that are important to creativity. First, novelty spurs the development of more hierarchically complex behaviors, and second, creativity requires an original response to novelty. People who are overwhelmed by novelty are precluded from creative discovery. In this section, we discuss how novelty is involved in stage change. Such stage change is quite often necessary for the truly creative act.

Novelty is the psychological dimension of an individual's response to a new or strange situation. Such a situation may consist of a sudden or unpredictable change in a known state of affairs. It has been shown that novelty greatly aids, if not induces, continuous intellectual development within domains and discontinuous development across domains by forcing transitions between lower and higher stages (Grotzer et al., 1985). Furthermore, this development is dependent on "new," more hierarchically complex behavior obtaining outcomes that the individual prefers. Novelty in ordinary problem solvers often produces some development. Strikingly similar in some aspects, but just as strikingly different in others, is the problem solving of "truly innovative" thinkers. The former type of novelty leads to development that is ordinary in the society and to actions that are also ordinary. The latter, by comparison, is characterized by originality and not limited by the hierarchical complexity of thinking that is near the social norm. A tangible and full-bodied historical example of this latter type can be found in the creative work of Charles Darwin.

Novelty and Creative Behavior

Creative behavior is always novel. The behavior responds to some novel aspect of the environment that others have missed. Take the example of Darwin's observation of finches as discussed earlier. Many people had been exposed to just such novel situations but made nothing of them. This is an example of discovering a phenomenon. The discovery itself did not have much impact on Darwin's conceptualization, but years later he made sense of the phenomenon by proposing his theory of evolution. The finches had evolved and now filled the same niches that mainland species of birds of much greater variety had filled. In one case, the niches were filled by a variety of finches (system 1) and in another by many separate mainland species (system 2). Darwin saw that evolutionary forces had transformed the birds differently (a metasystematic comparison of systems 1 and 2). But, he understood this phenomenon without support. Hence, this is cross-paradigmatic. Creative innovations, to have social impact, must be a part of a chain of transformations in which later ones progressively build on earlier ones. The progressive nature of such transformations distinguishes such creative innovation from mere stylish variations. Styles come and go, but science tends to be progressive.

THE PERSONALITIES OF MAJOR INNOVATORS

Necessary (but not Sufficient) Traits of Environments and History That Allow for True Creativity

Many tendencies to act in particular ways can be directly related to major innovation. In traditional personality theories, when tendencies remain somewhat stable over time, they are called *traits*. Although some of these tendencies are partially inherited, some portions are acquired. When we assess these tendencies, we cannot tell which it is without doing twin studies or similar studies. In either case, in the present no one has access to what created these tendencies. Traits are not causes of behavior, however. They are just intermediate results. Behavioral-analytic theories would tend to explain these tendencies with respect to the individual's history and present circumstances. Behavioral momentum theory (Mace, Charles, Lalli, Shea, & Nevin, 1992; Nevin, Tota, Torquato, & Shull, 1990) describes two types of histories that produce persistence and independence: a resistance to influence by social controls and high risk taking. The first history is one of plenty or independent wealth. Let us take the case of Darwin again; he was independently wealthy. Darwin's quest for the truth was unfettered by concerns for employment. Although some were extremely upset by what he was doing, he could not be fired and lived quite well. Einstein describes the life of a patent officer as ideal, getting paid for doing what he liked. There was little work in that position he did not enjoy. And, it left him with plenty of time to work on his own theories. Hence, again, his discovery behavior was not under the control of an employer or social institution.

Personalities That Withstand Social Conformist Influences

Innovators do not have nonconforming personalities in general, but they do withstand social conformist influences. To spread their innovations they are highly connected to society as opposed to the nonconformist who, to a large degree, lives outside of society, such as Raskolnikov in Dostoyevsky's (1914) *Crime and Punishment.*

Cognitive styles

Field independence is associated with creative functions in adults (Minhas & Kaur, 1983). This classically defined cognitive style has been measured by the rod and frame task (Witkin, 1949; Witkin et al., 1954). The degree to which people are field-independent correlates with their ability to resist social pressure and the influence of social cues. Field-independent people are more likely to exhibit creativity and are more likely to resist the social pressure to conform to tradition.

Minhas and Kaur's (1983) research supports the idea that field-independent individuals display a penchant for novel types of acts. They also find an overlap between field-independence and intelligence. Ohnmacht and McMorris (1971) found that neither field-independence nor lack of dogmatism alone is useful in explaining variations on a task presumed to reflect creative potential. However, when considered together, these variables become significant. Using the proclivity to produce transformations of visual information as a measure of creativity, Ross (1977) also found a high correlation between creative behavior, locus of control, and field-independence.

Detachment From the Social Order

But traits are not enough. The major innovators act in ways that insulate them from social pressures rather than just resisting the social pressure to conform. Major innovators tend to be noncompetitive with others because they do not use others as a frame of reference. They are not really concerned with other people's opinions of them and do not compare their own "success" with others'. Instead, in terms of *social comparison theory*, the comparison may be to one's own performance or the performance of some historical figure. Therefore, creative actions often *require* that there be a certain detachment from the social order and social approval.

To be creative, individuals also must be able to withstand rejection. Smith, Carlsson, and Sandstrom (1985) found that creators use fewer compulsive or depressive defenses and are free from excessive anxiety. They also found that creative individuals have access to their dream life and their early childhood more often than noncreative individuals and tend to remember both positive and negative qualities of these life experiences. Finally, creativity requires one to separate oneself from one's creations. Otherwise one would rarely be self-critical of one's creative output. If one were always satisfied, there would be no development, no striving for more. Being challenged by, rather than upset at, not knowing the details or the direction of one's enterprise seems essential, as does the ability to withstand and overcome disconfirmation or failure at a particular step in the enterprise. All of these require risk-seeking behavior. The passion involved is for the enterprise of discovery, not for the self, a particular act, or a need for social approval. This independence may lead to a sense of isolation from others, while—though painful—it may also prove to be surprisingly necessary.

Timing of Creative Acts

Even with all of the personal traits mentioned above, creative acts require a certain timing. Timing of creative acts may have three sources, each conflicting with the others. First, development of higher-order hierarchical complexity takes time. As we show, some of the most integrative and highest-order acts may not take place until middle age or later. Second, one needs a lot of time to develop one's own ideas, and an arena within which those ideas will not be demolished before they can attain integrations. Third, there is a long social agenda of what work one is supposed to carry out rather than going down one's own creative path. This social agenda entails diversion of a certain amount of time and energy to work on other people's problems. One might then simply adopt their frame of reference.

Tolerance of Ambiguity and Risk Taking

Tolerance of ambiguity and the taking of risk are necessary for creativity. Students doing research often ask why the professor does not simply give them the right method for understanding a new problem the first time. The professor then says that "if I knew the right method for solving this problem, I would have learned it from somebody who had already answered the question." Ambiguity is more tolerable for older adults, making the ambiguity in the creative process less of a threat. Gisela Labouvie-Vief (1985) noted that older adults were at ease when working with ambiguity creatively (also see Labouvie-Vief, Adams, Hakim-Larson, & Hayden, 1983). Younger adults focus on reaching a conclusion that makes sense when presented with logically inconsistent statements, whereas older adults concentrate on the problems inherent in the premises. They comment on the inconsistencies, question them, and sometimes introduce ideas that might resolve them. They go beyond the information given in the problem on the basis of their own personal experience and knowledge.

The Integration of Postformal Scientific Actions with Adult Social Actions

The exposure to a broad range of societal ideas through integrating career with societal activities prompts greater creativity based upon higher stages. Integration of social and scientific acts primarily occurs in early adulthood and after. Whereas people meet the peak of their stage development in early through late middle age, some great innovators reach the highest orders of development earlier over a greater range. Mathematicians often reach their peak in their 20s. For active individuals, developmental stage peaks between the 50s and late 60s. Generally, it is not until middle age (40s or so) that people can recognize that they are not only underneath a social structure and climbing within it, but that they also create and maintain that system. Active people engage in the process within their families, workplaces, professions, and communities. They come to see themselves as responsible parts of society. It is at this time, for example, when many men become more active in their families by exhibiting more nurturing behavior. Many women become more active by pursuing careers, additional education, and so on. Both genders thus become more similar to each other.

Such increased activity for women, and engaging more in the family process for men, exposes them to a broader range of societal demands. These demands press for development. Even so, adult-developmental researchers find very few individuals who engage in the metasystematic performance necessary for creativity. Some examples are: Armon (1984), who found 9% (3 out of 32) on the Good-Life Interview, and 15% (5 out of 32) on the Moral Judgment Interview; Richards and Commons (1984), who found only 14% (10 out of 71 participants) on the Multisystems Task; Demetriou and Efklides (1985), who found 11% (13 out of

114) on the Metacognitive Task; Kohlberg (1984; Colby & Kohlberg, 1987), who found 13% (8 out of 60 aged 24 and older) used stage 5 reasoning on the Moral Judgment Interview; and Powell (1984), who reported 9% (4 out of 44 participants) performed metasystematically.

Social Control

A society that promotes as well as tolerates creativity produces more creative acts. Nemeth and Kwan's (1985) study on originality in word associations found that participants who are exposed to persistent minority views tend to reexamine issues and engage in more divergent and original thought. On the other hand, participants exposed to persistent, fairly exclusive, majority views tend to concentrate on the position proposed, have convergent thinking, and tend to be less original.

General Characteristics of "Truly Creative" Individuals

A creative innovator cannot do society's bidding for long. One has to work on one's creative acts early on. True adult creativity requires building on current knowledge and then transcending it. It requires that innovators or creators have novel insights into complex problems. This often requires that there be created a new synthesis of systems (metasystematic), or a new paradigm (paradigmatic order) or field (cross-paradigmatic order) on the part of such an individual. Again, Charles Darwin provides us with an excellent example of the truly creative individual.

IMPLICATIONS OF VALUING THE HIGHER STAGES

As evolutionary forces have generally increased the stage of reasoning from the concrete to the cross-paradigmatic, we may wonder whether such forces will actually increase the number of people functioning at the cross-paradigmatic stage over time. How soon might this begin to happen? Might someone even function at stages beyond the cross-paradigmatic?

As revealed in introductory psychology books, a self-reflective understanding of postformal stages is developing widely. In this context, we find tremendous differences arising among social groups—differences that seem to be related to education levels and the power of reasoning (Kegan, 1995). Will this trend continue? Given the degree to which certain peoples and groups seem to value higher-stage development, one must wonder how far some might go in their efforts to produce intellectually advanced individuals—those who, for example, could function at the cross-paradigmatic stage. Might the trend in this direction be illustrated in part by the fact that people are now paying huge sums to educate their children at top universities, in graduate and professional schools? Might some go even further in this direction and attempt to push the limits of evolution and natural selection through humanly engineered means? How far will people go in this direction?

Innovation, as we have posited it, is usually dependent on highly educated individuals who function at the cross-paradigmatic stage. Cultural evolutionary theory suggests that powerful innovations lead to tremendous advantages for both the individual and for society. Historically, creative people functioning at the cross-paradigmatic stage have been extremely influential and powerful. Power and influence are highly selected for, both genetically and culturally. This seems to be true whether we are in favor of this reality or not. Where might this tendency lead us? Some extremely controversial predictions are to be made in this context. Please keep in mind that we, the authors of this chapter, do not advocate these scenarios, but merely describe their possibility and ponder their implications. At the same time, we believe we must marvel at the degree to which some people might just push the envelope of selection in their efforts to achieve some kind of competitive edge, creative edge, or some unique version of self-transformation. As we write about these things, we are aware that some of these ideas might sound like the plot lines from various science fiction novels. When we push the limits of this kind of thinking, and translate it into practice, we might obtain very interesting, but sometimes sobering or even frightening, results.

As mentioned earlier, evolution itself is not teleological. It is not directed by moral or ethical considerations. For this and related reasons, people should pay attention to the tremendous ethical controversies surrounding these issues. Our entire society should wrestle with these ethical dilemmas and address them adequately. There is the daunting task of showing respect for all, while recognizing the inequities promulgated by the interplay of nature and nurture. How these differences should be handled in the future should be widely discussed. The consequences of such matters should be vigorously debated, and ethically informed policies must be formulated.

With these ethical considerations in mind, we review three mechanisms through which one can imagine that the number of higher-order creative innovators might increase: a) cultural evolution, b) biological evolution, and c) computer and robotic hardware and software evolution.

Cultural Evolution

With the increase in demand for people with the highest stages of post-formal reasoning, certain forces have come to bear. Our society is rapidly acquiring the technological know-how that permits experts to engage in human engineering and cloning. Might people begin to use these mechanisms to produce intellectually superior individuals? This could lead to further assortativeness. Assortativeness has always been a force in human cultural and biological evolution. Assortativeness means that there is a demand for separation from the rest of the population (accomplished by means of clubs, zoning, rules promoting intragroup marriage, career specialization by groups). The evidence suggests that many will be tempted to move in this direction, as those with high intelligence already do by joining the Mensa organization.

Biological Evolution

Biological evolution, as described by Darwin, requires isolation among individuals, groups, within species. It also requires forces for selection. It is predicted that speciation in humans is likely soon, however controversial it is. That is, we might begin to find the differentiation of humans into more than a single species. Some groups might begin to engage in genetic engineering in order to isolate their group from the rest of humanity. It is this isolation from the rest of humanity that can cause speciation.

If these individuals are sufficiently different enough and brighter, and can survive inbreeding, some would argue that a new species might evolve. This new species might be more capable of creativity in general and especially in science, if some of the relevant traits discussed above, as well as highest postformal stages, are selected for.

Computer and Robotic Hardware and Software Evolution

There is another way that people might attempt to create the extra-human or super-human levels of achievement: by somehow linking advanced humans with superior reasoning and creative proficiencies with hierarchically complex neural-net computers. The "product" or "offspring" might be able to solve problems in science that are not solvable by ordinary high-functioning humans. The motivation for "supercomputers," on the other hand, seems to differ from speciation. The development of computers is relentless with most people cheering the changes. Computers, like all technology, are used for good *and* evil (remember "Hal" in Arthur Clarke's (1968) *2001*). Such super-computers likely could be built from stacked neural nets, and in turn, reason like humans and not be limited in the number of layers. This is an important consideration, because we speculate that the number of layers is related to the order of hierarchical complexity at which such machines will perform. It might be interesting to assess their stage of development with our MHC scoring system.

Again, the consequences of all these possibilities must be thoroughly debated and policies formulated with an ethical standard in mind. Furthermore, we argue that the debate must be spirited and it should begin soon. The doggedness with which individuals and groups may pursue such revolutionary intellectual and creative transformations as these may prove to be truly remarkable. Could Darwin have had any idea where some of his early theorizing might lead?

CONCLUSION

The creation of major cultural innovations is multidimensional. These innovations are often accomplished by distinct groupings of individuals who display an assortment of specific traits. Charles Darwin was chosen as an example of one with the requisite traits. Most major innovators display the essential traits or characteristics discussed throughout this chapter. There were a few characteristics that have been found to be absolutely necessary. Most important was the order of hierarchical complexity of tasks with which such a person could deal. This included the complexity in the area of work as well as commensurate complexity in the social system. When these two dimensions work together, the likelihood of a major creative innovation is enhanced.

REFERENCES

Arlin, P. K. (1975). Cognitive development in adulthood: A fifth stage? *Developmental Psychology, 11*, 602–606.

Arlin, P. K. (1977). Piagetian operations in problem finding. *Developmental Psychology, 13*, 247–298.

Arlin, P. K. (1984). Adolescent and adult thought: A structural interpretation. In M. L. Commons, F.A. Richards, & C. Armon (Eds.), *Beyond formal operations: Vol. 1. Late adolescent and adult cognitive development* (pp. 258–271). New York: Praeger.

Armon, C. (1984). Ideals of the good life and moral judgment: Ethical reasoning across the life span. In M. L. Commons, F. A. Richards, & C. Armon (Eds.), *Beyond formal operations: Vol. 1. Late adolescent and adult cognitive development* (pp. 357–380). New York: Praeger.

Cavalli-Sforza, L. L., Feldman, M. W., Chen, K.-H., & Dornbusch, S. M. (1982). Theory and observation in cultural transmission. *Science, 218,* 19–27.

Clarke, A. C. (1968). 2001: a space odyssey. New York: New American Library.

Colby, A., & Kohlberg, L. (1987). *The measurement of moral judgment: Vol. 1. Theoretical foundations and research validation.* New York: Cambridge University Press.

Commons, M. L., & Goodheart, E. A. (1999). The philosophical origins of behavior analysis. In B. A. Thyer (Ed.), *The philosophical legacy of behaviorism* (pp. 9–49). Boston: Kluwer.

Commons, M. L., Richards, F. A., Trudeau, E., Goodheart, A. E., & Dawson, T. L. (1997, May). *Psychophysics of stage: Task complexity and statistical models.* Paper presented at the Ninth International Objective Measurement Workshop, Chicago, IL.

Commons, M. L., Krause, S. R., Fayer, G. A., & Meaney, M. (1993). Atmosphere and stage development in the workplace. In J. Demick & P. M. Miller (Eds.), *Development in the workplace* (pp. 199–218). Hillsdale, NJ: Lawrence Erlbaum.

Commons, M. L., & Miller, P. M. (1998). A quantitative behavior-analytic theory of development. *Mexican Journal of Experimental Analysis of Behavior, 24*(2), 153–180.

Commons, M. L., & Richards, F. A. (1984a). A general model of stage theory. In M. L. Commons, F. A. Richards, & C. Armon (Eds.), *Beyond formal operations: Vol. 1. Late adolescent and adult cognitive development* (pp. 120–140). New York: Praeger.

Commons, M. L., & Richards, F. A. (1984b). Applying the general stage model. In M. L. Commons, F. A. Richards, & C. Armon (Eds.), *Beyond formal operations: Late adolescent and adult cognitive development* (pp. 141–157). New York: Praeger.

Commons, M. L., & Richards, F. A. (1995). Behavior analytic approach to dialectics of stage performance and stage change. *Behavioral Development, 5*(2), 7–9.

Commons, M. L., & Rodriguez, J. A. (1990). "Equal access" without "establishing" religion: The necessity for assessing social perspective-taking skills and institutional atmosphere. *Developmental Review, 10,* 323–340.

Commons, M. L., Trudeau, E. J., Stein, S. A., Richards, F. A., & Krause, S. R. (1998). The existence of developmental stages as shown by the hierarchical complexity of tasks. *Developmental Review, 18,* 237–278.

Darwin, C. (1855). *On the origin of the species.* London: Murray.

Darwin, C. (1897). *Expressions of the emotions in man and animals.* New York: D. Appleton.

Dawkins, R. (1976). *The selfish gene.* New York: Oxford University Press.

Dawkins, R. (1981). In defense of selfish genes. *Philosophy, 56,* 556–573.

Demetriou, A., & Efklides, A. (1985). Structure and sequence of formal and post-formal thought: General patterns and individual differences. *Child Development, 56,* 1062–1091.

Dostoyevsky , F. (1914). *Crime and punishment* (Contance Garnett, Trans.). London: William Heinemann.

Erikson, E. H. (1959). Identity and the life cycle. *Psychological Issues Monograph, I*.

Erikson, E. H. (1978). *Adulthood*. New York: Norton.

Feldman, D. H. (1980). *Beyond universals in cognitive development*. Norwood, NJ: Ablex.

Feldman, D. H., Csikszentmihalyi, M., & Gardner, H. (1994). *Changing the world: A framework for the study of creativity*. Westport, CT: Praeger/Greenwood.

Fischer, K. W., Hand, H. H., & Russell, S. (1984). The development of abstractions in adolescents and adulthood. In M. L. Commons, F. A. Richards, & C. Armon (Eds.), *Beyond formal operations: Late adolescent and adult cognitive development* (pp. 43–73). New York: Praeger.

Grotzer, T. A., Robinson, T. L., Young, R. M., Davidson, M. N., Cohen, L., Rios, M. L., Eddy, S., Rodriguez, J. A., Lewis, T. S., Gauthier, A. M., Shapiro, J. M., Miller, P. M., & Commons, M. L. (1985, June). *The role of repeated presentation of a formal operational problem, feedback, and social reward: An examination of Piaget's equilibration theory of stage transition*. Paper presented at The Jean Piaget Society, Philadelphia.

Inhelder, B., & Piaget, J. (1958). *The growth of logical thinking from childhood to adolescence: an essay on the development of formal operational structures*. (A. Parsons & S. Milgram, Trans.). New York: Basic Books. (Original work published 1955).

Kegan, R. (1995). *In over our heads: The mental demands of modern life*. Cambridge: Harvard University Press.

Kohlberg, L. (1984). *Essays on moral development: Vol. 2. The psychology of moral development: Moral stages, their nature and validity*. San Francisco: Harper & Row.

Labouvie-Vief, G. (1985). Intelligence and cognition. In J. E. Birren & K. W. Schaie (Eds.), *Handbook of the psychology of aging* (2nd ed, pp. 500-530). New York: Van Nostrand Reinhold.

Labouvie-Vief, G., Adams, C., Hakim-Larson, J., & Hayden, M. (1983). *Contexts of logic: The growth of interpretation from pre-adolescence and adult thought*. Paper presented at the meeting of the Society for Research in Child Development, Detroit, MI.

Mace, F. C., Lalli, J. S., Shea, M. C., & Nevin, J. (1992). Behavioral momentum in college basketball. *Journal of Applied Behavior Analysis, 25*(3) 657–663.

Minhas, F. C., & Kaur, F. (1983, January). A study of field-dependent-independent cognitive styles in relation to novelty and meaning contexts of creativity. *Personality Study and Group Behavior, 3*(1), 20–34.

Nemeth, C. J., & Kwan, J. L. (1985). Originality of word association as a function of majority versus minority influence. *Social Psychology Quarterly, 48*, 277–282.

Nevin, J. A., Tota, M. E., Torquato, R. D., & Shull, R.. (1990). Alternative reinforcement increases resistance to change: Pavlovian or operant contingencies? *Journal of the Experimental Analysis of Behavior, 53*(3), 359–379.

Ohnmacht, F. W., & McMorris, R. F. (1971). Creativity as a function of field independence and dogmatism. *Journal of Psychology, 79*(2), 165–168.

Overton, W. F. (1990). Competence and procedures: Constraints on the development of logical reasoning. In W. F. Overton (Ed.), *Reasoning, necessity and logic: Developmental perspectives*. (pp. 1–32). Hillsdale, NJ: Lawrence Erlbaum.

Powell, P. M. (1984). Stage 4A: Category operations and interactive empathy. In M. L. Commons, F. A. Richards, & C. Armon (Eds.), *Beyond formal operations: Vol. 1. Late adolescent and adult cognitive development.* (pp. 326–339). New York: Praeger.

Richards, F. A., & Commons, M. L. (1984). Systematic, metasystematic, and cross-paradigmatic reasoning: A case for stages of reasoning beyond formal operations. In M. L. Commons, F. A. Richards, and C. Armon (Eds.). *Beyond formal operations: Vol. 1. Late adolescent and adult cognitive development* (pp. 92–119). New York: Praeger.

Rodriguez, J. A. (1989). *Exploring the notion of higher stages of social perspective taking* Unpublished qualifying paper, Harvard University Graduate School of Education, Cambridge, MA.

Ross, B. L. (1977). Interrelationships of five cognitive constructs: Moral development, locus of control, creativity, field dependence-field independence, and intelligence in a sample of 167 community college students. University of Southern California.

Smith, G. J., Carlsson, I., & Sandstrom, S. (1985). Artists and artistic creativity— elucidated by psychological experiments. *Psychological Research Bulletin, 25,* 9–10.

Trivers, R. (1985). *Social evolution.* Menlo Park, CA: Benjamin/Cummings.

Witkin, H. A. (1949). Perception of body position and of the position of the visual field. *Psychological Monographs: General and Applied, 63*(7) #302.

Witkin, H. A., Lewis, H. B., Hertzman, M., Machover, K., Meissner, P. B., & Wapner, S. (1954). Personality through perception: An experimental and clinical study. New York: Harper.

chapter 10

Lifelong Learning and the Good Life: Reconceiving Adult Education for Development

Stephanie Glass-Solomon
Antioch University Los Angeles

Cheryl Armon
Antioch University Los Angeles

Adult development has received increasing attention among researchers, educators, and professional consultants over the last two decades. Since 1990, an array of books, textbooks, articles, and a professional journal devoted exclusively to theory and research about progressive development in adulthood have appeared (Alexander & Langer,1986/1990; Commons et al., 1990; Commons, Richards, & Armon, 1984; Commons, Sinnott, Richards, & Armon, 1989; Demick, 1999; Rybash, Roodin, & Santrock, 1991; Stevens-Long & Commons, 1990). At the same time, adult education programs are proliferating.

Adult developmental theory, however, is consistently disregarded in the design of typical adult education programs. This disregard is exemplified by a recent national agenda advanced by the Commission for a Nation of Lifelong Learners. This is group was appointed by a consortium of organizations, including leading institutions in adult education, and represents the interests of business, labor, education, government, and philanthropy to study and make recommendations concerning the country's need for adult education. The commission proposed "a nation of lifelong learners" and a system of "lifelong learning" (Commission, 1997). This agenda appears to have been put forth in response both to the need for the United States to remain competitive in the global marketplace and to the negative psychological and economic effects that globalization and technology have had on adults. The intent is to promote better lives for adults and to enhance adult life satisfaction.

In this chapter, we examine and challenge this agenda. We begin by briefly presenting a developmental model of the Good Life. If an educational agenda is to be presented to better the lives of adults, it is necessary to have some ideas about how adults themselves conceptualize the Good Life and how they develop these concepts. One of the first problems with the work of the Commission, from our point of view, is that it failed to consider how adults themselves conceptualize the Good Life. The Good Life model contains such ideas and provides useful criteria for examining the objectives of this national educational agenda.

Different models could be used to study and describe adult development, including structural and functional types, and life span approaches. We have chosen to use a structural-developmental model of evaluative reasoning[1] because it specifically addresses adult conceptions of the Good Life. While we are well aware of varied critiques of Piagetian and neo-Piagetian models (e.g, Vuyk, 1981; cf. Bond, 1994), for us, the structural approach retains value. Moreover, the developmental information gained from the evaluative reasoning model is particularly pertinent to adult education.

After a review of the Good Life model, we explore the nature of "lifelong learning," as it is described by the Commission. We contrast that concept with stage-related notions of the Good Life and with the ideals of liberal arts education. We conclude that the Commission's agenda supports neither adults' development nor their construction of meaningful and worthy lives. Instead, lower-stage reasoning about the Good Life is rewarded and opportunities for development are restricted. We suggest that the Commission's agenda is naïve and misguided. While it might benefit the existing corporate sector, it will actually exacerbate the problems of adult life. "Lifelong learning" is merely continuous training and retraining for work. We suggest that it is a guise that serves the corporate hegemony of education.

To support these claims, we trace some of the competing aims in the history of undergraduate education. We attempt to show the importance of liberal arts education for adult development, and that this form of education is threatened by corporate interests that define educational aims for the 21st century. We conclude by proposing a model of adult education that is informed by adult developmental theory and political and social critique, and that would integrate the ideals of liberal education with professional preparation. It is our intention that this chapter serves as an argument for, and an invitation to, academics and others concerned with the lives of adult to become active in resisting the continued reduction of adult education to mere education for work.

DEVELOPMENTAL CONCEPTIONS OF THE GOOD LIFE

The Good Life stage model (Armon, 1984a, 1984b) has been empirically validated, brings together the philosophy and psychology of the Good Life, and is operationally defined as the combined set of values that persons affirm in normative, ideal-evaluative judgments about the Good Life, in general, and about good work, good friendship or relationship, and the good person, in particular. The domain of the Good Life is conceptualized as broad, including the *moral* good (e.g., ethical dimensions of persons, relationships, groups) and *non-moral good* (e.g., non-moral aspects of work, family, and community). The model contains five stages that develop sequentially, each a necessary precursor for the next. The model is considered to be normative; each higher stage is more complex and inclusive. Formal definitions of all stages can be found in Table 10.1. A brief narrative of the adult stages two through five follow.

Good Life Stages

- *Stage two*, which is the lowest form of reasoning found in normal adults, represents a Good Life that consists of activities, objects, and persons that meet the individual's needs and interests. Other people are valued primarily for what they bring to the self, and what is desired is not distinguished from that which is worthy of desire. Reasoners at this stage rely on concrete, preconventional, intellectual operations.
- At *stage three*, the Good Life is predominantly determined by positive *affective* experience and the absence of bad feelings. The Good Life consists of activities in accordance with stereotypical, conventional, interpersonal, and personal virtues of the society or group and takes place in a stable, interpersonal context. The Good Life is experienced in the maintenance of mutual, face-to-face relationships that provide the self with value and meaning. Intellectual reasoning consists of a limited form of abstract, or hypothetical, reasoning skills.
- At *stage four* (which, *if* it develops only does so after the late 20s), the Good Life consists of activities that express the individual's *self-chosen*, internalized interests and values. The good is found in those activities perceived as personally meaningful. Life satisfaction and worthiness are often pursued over happiness or pleasure *per se*, and require an orderly societal context that allows interests to be pur-

Table 10.1. Comparison of Developmental Sequences

Piaget (Inhelder & Piaget, 1958) Cognitive	Kohlberg (Kohlberg, Levine, & Hewer, 1983) Justice Reasoning	Selman (1980) Armon (1984) Perspective-Taking	Loevinger (1987) Ego	Damon & Hart (1988) Self-Understanding	Kegan (1982) Self	Gilligan* (1982) Caring	Fowler (1981) Faith
Pre-Operational	Stage 1: Heteronomous morality	Stage 1: Differentiated & subjective	1: Symbolic 2: Impulsive	Level 1: Categorical identifications	Stage 1: Impulsive		Stage 1: Intuitive-projective
Concrete Operational	Stage 2: Individualism, instrumental purpose, and exchange	State 2: Self-reflective	Δ: Self-protective	Level 2: Comparative assessments	Stage 2: Imperial	Survival	Stage 2: Mythic-literal
Early Formal	Stage 3: Mutual interpersonal expectations; conformity	Stage 3: Third-person mutuality	3: Conformist 3/4: Conscientious/Conformist	Level 3: interpersonal implications	Stage 3: Interpersonal	Goodness	Stage 3: Synthetic-conventional

Consolidated Formal	Stage 4: Social system maintenance; conscience	Stage 4: In depth & societal; Symbolic	4: Conscientious	Level 4: Systematic beliefs & plans	Stage 4: Institutional	Truth	Stage 4: Individuative-reflective
	Stage 4/5: Subjective relativism		4/5: Individualistic				
	Stage 5: Prior rights; Social contract or utility	Stage 5: Second-order reciprocity	5: Autonomous		Stage 5: Interindividual	Nonviolence	Stage 5: Paradoxical-consolidative
	Stage 6: Universal ethical principles	Stage 6: Second-order mutuality	6: Integrated				Stage 6: Universalizing

Note: *Gilligan may not agree with this characterization of her stages.

193

sued over time. Thus, emphasis is placed on maintaining a rational and predictable social system that permits pursuit of person's freedom and interests. Stage four reasoners use fully operational abstract reasoning skills.

• *Stage five* is a postconventional stage. The Good Life is conceptualized from a rational, consistent ideology (generalizable framework of values) that integrates personal ethics and social morality. General standards are used in the construction of the good, which means considering the good not only for the self but also for others. Thus, pursuing one's own Good Life requires pursuing the good life for others. At this stage, reasoners can conceive of the social world independent of extant systems and are able to reflect on and evaluate alternative systems, discriminating what is from what might be. Postformal operational reasoning is used.

As described, the Good Life model traces the philosophy and developmental psychology of adults' conceptions of the meaningful and worthy life and their ideal constructions of social, political, and spiritual conditions. In the higher, postconventional stages of adult reasoning about the Good Life, adults' ideas are similar to Good Life concepts of well-known Western philosophers in the liberal tradition, such as Aristotle, John Stuart Mill, and John Dewey. The stage model is a normative one; higher stages are considered superior to lower ones, other things being equal (Kohlberg, 1981). We are, therefore, primarily concerned with the higher stages as the content and structures of these stages would most likely yield adult capacities and interests that would allow consideration of social and personal conditions for the betterment of society as a whole.

At these higher stages, adults conceive of an ideal life that reaches out beyond the fulfillment of one's individual desires, talents, and interests. For these adults, a Good Life also includes an active acknowledgment of all persons' interdependence for the fulfillment of each person's full humanity. There exists a profound respect for nature and an appreciation of the important role of aesthetics in human experience. These adults also want to maximize the development of the Good Life for all adults.

Inevitably, the nature of higher-stage structural development also leads to a critique of social convention. These constructions of complex ideas rely on the intellectual development that is correlated with the development of Good Life reasoning. At the higher stages, complex, abstract, systems-oriented reasoning makes possible elaborate Good Life conceptions. Higher stages of development help adults to comprehend, interpret, and recreate the complex conditions in which we live.

It is precisely these qualities of higher-stage conceptions of a good human life that we would hope a national agenda for adult education would take into account. Not only do higher stage abilities allow adults to better understand and thus re-create social conditions, but the ethics of higher stages also motivate adults to create social conditions that benefit others as well as themselves.

Education is perhaps the most controllable variable in Good Life stage development. Research has for some time shown that college and graduate school experience are predictive variables in Good Life development as well as structural development in other domains (Armon, 1984a, 1984b; Armon & Dawson, 1997; Colby, Kohlberg, Gibbs, & Leiberman, 1983; Rest & Narvaez, 1991; Rest & Thoma, 1985). Particular educational activities considered relevant for development are engagement with new ways of thinking, addressing novel problems, and learning new ways to perceive one's relationship to others, as well as one's role in social and economic conditions. Although this is somewhat speculative, and researchers continue to deconstruct the education variable into its significant components, these ideas are consistent with assumptions in Piagetian and neo-Piagetian developmental models about what makes development happen. Importantly, these developmentally provocative activities are common in many contemporary liberal arts undergraduate curricula and most of the studies that have examined the role of education in development have taken place in colleges.

THE COMPETING AIMS OF HIGHER EDUCATION

Broadly speaking, education for adults is typically either liberal education or what we call education for work. Liberal education and education for work have had competing basic aims. One can find in the history of higher education its ideal liberatory purposes—freeing the individual to think critically about the self and its relationship with the social world. In contrast, the aim of producing workers to meet the needs of capitalist production has been dominant since before the turn of the century.

Ancient philosophers described the purposes of education as the development of internal capacities such as critical reasoning, ethical character, and aesthetic appreciation. Later, the Kantian notion of liberal education emphasized the purpose of freeing individuals from the constraints imposed by their origins to allow them to reconstruct the world in which they lived in terms of inspired aims and ideals. In the 20th century, the Deweyan reconstruction of that ideal suggested that reflection on "the good" was essential not only for elites but also for the masses who were needed to participate meaningfully as citizens in a democracy. He advocated that teachers should help students follow *their* interests in determining projects and courses of study and approach students from their own developmental positions. Today, research on social and intellectual development suggests that these ideal liberatory conceptions of education could indeed enhance the possibilities for realizing human potential.

In sharp contrast to a liberating force in human evolution, most of higher education in the United States can be more clearly seen as a production point within the capitalist system (Aronowitz, 1992). Corporate elites must socialize and secure workers at a reasonable cost through state support in educating the workforce. Simply put, universities and colleges produce workers to meet the needs of our corporate-dominated economic system. A most visible example is in the curricular content that includes the skills and knowledge that prepare persons for specific work roles. Less visible but equally powerful are the socialization practices embedded in education that prepare individuals for the social structure of most work roles. Hierarchically structured, authoritarian classrooms that require subordination; emphasis on individual, rather than group work, within a competitive rather than cooperative context; and the psychosocial constructions of self in which emotional and aesthetic dimensions are repressed in the service of external rewards all serve to prepare individuals for their roles in hierarchically structured corporations and societies.

These competing aims—liberation versus work preparation—have existed historically in higher education. In the United States, generally speaking, education for work has been dominant. While some educational philosophers and educators continue to uphold the ideal liberating notions of liberal education, new agendas in higher education threaten the existence of liberal education altogether. Insofar as liberal education supports progressive adult development, which we contend it can, any further movements to diminish its influence should be of concern to those interested in promoting higher-stage development and the building of meaningful and worthy lives for adults. The two aims, however, need not be opposed. A liberatory interpretation of a liberal arts education *could* be integrated with professional preparation. Such an integration could yield a form of education that would challenge the social conditions that give rise to exploitation and alienation—in other words, lower-stage development. Beginning thoughts on this type of educational model are described later.

THE AGENDA: EDUCATION FOR WORK AND ADULT LIFE

Furthering the movement away from liberal education, the Commission for a Nation of Lifelong Learners sets forth a comprehensive set of recommendations to realize their aims. We use aspects of its report to characterize the recent policy-making efforts in adult higher education to which we are opposed.

The Commission describes the current hazards of American adult life, particularly the enormous insecurities adults report about the future stability of the United States economy in the global marketplace and their work lives in this context.[2] They note the cynicism toward government and diminished political and civic participation in adult life. The Commission (1997) accurately acknowledges what compromises the ability of many adults to realize meaningful and worthy lives. For example, the report states that "Americans are uneasy about their own life situations and fearful about their children's futures" (p. 2). And, that the adult population manifests "a reservoir of doubt, diverted dreams, unmet challenges and, for some, a deep cynicism about America's promise for the future" (p. 9).

The Commission (1997) describes how the personal anxiety about economic security of today's workers has risen to "dangerously high" levels. Although there has been a net increase of 27 million jobs during the last 18 years, "only 35 percent of laid-off workers end up in equal or better paying jobs" (p. 13), and job loss has negatively affected 75 percent of all households. The Commission states:

> Workers' average real earnings have decreased over the last two decades, their health plan coverage has been reduced, and fewer of the unemployed are protected by unemployment insurance. Unrelenting fears about the future downsizings have shattered individuals' ideas about work and self-worth. (p. 13)

To their credit, the Commission attempts to address these problems by promoting an agenda of greater access to higher education for adults; new skills, they argue, particularly in technology, will help workers relieve their anxieties. But will they?

The Commission's recommendations suggest ways for workers to adapt to extant social and economic conditions. The problem is that the recommendations are predicated on the assumption that "market forces" are *"the natural state"*—that is, a priori conditions to which individuals must respond—rather than social conditions that people create, *and can change.* The worker described by the Commission does not see him or herself as an architect of the industry but, instead, an individual piece of machinery that must be continually honed in order to simply *maintain* a useful function. The adult is reduced to a commodity of exchange—dispensable and replaceable. Not only is higher-stage adult development antithetical to this view, but these aims can be placed in direct opposition to those of education as a liberating force.

The Commission recommends that "education" become a national priority. Indeed, they argue that education is the single most important way to address the growing despair experienced by adults as well as the decline in their economic conditions. Moreover, they contend that through education, workers are able to be competitive in the global marketplace, and thus are able to construct good and meaningful lives. But the definition of good and meaningful is tied to responding to constant changes and insecurities in this omnipresent marketplace. The Commission suggests that the worker must "continuously acquire skills, knowledge, and 'resilience' to move in the global labor market" (p. 11). The U.S. Department of Labor estimates that workers change jobs/careers an average of seven times during their work lives. Thus, the Commission recommends that the aim of higher education should be to produce "resilient workers."

The resilient worker can be seen as the concrete manifestation of the new educational agenda. This concept provides an opportunity for more detailed examination of some significant implications of the education proposed for adults. While resiliency in other contexts connotes a desirable quality, suggesting flexibility, responsiveness, and durability, its application in this context is euphemistic. The term, as used by the Commission, refers to an individual's ability to move easily from task to task, from job to job—to change careers smoothly —developing one's role in the global workplace. While *resilience* may be a desirable aim of the leaders of the corporate economy, will the new "resilient" worker have an opportunity for re-creating the social and material world so as to contribute to a Good Life for others? For themselves? Will this resilience truly diminish or eradicate the angst experienced by adults today? Or, will it ultimately prove to benefit only the lives of the corporate elite who depend on the dumbing down, insecurity, and passivity of workers to maintain their control over the economy?

DEFINING THE GOOD LIFE IN TERMS OF RESILIENCY: THE RESILIENT WORKER AND LOWER-STAGE DEVELOPMENT

The life plan for adults engaged in progressive developmental change includes the opportunity to develop their interests and life projects over time in the context of reasonable temporal, spatial, and financial stability. Higher-stage Good Life constructions involve perceptions of the self as part of a larger human community, the nature and visions of which are determined by those who participate in it. Social organizations, such as workplaces or economies, are also seen as social constructions, not "givens." They can be constructed fairly or unfairly, depending on the wills of those who participate in them, and are affected by them.

These perceptions are contrary to the very underpinnings of the new educational agenda, which furthers lower-stage reasoning by training workers to adapt to social conditions in the context of financial instability, rather than to educate them to critique and re-create conditions that would allow them the autonomy of self-determination and the opportunity to improve their conditions. Instead, the social environment for the resilient worker appears to be one in which individuals compete with one another for scarce jobs and/or resources, continuously retraining and/or relocating, while balancing family responsibilities and financial problems. Fewer and fewer workers today can rely on secure employment simply because they work hard and remain loyal to their employers. Ultimately, secure employment is rendered impossible when workers are made expendable by a system motivated by profit and accumulation which, in the process, generates new forms of exploitation.

While change can certainly be invigorating, the idea that one cannot and should not attempt to envision a stable future is frightening. The social conditions of constant flux and uncertainty, already apparent in the lives of many adults, are likely to produce anxiety, leading to self-protection, high stress, and fear, as well as alienation from others and one's self. These are the personal, emotional, and social conditions that are characteristic of lower-stage Good Life development.

At stage two of the Good Life, reasoners must rely on Piagetian concrete operations, which restricts the individual's capacities for hypothetical reflections, such as envisioning options and possibilities, or conceiving of rational systems. Work at this stage is evaluated in terms of its exchange value, rather than the nature of the labor itself. Successful competition often relies on the self-interest and ego-centrism of stage-two reasoning. The preconventional nature of stage-two reasoning makes impossible any meaningful engagement in organized groups with sustained purposes over time. Similarly, abilities to work collaboratively in groups or teams are severely diminished.

The Good Life at stage three focuses on immediate relationships with others in the home, workplace, and community. Good Work at this stage is determined primarily by the nature of the interpersonal relationships one experiences in the workplace. Good is determined by adherence to the conventional, accepted norms and virtues of the mainstream culture. The tendency is to maintain the status quo because the self is identified by that which currently exists. Resiliency, however, minimizes the opportunities to maintain connections with coworkers or, often, members of local communities. Confronted with mergers, downsizing, the increase of part-time work and, at times, the expectation of relocation, the players are always changing. Individuals cannot develop trusting relationships over time, an aspect that, among other things, is associated with social pathologies. Moreover, these conditions so fragment one's life, that there is little, if any, time for community participation. Even stage-three conventional-level development is not supported by the new agenda.

In the United States, there are many aspects of fragmentation and contradiction apparent in today's adult lives. For example, in their roles as workers, adults may deplore low wages, part-time employment, and the effects of jobs going abroad or given over to technology. In their role as consumers, however, adults are complicit in jobs going overseas because products are produced at lower costs and, therefore, can be sold back to them more cheaply. In their roles as investors, they may feel they have to support global expansion, downsizing, and the reduction of a higher-wage force since this maximizes profits from their investments, even while it carves away their opportunities for a living wage and career advancement. These contradictions cannot support, much less promote, development; more frustration and alienation are likely outcomes.

Looked at another way, higher-stage notions of the self and social identity are unlikely in the society prescribed by the new agenda. Higher-stage constructions of Good Work rely on the individuals' opportunities to pursue their emotional and intellectual interests in their work. If the nature of labor is determined exclusively by market forces rather than cultivated curiosities, individuals will become disaffected and cynical about government and labor. They will turn their personal, intellectual, and ethical investments away from public life and pursue interests only in the private realm when and where that might be possible.

Higher-Stage Good Life development for adults is, therefore, undermined in a society dominated and structured by the global corporate order as it is currently organized. Similarly, an educational system predicated on this economic basis and designed to adapt adults to it raises serious questions and concerns for those interested in promoting adult development and the Good Life for members of our society.

AMERICAN INSTITUTIONS AND LOWER-STAGE DEVELOPMENT

Why would the adult-oriented universities, labor leaders, government, and major corporations (as represented in the Commission for a Nation of Lifelong Learners), for example, support an educational approach that promotes lower-stage development, as well as social conditions so destructive to adult life? One possibility is that policy makers are not aware of adult developmental research when they make educational recommendations. If they were, perhaps other options would be considered. However, many educators of adults *are* aware of this research. Why then is it ignored? Perhaps the reason is that education for work addresses some very real needs of government and capitalist corporations and this is of greater concern than the Good Life for adults. After all, the government has a primary interest in United States global hegemony and is ultimately linked in this aim to these corporate interests. These interests, as we discussed above, in many ways create social conditions that diminish opportunities for adult development, for adults' opportunities to create meaningful lives, and for them to be civically active. Yet, there are clearly benefits to the elites in the corporate and government sectors in keeping adults at the lower stages.

Consumed with fear of power, while simultaneously attempting to compete for it, stage-two reasoners are less likely or less able to participate in political reform or to join with others to promote the general good. They find it virtually impossible to organize themselves for interests beyond their immediate needs. Thus, the status quo is maintained. Whether defined by self-interest at stage two or the struggle to maintain the status quo and identify with it in stage three, lower-stage reasoners are more likely to support and to be reliant on mass culture, the government, and the corporation in defining and explaining the nature of reality and their choices. Unable to construct a shared reality concerning possibilities at stage two, or seeking the affirmation of the group at stage three, lower-stage reasoning adults are more prone to manipulation and control by external forces. The mass media, part of the global corporate sector, can therefore become a strong socializing force. Finally, the never-ending consumerism promoted as a source of gratification further serves these interests by directing individuals to seek extrinsic satisfaction through accumulation ("stuff"), rather than through meaningful work, intrinsic pleasures, and positive social change.

As educational institutions become more reliant on corporate and state partnerships for funding, as has occurred in the late 1990s, educators themselves must support the aims as defined by the state and the corporate sectors in order to receive funding. Crudely put, educators must support the status quo to benefit from it.

However, if workers were to obtain the skills and knowledge of advanced human development, such as postformal operational thinking and postconventional ethical reasoning, it would likely undermine the class society, social stratification, and the unequal distribution of wealth and opportunities that currently exist. Abilities that include systems-oriented evaluations, flexible problem solving, and advanced conceptions of persons, nations, and nature might provide impetus for a thorough reexamination and reconstruction of these conditions. Clearly, this would not benefit those who would maintain current social, political, and economic realities.

LIBERAL EDUCATION FOR ADULT DEVELOPMENT AND THE GLOBAL ECONOMY

Throughout this chapter we claim that recently proposed educational agendas not only encourage the lowest stages of adult development, but are also antithetical to higher-stage development. Further, we have said that an ideal liberal education would be more appropriate to help adults develop to higher stages and construct more meaningful lives. In addition, we argue that a developmentally oriented liberal education helps adults to address variable social conditions. As discussed, the aims and practices of liberal arts education have evolved over centuries.

Here, we offer our vision of an integrated model of liberatory education for adults. It is a model that renews, revitalizes, and advances the ideals of liberal arts education, informs its goals with adult developmental theory, addresses adults' needs for professional skills and knowledge, and advances a social critique of the conditions that diminish opportunities for meaningful lives. We invite our colleagues to consider this ideal construction.

Primarily, this model of liberal arts education for adults is built on adult developmental theory. The fundamental practices influence development by drawing on students' interests to enhance motivation, while promoting challenges to their current ways of thinking. The educational objectives are to develop analytic skills, critical thinking, ethical reasoning, perspective-taking, and creativity.

The model's pedagogy requires the student to be engaged with both the learning material and each other. Learning is motivated by students' curiosities and interests. Cooperative learning and dialogue permeate nonauthoritarian classrooms. Shared projects, interdisciplinary studies, civic internships, and individualized evaluation replace isolated work, rote memorization, fragmented knowledge, irrelevant study, and competition for grades. Hands-on experiences permit students to act on knowledge, which requires them to internalize and organize what they learn.

A constructivist dimension encourages the continuous reconstruction of the self and the social world. This includes the examination of the self and the role of the individual in the creation of social conditions, particularly political and economic systems. Reconstruction of oneself and the world acknowledges the very human desire to transcend human conditions toward liberation. Therefore, rather than cynicism and withdrawal from civic and political life, adult students are encouraged to explore the role that social and economic conditions play in the professional and public domain. They are asked to envision and act toward the construction of alternative social models. These activities are linked to higher-stage notions of self and other, and in particular, an expanded consciousness of the organic connection between private, work, and civic life.

Preparation for work and career is integrated into the curriculum because meaningful work is inherent in the construction of a meaningful life. Emphasis is placed on generalizable skills in problem solving and ethical reasoning, while including current knowledge and expertise required by particular career directions. Generalizable skills allow students to respond to the changing nature of the workplace, not only to critique the workplace but also to remake it under conditions of increasing humanity. Adults are encouraged to use their own workplaces as experiential learning sites. While skill development is emphasized, students are guided toward an examination of their workplaces in terms of their justice structures, power relations, and distributions of resources and privileges. Moreover, students study the way in which this work realm intersects with the personal and civic realms to further diminish meaningful participation in these other areas of life.

The curricular content emphasizes historical, cultural, and political material, which develops civic literacy and equips adults to construct their social and political identity and actively participate in social change. Moreover, the study of traditional disciplines serves developmental purposes. Alternative ways of thinking and valuing (e.g., philosophy, spirituality, political science), different interpretations of events (e.g., sociology, history), different modes of expression (e.g., the arts, creative writing), and interpretations of nature (e.g., mathematics, science) enhance perspective-taking and critical thinking.

We suggest this concept of liberal arts education for adults would enhance the probability for higher-stage development and it would also more effectively address the problems of adult life so aptly described by the Commission. Higher intellectual development permits more discrete distinctions to be made, and for persons to reflect more effectively on conflicting claims and desires. These abilities better enable adults to confront the problems we as a society face, including insatiable consumerism, destruction of the environment, and the marginalization of various groups.

Civic participation and concern for citizenship would also be effectively addressed by this ideal form of adult liberal education. Predicated on the idea that transcendence is the essential praxis of human life—that is, humans participate in the creation of the world and are thereby created by it—true democratic practice might become the norm of higher-stage reasoners. Higher stages of reasoning include concern for the greater good over the self; adults at these stages are more likely to perceive the purposes of engaging in the reconstruction of social systems. Therefore, the liberally educated adult would be better prepared to affect the political process because they would have a greater vision of organic, civil society and a more complex picture of the social order. Importantly, too, higher-stage reasoners would not only construct new and innovative solutions to social problems, they would also contribute to our cultural wealth through expanded creativity and self awareness.

In terms of the greater social good, it might be the case that higher-stage reasoners would be able to contain the contradictory and complex nature of human life. For example, while economic life may always change, a modicum of stability seems necessary in human life. This could be accomplished if economic life were embedded in a stable community life. Global markets require accommodation to differences, yet intractable religious and political differences threaten global expansion. Higher-stage reasoners might see the value in and have the ability to create a global community with a civic "religion," based in democracy and world citizenship, to reinforce and better articulate self and society, economy, and community. As a greater understanding of the nature of the physical world might challenge deistic religions and artificial concepts of difference and separation, overall, the "resilience" truly needed and achievable for higher-stage reasoners is one that can sustain difference yet maintain community and the environment.

TAKING THE LEAD: EDUCATION FOR THE 21ST CENTURY

We urge our colleagues to take the lead to resist the false promise of the Commission's agenda for adults—what we have described as education for work. Education must be an opportunity for all students of all ages to develop their abilities as authors of social and personal change. Adults need to recapture their citizenship potential to remake public life, to reinvent the workplace to serve persons, not profits, and to be able to envision change and a future that is one of hope and promise. Education needs to promote the conditions that allow adults to develop to higher stages.

Ideally, higher-stage reasoners would be more likely to work for an inspired life in which all humans are treated as persons, the world of nature is respected and loved, and aesthetics and beauty are highly revered. Rather than restricted by aspirations for accumulation, self-aggrandizement, and singular egoistic interests, higher-stage reasoners could raise the threshold for what is possible in terms of the Good Life and begin to construct the conditions for *the good human society*. The more that adults conceptualize the Good Life as one that upholds the potential and dignity of all living things, the more likely we will ensure a future of increased opportunities for all people to have a Good Life. Ultimately, this supports the continued evolution of human life and the planet.

We must oppose the waste of human and environmental potential apparent when adult education is reduced to the needs of a corporate sector designed to benefit the few. Educators, and the education they provide, can be effective in stimulating intellectual controversy and positive social change. We urge a commitment to this purpose.

NOTES

1. There are a number of structural models (Alexander, Drucker, & Langer, 1990; Kohlberg, 1981; also see Commons, Richards, & Armon, 1984) as well as lifespan approaches (e.g., Baltes, Hayne, & Lipsitt, 1980; Ryff, 1989; Stock, Okun, & Benin, 1986). Although certain assumptions differ, most of these models have significant commonality with the stages described here. For a complete explanation of the Good Life model, see Armon, 1984a, 1984b.

2. It is not that a global econmic order is by definition exploitative and oppressive. Rather, we refer to the current arrangements, which include exploiting workers around the world, moving capital across borders at accelerated rates through financial institutions, and creating a wealthy class of elites that control these conditions.

REFERENCES

Alexander, C., & Langer, J. (1990). *The higher stages of human development*. New York: Oxford University Press. (Original work published 1986)

Alexander, C., Drucker, S., & Langer, E. (1990). Introduction: Major issues in exploration of adult growth. In C. N. Alexander & E. J. Langer (Eds.), *Higher stages of human development*. New York: Oxford University Press.

Armon, C., (1984a). Reasoning about the good life: Evaluative reasoning in children and adults. Unpublished doctoral dissertation, Harvard University.

Armon, C. (1984b). Ideals of the good life and moral judgment: Ethical reasoning across the lifespan. In M. Commons, F. Richards, & C. Armon (Eds.), *Beyond formal operations: Late adolescent and adult cognitive development*. New York: Praeger.

Armon, C., & Dawson, T. (1997). Developmental trajectories in moral reasoning across the life span. *Journal of moral education, 26*(4), 433–453.

Aronowitz, S. (1992). *False promises: The shaping of American working class consciousness.* Durham, NC: Duke University Press.

Baltes, P., Hayne, R., & Lipsett, L. (1980). Life-span developmental psychology. *Annual Review of Psychology, 31,* 65–110.

Bond, T. (1994). Piaget and measurement II. Empirical validation of the Piagetian model. *Archives de psychologie, 63,* 155–185.

Colby, A., Kohlberg, L., Gibbs, J., & Lieberman, M. (1983). Report on a 20-year longitudinal study of moral development. *Monograph of the society for research in child development, 48,* 1–124.

Commission for a Nation of Lifelong Learners. (1997, November). *A nation learning: Vision for the 21st century.* Washington, DC. (Available from Regents College, Dept. NLL, 7 Columbia Circle, Albany, NY 12198)

Commons, M., Armon, C., Kohlberg, L., Richards, F. A., Grotzer, T. A., & Sinnott, J. D. (Eds.). (1990). *Adult development, Vol II: Models and methods in the study of adolescent and adult thought.* New York: Praeger.

Commons, M., Richards, F., & Armon, C. (1984). *Beyond formal operations: Late adolescent and adult cognitive development.* New York: Praeger.

Commons, M., Sinnott, J., Richards, F., & Armon, C. (Eds.). (1989). *Adult development, Vol. I: Comparisons and applications of developmental models.* New York: Praeger.

Damon, W., & Hart, D. (1988). *Self-understanding in childhood and adolescence.* New York: Cambridge University Press.

Demick, J. (Ed.). (1999). *The Journal of Adult Development.* New York: Plenum.

Fowler, J. (1981). *Stages of faith: The psychology of human development and the quest for meaning.* San Francisco: Harper & Row.

Gilligan, C. (1982). *In a different voice: Psychological theory and women's development.* Cambridge: Harvard University Press.

Inhelder, B., & Piaget, J. (1958). *The growth of logical thinking from childhood to adolescence.* New York: Basic Books.

Kegan, R. (1982). *The evolving self: Problem and process in human development.* Cambridge: Harvard University Press.

Kohlberg, L. (1981) *The philosophy of moral development.* New York: Harper & Row.

Kohlberg, L., Levine, C., & Hewer, A. (1983). Moral stages: A current formulatino and a response to critics. *Contributions to Human Development, 10,* 174.

Loevinger, J. (1976). Ego development: Conceptions and theories. San Francisco: Jossey-Bass.

Rest, J. R., & Narvaez, D. (1991). The college experience and moral development, In W. M. Kurtines & J. L. Gewirtz (Eds.), *Handbook of moral behavior and development. Vol. 2: Research,* 229–245. Hillsdale, NJ: Erlbaum.

Rest, J. R., & Thoma, S. J. (1985). Relation of moral judgment to formal education. *Developmental Psychologist, 21*(4), 709–714.

Rybash, J., Roodin, P. & Santrock, J. (1991). *Adult development.* Dubuque, IA: W. C. Brown.

Ryff, C. (1989). In the eye of the beholder: Views of the psychological well-being among middle-age and older adults. *Psychology and Aging*, *4*(2), 195–210.

Selman, R. L. (1980). *The growth of interpersonal understanding: Developmental and clinical analyses*. New York: Academic Press.

Stevens-Long, J., & Commons, M. (1990). *Adult life: Developmental processes* (4th ed.). Mountain View, CA: Mayfield.

Stock, W., Okun, M., & Benin, M. (1986). Structure of subjective well-being among the elderly. *Psychology and Aging*, *1*, 91–102.

Vuyk, R. (1981) *Overview and critique of Piaget's genetic epistemology 1965–1980*, Vols 1 & 2. New York: Academic Press.

chapter 11

The Transpersonal Orientation as a Framework for Understanding Adult Development and Creative Processes

Marcie Boucouvalas
Virginia Tech/University of Virginia Northern
Virginia Center

Humans mature, and an understanding of the maturing self forms the focus of this book. One hallmark of maturation is the development of a strong, independent, autonomous, separate self-sense. Some caches of literature would refer to such a phenomenon as a strong, well-developed ego. For the most part, Western psychology has almost exclusively embraced this conceptualization of self as a framework for theorizing and research as well as good practice. This "separate self" identity is quite important in navigating life and living on this planet. It also serves a protective function for the individual and the species where the law of the jungle (i.e., eat or be eaten) may still prevail in human civilization.[1] Over the past 30 years, however, a movement has arisen within Western psychology (now spreading around the globe) named *transpersonal psychology* which bemoans the limited rendition of selfhood which such a conceptualization affords.[2] This movement has developed into a field of both study and practice which recognizes that for millennia ancient wisdom traditions, indigenous cultures, poets, philosophers, and literary genres have viewed the separate self identity as only a partial version of what it means to be human. Also pursued now, however, is a scientific understanding of the territory. Consequently, a deeper science is being born.

A main aim of this chapter is to offer the transpersonal as an organizing framework for understanding the unfolding of the "maturing self" while, at the same time, clearing up misconceptions of the transpersonal. As part of this process, an understanding of creativity from a transpersonal perspective is also addressed.

THE TRANSPERSONAL ORIENTATION:
AN ORGANIZING FRAMEWORK

The transpersonal orientation offers a broadened, deeper framework from which to consider the maturation process as well as the meaning and manifestation of creativity in life and living. It deals with the domain of human functioning as well as motivation that extends beyond the purely personal individual "I" or "me" which has been the primary domain of Western psychology.

From a transpersonal perspective, humankind and the related maturation process of individuals, groups, organizations, societies, and cultures includes a balance between a separate self sense and a deeper broader sense of self that is "connected," to use a current term.[3] Guided by what is referred to as the "transpersonal Self," the transpersonal dimension of selfhood purportedly unfolds as part of the greater developmental process in adulthood (see, for example, Cook-Greuter, 1990, 1994; the seminal works of Wilber referenced throughout; as well as Washburn, 1995).

The "transpersonal Self" is generally acknowledged by those in the field as a center of pure awareness that can observe and transcend ego conflicts, being both independent of and unaffected by fluctuations in feelings and thoughts. As I have stressed in earlier papers, the transpersonal Self tends to perceive the unity and interconnectedness of all things and often causes one, as a result, to see the personal ego (that is, the separate self identity) as a useful but limited vehicle or satellite rather than the axis upon which one's world turns. It is important to note that the perception of unity and interconnectedness is not just a cognitive understanding. Individuals who have developed to the point of identifying themselves as members of the planet feel connected with all humans, not just those of one's own race, gender, culture, nationality, and so on. This expanded identity enables one to increasingly transcend a purely "what's in it for me" kind of motivation.[4]

This transpersonal developmental potential can also be glimpsed and experienced as a special "state" by individuals at many "stages" of development. In such states "the individual feels that consciousness has expanded beyond the usual boundaries and limitations of time and space," to use Grof's (1976, p. 154) widely acknowledged description and definition. Some of these states of awareness have not been systematically studied in modern Western psychology previously.

Those who have caught glimpses of transcendent realities in various states of consciousness are awakened and aware but are often unable to explain or sometimes even understand the state-specific nature of the experience or the knowledge gleaned when they return to what has been termed "ordinary reality." Continual exposure to transpersonal states can act as a catalyst to further inquiry and interest regarding transpersonal development. These experiences benefit from supportive environments and relationships but can also atrophy or be led awry without such support, particularly during incipient awakening and development.

It is important to understand, however, that individuals at any level of health or pathology can have transpersonal experiences (Wilber, 1984a, 1984b). One must recognize that getting outside of and beyond one's own separate self-identity can manifest in developmental *or* pathological forms. Thus, we have the old adage about the fine line between "creative genius" and the "madman." Joseph Campbell (1972), philosopher and mythologist, recognized the transpersonal terrain as a sea in which mystics, for example, were swimming with delight, while psychotics were drowning. Equally noteworthy is the caveat about ingestion of psychotropic chemicals without guidance, since one may be stripped of ego "defenses" and protection and be catapulted into a "state" with which one is ill-equipped to deal or for which the personality may be too unstable. Transpersonal experiences can also coexist with psychopathology. Since people at any level of health or pathology can have transpersonal experiences, a major challenge and issue is differentiating the pathological from the nonpathological and integrating the experience into development in a meaningful way. There is another intriguing question that is central to both the development of the individual and the evolution of human species: how can transpersonal experiences be integrated into one's life and developmental trajectory.[5]

The meaning of all these descriptions should become clearer as the chapter progresses. Do remember that while much of the transpersonal must be experienced to be understood deeply, one can still appreciate the importance of this territory to the further development of the human species. Healthy skepticism helps us question the "reality" of something we may not have experienced. Rigidity in thinking, on the other hand, denies the existence of anything that lies outside our experiential reality. With this distinction in mind, welcome to the journey and our quest to understand what it means to be a maturing human.

From a transpersonal point of view, it is important to not consider unfolding and maturation only as a process of becoming more intelligent in the cognitive sense, or more developed in the emotional or moral sense, and so on. More important is the quality of how one experiences the world and one's place in it—how one "acts" in the world and reacts to it in a qualitatively different manner. I suggest this is so because one's consciousness of the world and one's place in it has shifted. This is the notion of maturation that guides my discussion and dialogue.

Kegan (1994) has made it clear that it is not cognitive intelligence per se but the "order of consciousness" from which one exercises one's intelligence that constitutes development. Moreover, Miller (1981, 1994) has offered longitudinal research in this regard as to how worldviews evolve and unfold and how they affect one's way of being in the world. These penetrating examples, as well as other relevant studies, emanate from a cognitive-developmental framework; however, glimpses of transpersonal nuances are already evident as will become clearer.

First, a brief historical understanding of transpersonal origins and roots is in order, followed by an updated overview of the scope of the movement and "field," and articulation of some common misconceptions. Such an overview should lay a groundwork for better understanding the relationship of the transpersonal terrain to creativity, broadly defined, as well as transpersonal challenges inherent in both individual and societal domains.

THE TRANSPERSONAL ORIENTATION: A BRIEF HISTORY

The idea of transpersonal aspects to humanity is millennia old. New is the organized movement to study the arena, catalyze and understand its theoretical as well as practical components, and an infrastructure to professionalize and promote such an inquiry as a field of study and practice.

The beginning of the movement is generally dated to the late 1960s, with the establishment in the United States of the *Journal of Transpersonal Psychology* (JTP) in 1969 and the Association of Transpersonal Psychology in 1970. A fuller understanding of the discussions and dialogues surrounding the formative years is available in the early volumes of the *Journal of Transpersonal Psychology*. The transpersonal movement has grown in intensity and scope over the past few decades. Associations and journals as well as networking groups have been established around the globe, including regional groups such as the European Transpersonal Association. During the 1970s, momentum grew as the journal and association flourished and national, as well as international, conferences took place. During the 1980s, the *Australian Journal of Transpersonal Psychology* was launched in 1981 and a German journal (*Zeitschrift fur Transpersonale Psychologie*) in 1982. During the 1990s, a Polish journal and association were founded, a Japanese association, British and Italian groups, and another German journal (on transpersonal psychotherapy— *Transpersonale Psychologie und Psychotherapie*) were introduced. In addition, during the past three decades the emergence of the transpersonal orientation in Russia has been evolving, at first silently and even underground, then in a more vocal manner (note the publication of books by Nalimov [mathematician/transpersonalist] in English by an American publisher beginning in the 1970s and the employment of transpersonal metaphors and musings by Russian geneticist Tonu Soidla [see, for example, a most recent Soidla, 1998]). Perhaps one of the most significant events of the 1990s was the name change in Australia from the *Australian Journal of Transpersonal Psychology* to the *International Journal of Transpersonal Studies* (IJTS),[6] thus recognizing both the global nature of the movement and its influence beyond the discipline of psychology. As we now enter the new millennium, I view the movement of the transpersonal perspective into other disciplines and fields of professional practice as one of the most promising advances to watch.

Of course, a host of sages, saints, philosophers, and poets precede this modern movement. Moreover, widely acknowledged as precursors are the following historical figures: Emanuel Swedenborg, William James, and Carl Jung, although differing positions exist as to the unique contributions of each. The interested reader is further referred to several historical reviews of the movement such as those by Sutich (1976), Walsh (1993), and Moss (1998).

There is one potential precursor who seems to have gone almost unnoticed. As early as the 1940s, the work of Andreas Angyal (1941), addressed to those disciplines working in the human realm, implored researchers and practitioner/professionals alike to frame their endeavors with an understanding of the complementarity between autonomy (the separate self sense) and homonomy (the meaning derived in life by feeling and being parts of greater wholes). His work, however, is never noted in the transpersonal literature (unlike the familiar figures of Swedenborg, James, and Jung listed above). I was first alerted to the work of Angyal from an obscure footnote in Maslow's book *Toward a Psychology of Being* (2nd ed.) published in 1968, one year after his now-famous speech in which he publicly referred to transhumanistic (later named transpersonal) psychology for the first time.

Just as the autonomous, separate self-sense has a developmental trajectory, likewise with the homonomous self-sense that focuses on the supra-individual unit with which one identifies. Manifesting throughout the developmental trajectory, it begins with the family, extends out to the "group(s)" to which one belongs, to one's culture, then moves toward an identity as a planetary citizen, and into the numinous (experience of the divine). Note the famous Socratic maxim: "I am neither an Athenian nor a Greek but a citizen of the world." As our sense of identity and belonging tends to include greater and greater wholes of which our smaller identities are a part, the objectionable "other" tends to recede and we are simultaneously able to embrace the "common good" (not just our own good) naturally as a result of this development. This internal developmental shift is different in quality from the externally imposed "shoulds" and "oughts" of proper behavior or political correctness. I have explored in more detail elsewhere a discussion of the autonomous and homonomous dimensions of selfhood as informed by Angyal (Boucouvalas, 1988, 1991). For present purposes I employ his term of homonomy as an identification that transcends the individual, separate self identity. There is a difference, though, between a cognitive/intellectual recognition that one "belongs" in a social sense to a particular group and a transpersonal awareness/identification that enables one to consider the larger unit, not just one's own needs.[7] Let us now move to a more in-depth inspection of the scope of the transpersonal terrain, including main themes, misconceptions, and caveats. I also discuss my own involvement in, and contribution to, this movement.

THE TRANSPERSONAL SCOPE

As a field of both study and practice, the transpersonal orientation contributes to the development of a knowledge paradigm that integrates both Eastern and Western ideas about humankind and the universe. Consequently, it is capable of accommodating areas such as human and cosmic energy systems; alternative methods of communicating, knowing, healing, and so on in local and nonlocal modes; reason, intuition, and in general a broader, deeper way of perceiving. This approach affirms a complementary relationship between science, humanities, and religion, and a more inclusive view of human nature.

The transpersonal arena is concerned with better understanding the most highly developed of the human species, those who tend to be motivated by needs that transcend their own skins and are living ontologically at a "level" of self-transcendence. Often these individuals are in touch with the "source"[8] of all creation and living an increasingly spiritual life. Albeit a small percentage of the population, they represent the "growing tip" of the human species and model what we might become. This is the transpersonal meaning of unfolding or maturing.

The transpersonal arena is also concerned with transpersonal states or glimpses in the lives of all humans. Transpersonal states are "temporary fluctuations" in awareness and knowing; temporary access to the "source." Perhaps the most recognized transpersonal pioneer who has extensively researched the quality and meaning of states of consciousness is Charles Tart. His first groundbreaking work in the 1960s (Tart, 1963/ 1969) illuminated many modes of functioning outside of our "ordinary waking" state of consciousness and addressed the phenomenon of state-specific knowledge. He observed that we have only a "one state" science while state-specific sciences are called for instead. A seminal article on the topic was published in *Science* (the periodical of the American Association for the Advancement of Science) (Tart, 1972).[9]

Understanding and experiencing states other than what we have become accustomed to calling our "ordinary waking" consciousness, then, forms an integral part of transpersonal studies. These states are not always spiritual in nature but offer a glimpse of what it might be like to get outside and beyond our encapsulated selves.

Transpersonal studies, then, address human consciousness in both spiritual and secular aspects. As Valle (1998) rightly reminds us, this distinction between spiritual and nonspiritual could lead to a fifth force or a more "purely spiritual" psychology (p. 276).

It has been about 20 years since I first began to explore the transpersonal arena. After years of immersion in reading, analyzing, and "experiencing" the then-extant literature in this domain and dialoguing with researchers, writers, and practitioners, I offered a conceptualization of the transpersonal based on my earlier research (Boucouvalas, 1980, 1981). This view of the transpersonal was adapted and augmented by some to develop courses (e.g., Davis & Wright, 1987) and by others to explain the scope of the transpersonal arena (e.g., transpersonal anthropologist Charles Laughlin).

More recently, when invited to update my earlier work, it became apparent to me that what began as transpersonal psychology has now expanded to other disciplines and has become the transpersonal orientation (Boucouvalas, 1995).[10] What follows, therefore, is an articulation of the expanded transpersonal orientation as elucidated over the past several decades and the potential trajectory of self in the mature years that such a framework offers. Were I writing this piece 20 to 30 years ago, I would have said "it is hypothesized that . . . "; 10 years ago, "it is theorized that. . . . " Today, however, I can claim that it is indeed increasingly noted or found that transpersonal research is changing our vision of what it means to be human.

My earlier analysis of 20 years ago suggested that the transpersonal domain, as an arena of both study and practice, could be articulated on four levels: (a) individual, (b) group, (c) societal, (d) planetary/cosmic. My more recent analysis confirms the currency and value of this basic scheme, but it has been fleshed out with the involvement of other disciplines. Now, the transpersonal orientation is broadening to include areas such as transpersonal anthropology, sociology, ecology, social work, art, music, literature, healing (including nonlocal), law, entrepreneurship, acting, and others. Since an understanding of the nature, development, and structure of human consciousness has always been a vision of the transpersonal movement, expanding to a multidisciplinary base affords a much more solid foundation for the knowledge claims.

Also better illuminated through such a collective lens are the complementary contributions of modern science and ancient wisdom (including present day indigenous cultures). In the following discussion of the different levels of focus in the transpersonal field, keep in mind that the transpersonal arena cannot be studied well with the intellect alone or fully appreciated from the space of ordinary consciousness alone. Actual transpersonal experience is a definite benefit. For that reason, transpersonal anthropology aims at training "polyphasic" researchers—those who are capable of entering and exiting different levels and states of consciousness at will to study an event, individual or group experience, or phenomena from the inside.

Levels of Focus in the Transpersonal Field

Individual level

Concern is with understanding, nurturing, and studying *both* stages of transpersonal development and states of transpersonal awareness; both spiritual aspects that lead to increased moral and ethical concerns and secular aspects that usher one into sources of knowledge and being outside ordinary separate self consciousness. Examples include:

A. developmental trajectories of saints, sages, mystics, and others in nonegoic realms and the place of ego in life and in the evolutionary development of humanity;
B. pathways and methods to encourage transpersonal awakening;
C. pathological and nonpathological transpersonal experiences and the difference between psychoses and spiritual emergencies (see note #5); the nature of and attitude toward the experiences and the way they are integrated (or not) into life;
D. development of inner experiential empiricism.

Cautions, caveats, and challenges for the individual, however, include the fact that the transpersonal path is studded with distractions, deterrents, and deceptions (self and other, as in charlatans); traps of spiritual pride, hyper-introspection, and so on; fixation at good feelings, power, esteem (including paranormal powers); danger of "quick fix" programs;

belief in a rapid path; misuse of power (and development of a superior attitude); and depression/withdrawal masked as detachment.

Group and societal levels

Examples include concern with understanding, nurturing, and studying:

A. synergistic, interbeing, relationships as pathways to transpersonal development (in the family, workplace, community, etc.);
B. the potentials and pitfalls of group consciousness (e.g., the helpful aspects of group intuition, the harmful effects of cultism);
C. the promotion of environments, organizations, institutions, and communities that facilitate transpersonal awakening and being and that stress service as well as individual learning;
D. the unfolding movement of transpersonal social work and sociology;
E. the movement toward transpersonal ecology; and
F. the attention of transpersonal anthropology to the relationship between consciousness and culture.

Planetary/cosmic level

Examples include our concern with understanding, nurturing, and studying:

A. the contribution of the transpersonal orientation to the developmental process of consciousness, including humanity's place in the evolution of the planet; and
B. the "planetary field of mind," and geopsychology—the relationship of human, planetary, and cosmic energies (including the emerging area of bioelectromagnetism both in the cosmos as well as in the human organism).

Cautions, caveats and challenges for the field include:

A. social and cultural skepticism due to the fact that transpersonal experiences are outside the experiential world of many, and
B. semantic difficulties that arise when explaining and contrasting transpersonal states from the perspective of "ordinary" consciousness. Braud and Anderson (1998) have done much to educate researchers in dealing with this methodological challenge.

Equally germane, though, is the recognition of misconceptions and incomplete understandings of the transpersonal field that proliferate.

Therefore, the next section is devoted to illuminating and clarifying these misconceptions.

Misconceptions

First, the transpersonal orientation is *not* entirely new. The concepts and practices are millennia old. What is new is an organized, worldwide movement, a recognized complementarity of ancient wisdom and modern science, and incipient development of social structures and support. Further, the transpersonal is *not* restricted to Eastern philosophy, but an integration of Eastern and Western worldviews. Mysticism is only *part* of the territory, and that part recognizes Western as well as Eastern mysticism. The transpersonal terrain is *not* restricted to gurus, saints, and sages only, but is a province of all humanity. It is *not* antagonistic; rather it is complementary, to the first three forces (psychoanalytic, behavioristic, humanistic) in the discipline of psychology. It is no longer, however, restricted to the discipline of psychology. Consequently, the unit of focus is *not* just the individual.

Perhaps one of the greatest misunderstandings in this field of study is what Wilber has termed the pre/trans fallacy. Epistemologically, from a transpersonal perspective, the rational way of knowing (via reasoning), while acknowledged as important, is not considered the only or most valid way of knowing, nor is it considered the pinnacle. The crux of the dilemma is that "nonrational" states of knowing and being occur before (pre)development of mature reasoning as well as after (beyond, post, or trans) the ability to engage in postformal logic and reasoning manifests itself. The assumption inherent in Wilber's position is that one must first develop mature reasoning capacities before achieving mature benefit from the more subtle pathways of knowing and being that are nonrational in nature. However, there is some controversy among transpersonalists as to the degree to which personal maturity helps one assimilate transpersonal experiences.

When logic is called for to analyze or understand a situation and rational thinking is not employed, a person's thinking is considered irrational. When logic is superseded because a deeper or more subtle form of understanding is present, then one is said to be engaged in a legitimate nonrational pathway. This distinction is important.

If, however, one believes that rationality is the highest form of human knowledge, then very likely anything nonrational is reduced to a "lower" realm and an individual might even be considered as regressing to a prerational state. This, according to Wilber, is one of two fallacies that comprise the pre/trans fallacy.

The superconscious is reduced to the subconscious, the transpersonal collapsed to the pre-personal, the emergence of the higher is reinterpreted as an irruption from the lower. All breathe a sigh of relief, and the rational worldspace is not fundamentally shaken. (Wilber, 1995, p. 206)

The other side of the pre/trans fallacy occurs when anything nonrational is "glorified" and "rationality is debased as inferior." Wilber calls this the "elevationist position." Confusing the "pre" and the "trans," one will "elevate all prerational states to some sort of transrational glory" and in such a case "rationality is (considered) . . . the low point of human possibilities, as a debasement, as the cause of sin and separation, and alienation." As a result, "anything nonrational gets swept up and indiscriminantly glorified as a direct route to the Divine" (pp. 206–207).

With these misconceptions and distinctions in mind, we can begin to explore the meaning of creativity from a transpersonal perspective.

THE TRANSPERSONAL ORIENTATION AND CREATIVITY

The transpersonal orientation enables us to view creativity from a broader perspective. As is evident, the transpersonal deals with the vast potential inherent in human experience in all levels and states of consciousness: ordinary and extraordinary. In nonordinary states, in which the ego's censoring function is suspended, lies the potential of discovering and expressing many creative impulses. For instance, Harman and Rheingold (1984) help us understand that creativity is a spectrum ranging from the "mundane to the miraculous." They draw an analogy to the electromagnetic spectrum, discovered this century, in which only a small band is visible to the human eye. Their claim is also consistent with Wilber's thesis that consciousness is a spectrum ranging from matter to mind to spirit. Only a small band may be "visible," understandable, or experienced currently by most of the human species.[11] As a species, we are still in the midst of understanding and articulating that spectrum.

The sources of knowledge or insights that emerge from the transpersonal terrain are often referred to as "breakthroughs." For the interested reader, Harman (in Harman & Rheingold, 1984) shares his own unfolding experiences, while Ferrucci (1990) speaks to the "breakthroughs" in the lives of scientists and artists throughout history who are well known for their contributions to society. The mode of knowing is often called "direct experience" of knowledge (alternatively inner knowing or knowing from a deep sense within, sometimes imperceptible to the senses).

Any knowledge is embedded in the environment from which it unfolds. Consequently, when the emergence of such special knowledge is judged from a rational stance (either by the creators themselves or by the observers/consumers) its validity is sometimes questioned. Thus, it may take courage to remain with one's convictions. In the end, a profound inner sense of certainty persists, as has been the case with inventors and sages throughout the ages. Often such experiences have a transformative effect on individuals, raising their awarenesses and expanding their perspectives. Sometimes such awareness has a deep lasting effect that might lead to developmental changes. Other times it provides attunement for transpersonal "states" of being, along with nonrational ways of knowing.

With regard to artistic "products" fueled from transpersonal origins, the transformative effect is often not only the purview of the creator but also extends to those viewing, hearing, or more generally experiencing the creation. Funk (Chapter 4 in this volume, and in previous writings) has devoted much energy to helping illuminate such experiences in the world of music and composition. Sometimes, however, one has to develop a capacity for "inner listening." This thesis was explored several decades ago by Bonny and Savery (1973) who invited their readers to (as they termed it) "listen with a third ear." Readers are provided with a hands-on approach to experiencing various states of consciousness through a "mood wheel," a guide offered whereby one can play selected pieces of classical music in a specified sequence.

These practices hone one's capacity for "inner knowing." Throughout history, inner voices have been a familiar manner through which such inner knowing has been manifested. Both in art and science inner voices have been influential. The example of Socrates who followed and was guided by what he called his "daimon" is most well known. As I have noted elsewhere (Boucouvalas, 1997a, p. 7), the notion of daimon, chronicled throughout history by both modern civilizations and indigenous cultures, receded in the West around the 19th century as educated people began to embrace the advent of scientific "knowing." The concept of daemon (Latin) and daimon (Greek) gave way to the English "demon," interpreted as evil influences. (See Inglis, 1987, for a more extensive discussion couched within the framework of intuition.) Given that individuals at any level of health or pathology have heard "inner voices," a discussion of such experiences vis-à-vis creativity fell out of favor until transpersonal researchers and writers began to reexamine them.

In this regard, Liester (1996) offers criteria to differentiate the "transpersonal" from the pathological or regressive inner voices. He offers a "hallucination-revelation" continuum and, following Wilbers's pre/trans fallacy, warns that prepersonal perceptual distortions such as hallucinations and illusions not be confused with transpersonal experiences and revelations. While similarities exist, the knowledge of some clear differences can guide us in our pursuit of better understanding the transpersonal sources of creativity. Liester offers the following (p. 22):

1. Pathological voices tend to be "judgmental, critical, and condemning" while transpersonal voices are "supportive."
2. Pathological voices "have a reality only in the mind of the individual who hears them," while the transpersonal "offer truths with a validity that can extend beyond the limitations of ego." (Discernment is important here since corroboration by others is extremely difficult.)
3. In contrast to voices that "interfere with personal, interpersonal, and social functioning," the transpersonal voices "lead to benefits" in functioning in all three spheres.
4. Transpersonal voices "speak in complete sentences or long discourses" which is not the case with the pathological.
5. Transpersonal inner voices do not "result from brain malfunctions" whereas the pathological often do.

The author also offers guidance to those interested in attuning to transpersonal inner voices. The two prerequisite conditions are: (a) receptive awareness and (b) inner silence. Both of these involve practices that must be cultivated over time (p. 23).

In the realm of visual art, Wilber (1996b) discusses what he terms the power of "great art" to pull one into a contemplative state. In his words:

> Great art grabs you, against your will, and then suspends your will. You are ushered into a quiet clearing, free of desire, free of grasping, free of ego, . . . through that opening or clearing in your own awareness may come flashing higher truths, subtler revelations, profound connections. For a moment you might even touch eternity; who can say otherwise, when time itself is suspended in the clearing that great art created in your awareness? (p. 90)

Wilber continues: "In that contemplative awareness, our own egoic grasping in time comes momentarily to rest" (1998b, p. 145).

This description resonates with Grof's widely accepted description of transpersonal states (i.e., expansion of consciousness "beyond the usual boundaries and limitations of time and space" [p. 154]). It also illustrates Tart's conceptualization of what constitutes a "state," one characteristic of which was the sense of time (see note #9). The artist, as Wilber (1997) stresses, has access to and is "alive" to the transpersonal realm. It appears that the creator is sometimes able to transpersonally awaken the "consumer" as well. Transpersonally generated art is of a different quality, a phenomenon that has even prompted individuals such as Greenman (1990) to propose a new transpersonal model of art criticism. Moreover, authors such as Gold (1998) offer a more practice-oriented discussion by describing what the experience is like when one paints from the "Source" and by offering guidelines to help others in that direction.

Sometimes, however, creative impulses and experiences of a transpersonal nature and origin may be fragile when viewed in the light of "ordinary" consciousness. Yet, they are experienced as valid or "true" at a deep level. Addressing this dilemma becomes an important challenge as we explore and embrace a broader, deeper vision of what it means to be human. Other greater challenges of a societal nature also warrant our attention.

EMBRACING THE GREATER CHALLENGES

First, there are ethical considerations involved. Just because one might experience creative insights, fueled from nonegoic realms, we cannot be certain that altruism will follow. Such insights can be harnessed for destructive as well as constructive ends. Destructive phenomena, however, occur less so when one is maturing on a transpersonal trajectory of development, and not simply experiencing transpersonal states and spaces. Consequently, it is these individuals who experience a better understanding of integrity, wisdom, and spirituality in the mature years of their lives. As is implied in the title of this book, the context of maturity provides a platform for a richer dialogue among those in the domains of art, science, and spirituality. Such a process holds promise for a deeper understanding of our potential as a human species.

In order to make further progress, however, a new understanding of scientific inquiry is needed, as well as a reconciliation between science and religion. This is our greatest challenge. Discussing how these goals can be accomplished forms an integral part of the transpersonal movement. Nalimov[12] (1982), in an earlier work, attempted to consider the possibility of a complementarity between science and religion. Merely discussing parallels, he found, was insufficient. He recommended the development of a new paradigm. Toward this end he proposed that the primary tenets of modern science be revised in the following ways (pp. 278–279):

1. *On reproducibility*: The recurrence of states and behaviors is not as important as (and also no more important than) the "rare manifestations" that "reveal the hidden part of the consciousness spectrum."

2. *On separating the subject and object of research*: Some parts of the spectrum are "concealed from direct observation," so they have to be "entered, lived through consciously, and discovered within oneself."
3. *On overreliance on technology*: Humans (with special development & training) are capable of "discovering a reality concealed from physical instruments," and thus there is no need to rely only on that which can be "perceived by technical devices."

More recently, Wilber (1998a) has also embraced the challenge of reconciling science and religion. He differentiates two ways people experience religion.

1. Some may experience religion as a sociocultural experience that offers "connection" to a group of like-minded believers in a higher power. It also affords a deep internal security that can sustain and guide one in life and "create meaning for the separate self" (p. 140).
2. For others, religion may become a pathway to transpersonal awakening (p.140). I would add that reciprocally, an experience of transpersonal awakening (i.e., the experience that one's consciousness has "expanded beyond the usual limits of time and space") can likewise be a path toward religion. In this process one is also awakened to the smallness of one's own ego in light of the size of the cosmos in much the same way as the Copernican Revolution revolutionized our understanding of the earth. The geocentric theory was superseded by the heliocentric theory in which the earth was no longer the central axis around which all else revolved, but a satellite among other satellites that revolved around a more powerful body—the sun. For transpersonally awakened adults, the ego is a satellite, not necessarily the axis upon which one's world turns. The ego is deemphasized in favor of the transpersonal Self and its connection to the divine. Experiencing the sacred and moving into that experience as a way of living is a key element. This maturation process, however, (called transformative spirituality) entails a human capacity for suffering as one discovers the limits of the separate self. At the same time, this developing awareness leads to the kind of integrity and wisdom to which this book is addressed.

Wilber (1998c) deepened the discussion on these matters by suggesting an integrative approach between science and religion—one that recognizes the unique contribution of the ancient Greek categories of: the good (morals and ethics), the true (science), and the beautiful (aesthetics). Furthermore, Wilber noted that advocates of each category must acknowledge that their own, preferred way of knowing is not the only one, nor necessarily the best. Each needs to respect the other. All can benefit, he claims, from a broad empiricism that covers "all modes and awarenesses of consciousness," not just the sensory. Drawing from his earlier work, Wilber (1996a) discusses a related typology of "ways of knowing." Here, using a metaphor from Saint Bonaventure, he refers to the "Eye of the Flesh" which governs the external world and sensory data; the "Eye of Reason" which governs the mental world of philosophy, logic, and so on; and the "Eye of Contemplation," which governs spiritual and transcendent realities. No one way of knowing, it is argued, should make claim to or usurp the domain of the other. The eye of the flesh, for example, cannot claim to prove or disprove matters in the contemplative, spiritual realm. Wilber's suggestion, I believe, should guide our future explorations in these interrelated domains.

These are both the understandings as well as the challenges we are offered when the transpersonal framework is applied to our understanding of the human maturation process. Where will we go from here? The unknown beckons.

NOTES

1. This separate self identity may be applied equally to individuals, groups, organizations, nations, and so on. Without an understanding of the connection to the greater whole, however, "centrisms" often arise such as egocentrism, ethnocentrism, and so on. In today's world, in which many countries experience a newly found separate self identity, autonomous groups sometimes run the risk of truncating off, emphasizing their differences with others, but forgetting, ignoring, or sidestepping the greater whole of which they are part.

2. While the *term* transpersonal is now appearing around the globe, Eastern philosophies and some earlier Western writings (e.g., James, Swedenborg, Jung, etc.) were precursors. Since the Eastern philosophies, however, have heralded a nonegoic aspect of selfhood for millennia, this has led to a misconception that equates the transpersonal with Eastern philosophies. Moreover, the term mysticism (Eastern or Western) has often been equated with, but is only part of, the transpersonal.

3. In the transpersonal literature, the term "connected" is employed in a very broad deep inner sense and not restricted only to the social external sense of "connection" as appears in some caches of literature.

4. A strong, well-developed, and integrated ego is essential and enables one to discern and differentiate a cult from other kinds of spiritual or support groups. Sometimes, however, exclusive attention to the "separate self" can devolve into an ego-centered orientation that fosters excessive attention to the "what's in it for me" motivation. This should not be confused with self-centered egocentrism where one has not yet developed a strong well-integrated ego and may be operating more from a self-protective stance.

5. Increasing attention is focused on experiences that may overtly appear as psychotic, but are potentially transformative since they are not pathologically rooted. Called "spiritual emergencies" (see Grof & Grof, 1989), a valuable help network of professionals is operating. An example of such an experience is kundalini awakening (see Krishna, 1971; Sanella, 1978 on the experience; and Scotton, 1996 on treatment). Transpersonally oriented therapists are helping integrate the experience into development (since fear and anxiety can manifest) and are educating the public. The energy, awakened, is powerful and accompanied by alterations in consciousness and creative insights. The addition of a category on "religious and spiritual problems" to the DSM (Diagnostic and Statistical Manual of Mental Disorders) helps clarify such conditions that may be a focus of concern but are not attributable to a mental disorder.

6. The *IJTS* has recently moved to Hawaii, published by Panagada Press, and the Australian Society is publishing a new quarterly journal entitled *Consciousness*.

7. Balance between autonomy and homonomy is a key. When the separate self identity has not been well developed or when it has been affected by brainwashing, adherence to cults may occur. When the individual self identity becomes clouded or unimportant compared to the larger homonomous identification terrorists may also be born, ready to die for the cause (especially when the autonomous group is truncated off from the greater civilization of which they are part [see note #1]).

8. Throughout the chapter, the more popular term "source" is used to refer to what philosophers and theologians such as Paul Tillich and Huston Smith, as well as the Jungians, have referred to as the Ground of Being, the deep center and divine essence.

9. Gordon Globus had written a letter to the editors of *Science* in reaction against Tart's 1972 article. After experiencing a different "state," the article became clearer to him and he responded with a follow-up letter. Both letters are published (Globus, 1993) as an example of this challenge. In Tart's complex system model, a state (of consciousness) is comprised of ten subsystems (for example, sense of time, sense of space, etc.) Movement from one state to another involves alteration and restabilization in the constellation of the subsystem (for example, one's sense of time or space might expand or contract) (see also Tart, 1975, 1976). Those interested in education may want to explore Roberts (1989) who has developed a multistate educational model based on Tart.

10. My publications in the intervening years spoke more to applications of the transpersonal terrain and the broader field of consciousness studies to learning (see, for example, Boucouvalas, 1983, 1993, 1997b). At present, I am engaged in a systematic update of my earlier work that will include review and potential modification/verification by the same review panel used in 1979–1980. More recent leaders in the field will be added to the panel.

11. While the writings of Wilber are voluminous, the reader is especially referred to his early seminal book, *The Spectrum of Consciousness*, originally published in 1977, but updated and revised in 1993.

12. Nalimov (1974/1981, 1981, 1982, 1985), a highly respected mathematician, was an integral part of the transpersonal orientation in modern day Russia. Also of interest is a memorial issue of the *International Journal of Transpersonal Studies*

(Volume 16, No. 2, December, 1997–Voices of Russian Transpersonalism, No. 4) published upon the occasion of Nalimov's death.

REFERENCES

Angyal, A. (1941). *Foundations for a science of personality.* Cambridge: Harvard University Press.

Bonny, H., & Savery, L. (1973). *Music and your mind: Listening with a new consciousness.* New York: Harper & Row.

Boucouvalas, M. (1980). Transpersonal psychology: A working outline of the field. *Journal of Transpersonal Psychology, 12*(1), 37–46.

Boucouvalas, M. (1981). Transpersonal psychology: Scope and challenge. *Australian Journal of Transpersonal Psychology, 1*(2), 136–151.

Boucouvalas, M. (1983). Social transformation, lifelong learning, and transpersonal psychology: The fourth force. *Lifelong Learning: The adult years , 6*(7), 6–9.

Boucouvalas, M. (1988, July). An analysis and critique of the concept self in self-directed learning: Toward a more robust construct for research and practice. In M. Zukas (Ed.), *Proceedings of the Trans-Atlantic Dialogue Research Conference,* 56–61. Leeds, England: University of Leeds.

Boucouvalas, M. (1991, October). *The transcultural self.* Paper presented to the World Conference on Comparative Adult Education, University of Ibadan, Nigeria.

Boucouvalas, M. (1993). Consciousness and learning: New and renewed approaches. In S. Merriam (Ed.), *An update on adult learning theory.* San Francisco: Jossey-Bass.

Boucouvalas, M. (1995). Transpersonal psychology: Scope and challenges re-visited. In E. M. Neill & S. I. Shapiro (Eds.), *Embracing transcendence: Visions of transpersonal psychology* (pp. 1–25). Stafford Heights, Australia: Bolda-Lok.

Boucouvalas, M. (1997a). Intuition: The concept and the experience. In R. Davis-Floyd & S. Arvidson (Eds.), *Intuition, the inside story: Interdisciplinary perspectives.* New York: Routledge.

Boucouvalas, M. (1997b). Analysis and critique of transformation theory in adult learning: Contributions from consciousness studies. In P. Armstrong, N. Miller, & M. Zukas (Eds.), *Crossing borders, breaking boundaries: Research in the education of adults: An International Conference* (pp. 56–60). London: Birkbeck College, University of London.

Braud, W. & Anderson, R. (Eds.). (1998). *Transpersonal research methods for the social sciences: Honoring human experience.* Thousand Oaks, CA: Sage.

Campbell, J. (1972) *Myths to live by.* New York: Viking.

Cook-Greuter, S. (1990). Maps for living: Ego development. Stages from symbiosis to conscious universal embeddedness. In M. L. Commons et al. (Eds.), *Adult development Volume 2: Models and methods in the study of adolescent and adult thought.* New York: Praeger.

Cook-Greuter, S. (1994). Rare forms of self-understanding in mature adults. In M. Miller & S. R. Cook-Greuter (Eds.), *Transcendence and mature thought in adulthood*. Lanham, MD: Rowan & Littlefield.

Davis, J. & Wright, C. (1987). Content of undergraduate transpersonal psychology classes. *Journal of Transpersonal Psychology, 19*(2), 173–179.

Ferrucci, P. (1990). *Inevitable grace: Breakthrough in the lives of great men and women: Guides to your self-realization*. New York: St. Martin's.

Globus, G. (1993). Different views from different states. In R. Walsh & F. Vaughan (Eds.), *Paths beyond ego: The transpersonal vision*. New York: Jeremy Tarcher/Putnam.

Gold, A. (1998). *Painting from the source: Awakening the artist's soul in everyone*. New York: Harper-Collins.

Greenman, C. H. (1990). *A transpersonal model of art criticism*. Unpublished Ph.D. dissertation, Pennsylvania State University.

Grof, S. (1976). *Realms of the human unconscious*. New York: E.P. Dutton.

Grof, S., & Grof, C. (1989). *Spiritual emergency: When personal transformation becomes a crisis*. Los Angeles: Jeremy Tarcher.

Harman, W., & Rheingold, H. (1984). *Higher creativity: Liberating the unconscious for breakthrough insights*. Los Angeles: Jeremy Tarcher.

Inglis, B. (1987). *The unknown guest: The mystery of intuition*. London: Chato & Windus.

Kegan, R. (1994). *In over our heads: The mental demands of modern life*. Cambridge: Harvard University Press

Krishna, G. (1971). *Kundalini: The evolutionary energy in man*. Boulder, CO: Shambhala.

Liester, M. B. (1996). Inner voices: Distinguishing transcendent and pathological characteristics. *Journal of Transpersonal Psychology, 28*(1), 1–30.

Maslow, A. (1968). *Toward a psychology of being* (2nd ed.). New York: Van Nostrand Reinhold.

Miller, M. E. (1981). World views and ego development in adulthood (Doctoral dissertation, University of Pittsburgh, 1981). *Dissertation Abstracts International, 42* 08B, 3459.

Miller, M. E. (1994). World views, ego development, and epistemological changes from the conventional to the post formal: A longitudinal perspective. In M. Miller & S. Cook-Greuter (Eds.), *Transcendence and mature thought in adulthood*. Lanham, MD: Rowland & Littlefield.

Moss, D. (1998). *Humanistic and transpersonal psychology: A historical and biographical sourcebook*. Westport, CT: Greenwood Press.

Nalimov, V. V. (1974, 1981). *In the labyrinths of language: A mathematician's journey*. Philadelphia, PA: ISI Press.

Nalimov, V. V. (1981). *Faces of science*. Philadelphia, PA: ISI Press.

Nalimov, V. V. (1982). *Realms of the unconscious: The enchanted frontier*. Philadelphia, PA: ISI Press.

Nalimov, V. V. (1985). *Space, time, and life: The probabalistic pathways of evolution*. Philadelphia, PA: ISA Press.

Roberts, T. B. (1989). Multi-state education: Metacognitive implications of the mind-body psychotechnologies. *Journal of Tranpersonal Psychology*, *21*(1), 83–102.

Sanella, L. (1978). *Kundalini: Transcendence or psychosis*. San Fransisco: Dakin.

Scotton, B. W. (1996). The phenomenology and treatment of kundalini. In B. W. Scotton, A. B. Chinen, & J. R. Battista (Eds.), *Textbook of transpersonal psychiatry and psychology*. New York: Basic Books.

Soidla, T. (1998). Me and a giant kinesthetic bee: An attempt at a biographical and metaphoric study of a totalitarian psyche. *International Journal of Transpersonal Studies*, *17*(1), 19–34.

Sutich, A. (1976). The emergence of the transpersonal orientation: A personal account. *Journal of Transpersonal Psychology*, *8*(1), 5–19.

Tart, C. T. (Ed.). (1969). *Altered states of consciousness*. New York: Anchor. (Original work published 1963)

Tart, C. T. (1972). States of consciousness and state specific sciences. *Science*, *176*, 1203–1210.

Tart, C. T. (1975). *States of consciousness*. New York: Dutton.

Tart, C. T. (1976). The basic nature of altered states of consciousness: A systems approach. *Journal of Transpersonal Psychology*, *8*(1), 45–64.

Valle, R. (Ed.) (1998). Transpersonal awareness: Implications for phenomenological research. In Valle, R. (Ed.), *Phenomenological inquiry in psychology: Existential and transpersonal dimensions*. New York: Plenum.

Walsh, R. (1993). The transpersonal movement: A history and state of the art. *Journal of Transpersonal Psychology*, *25*(2), 123–139.

Washburn, M. (1995). *The ego and the dynamic ground*. (2nd ed.). Albany: SUNY Press.

Wilber, K. (1984a). The developmental spectrum and psychopathology: Part I. States and types of pathology. *Journal of Transpersonal Psychology*, *16*(1), 75–118.

Wilber, K. (1984b). The developmental spectrum and psychopathology: Part II. Treatment modalities. *Journal of Transpersonal Psychology*, *16*(2), 137–166.

Wilber, K. (1993). *The spectrum of consciousness* (2nd ed.). Boston: Shambhala. (Original work published 1977)

Wilber, K. (1995). *Sex, ecology, and spirituality: The spirit of evolution*. Boston: Shambhala.

Wilber, K. (1996a). *Eye to eye: The quest for the new paradigm* (3nd ed.). Boston: Shambhala.

Wilber, K. (1996b). Transpersonal art and literary theory. *Journal of Transpersonal Psychology*, *28*(1), 63–91.

Wilber, K. (1997). To see a world: Art and the I of the beholder. *Journal of Transpersonal Psychology*. *29*(2), 143–149.

Wilber, K. (1998a). *The essential Ken Wilber*. Boston: Shambhala.

Wilber, K. (1998b). *The eye of the spirit: An integral vision for a world gone slightly mad*. Boston: Shambhala.

Wilber, K. (1998c). *The marriage of sense and soul*. Boston: Shambhala.

About the Editors

Susanne Cook-Greuter is fascinated with how complex adult reality conceptions, language, meaning-making, and creativity interrelate. For the last 20 years she has been investigating mature ego development, first as an independent scholar, and more recently at Harvard University (Ed. M., 1979; Ed.D., 1999). Susanne grew up in Switzerland where she studied linguistics and English and Romance literatures as well as psychology at the University of Zurich Switzerland where she received the Lic. Phil. I., in 1974.

She has systematized and expanded Loevinger's ego development theory to more adequately reflect growth beyond self-actualization. Based on rare postautonomous responses from the Washington University Sentence Completion Test, she has posited two new distinctive postconventional stages at the transition from the personal to the transpersonal realm. Unlike most theories in this field, her distinctions are empirically grounded.

She is an active member of the Society for Research in Adult Development (SRAD), and the Guild of American Papercutters (GAP). As a linguist, she explores the nature and the limits of language and rational analysis in meaning making. She believes that new insights into the human condition will result from a synthesis of the self-psychology of the West and the wisdom literature of the East. She advocates an interdisciplinary approach to the study of human development that includes transpersonal, metalinguistic ways of knowing. She uses her artistic talents to express—in intricate scissorcuttings that celebrate nature—her fascination with contemplation as means of knowing, as well as to figuratively map complex ideas.

Melvin E. Miller has been interested in philosophy, narrative, and the creation of meaning for most of his life. His longitudinal research on the development of worldviews and religious perspectives naturally evolved from such interests. He received a Ph.D. from the University of Pittsburgh. Since then, in addition to postdoctoral clinical and psychotherapy studies, he has twice been a visiting scholar at Harvard Divinity School. He is presently Professor of Psychology, Director of Psychological Services, and Director of Doctoral Training at Norwich University. Among his publications is a book he coedited with Susanne Cook-Greuter entitled *Transcendence and Mature Thought in Adulthood: The Further Reaches of Adult Development*, and one recently coedited with Alan N. West: *Spirituality, Ethics, and Relationship: Clinical and Theoretical Explorations*. He is on the editorial board of the *Bulletin of the Boston Institute for Psychotherapy*. Mel has been actively involved in both the New England Psychological Association (NEPA) and the Society for Research in Adult Development (SRAD) over the past few years. He was president of NEPA in 1988, and SRAD Board of Directors member and executive director of SRAD for the past seven years.

About the Contributors

Cheryl Armon received her B.A. in liberal studies from Antioch University Los Angeles, and her master's and doctoral degrees in human development from Harvard University, with specializations in cognitive and moral psychology. There she worked with Lawrence Kohlberg on research in moral development, democratic education, and reasoning about the Good Life. In 1984, she won the Dissertation of the Year Award from both Radcliffe University and the Association for Moral Education. Currently, as a Professor of Human Development at Antioch University Los Angeles, Dr. Armon has designed and implemented various courses, training programs, and community interventions that involve the integration of structural-developmental psychology with educational theory, ethical philosophy, research methods, and clinical practice. She directs the Educational Assessment Project for Antioch's undergraduate program. Dr. Armon cofounded and is the current associate editor of the *Journal of Adult Development.* She has recently published three articles: "A Longitudinal Study of Adult Reasoning about the Good Life" in the *Handbook of Adult Development;* and "Adult Moral Development, Experience, and Education" and "Developmental Trajectories in Moral Reasoning Across the Lifespan" (with Theo Dawson) in the *Journal of Moral Education.* Currently, Dr. Armon is developing a new program in education for Antioch's Los Angeles and Santa Barbara campuses.

Marcie Boucouvalas is Professor of Adult Learning in the Department of Human Development at the Virginia Tech/University of Virginia Northern Virginia Center where she has been a resident faculty member since 1980. Prior to that she worked in a variety of contexts with adults as learners, broadly defined (e.g., physicians, in the criminal justice system, in urban and rural disadvantaged communities, etc.). She has been involved in researching, studying, and living within the transpersonal orientation since the late 1970s and serves a field editor for the *Journal of Transpersonal Psychology.*

Linda Marie Bresette received her undergraduate degree at Salem State College in Massachusetts where in 1997 she obtained a B.A. in psychology with honors. In 1999, she earned an M.S. in mental health counseling and psychological services with highest honors. Since 1997, she has been a psychotherapist in the Leland Psychiatric Detoxification Unit of Beverly Hospital and a research associate at the Dare Institute, Cambridge, MA. She is a member of both the Program in Psychiatry and the Law, and the Society for Research in Adult Development.

Ms. Bresette coauthored, with Eric Goodheart and Michael Commons, an article entitled "Formal, Systematic, and Metasystematic Operations with a Balance-Beam Task Series: A Reply to Kallio's Claim of No Distinct Systematic Stage." This article was published in the *Journal of Adult Development* in 1995.

Linda Bresette's research interests include: the effective provision of care during short-term inpatient hospitalizations, patient/provider relationships, postformal thinking in adult development, and mental health law.

Michael L. Commons did his undergraduate work at the University of California at Berkeley, and then at Los Angeles, where in 1965 he obtained a B.A. in both mathematics and psychology. In 1967 he earned an M.A. and M.Phil., and he received a Ph.D. in psychology from Columbia University in 1973. Before coming to Harvard University in 1977 as a postdoctoral fellow and then becoming research associate in psychology, he was an assistant professor at Northern Michigan University.

Since 1987, he has been lecturer and research associate at the Department of Psychiatry at Harvard Medical School, Massachusetts Mental Health Center, and research scientist for the Program in Psychiatry and the Law. Dr. Commons is also director of the Dare Institute, Cambridge, MA. He is cofounder of the Society for Quantitative Analyses of Behavior and The Society for Research in Adult Development, and founder of the *Journal of Adult Development*. Dr. Commons has numerous publications that include: an article with Gerhard Sonnert (1994) "Society and the Highest Stages of Moral Development," published in *The Individual and Society*. His seminal volume, *Beyond Formal Operations* (1984), coedited with Francis Richards and Cheryl Armon, has become a classic in the field of adult development.

Dr. Commons's research interests are primarily in the quantitative analysis of the construction, understanding, and experiencing of reality as it develops across the life span. He is interested in how these elements affect decision processes, life-span attachment, and alliance formation in a number of domains including the ethical, moral, epistemological, valuative, and evaluative.

Christopher Edwards is a writer, editor, and entrepreneur in Cambridge, Massachusetts. He owns and operates a consulting and coaching firm that helps people find greater satisfaction and productivity in their careers. Edwards holds a Ph.D. in literature and religion from Boston University and a B.A. in philosophy and psychology from Yale University. His doctoral work explored the spiritual dimensions of creativity among writers from various religious traditions.

In his current position, Edwards works with clients to help them discover their creativity and how they can channel it into their everyday lives. He has started a number of publications, cofounded a biotechnology company, and consulted for startup companies for 19 years. Edwards is the author of books in both biotechnology and religion, and he currently writes a column on career development for scientists.

Joel Funk received a B.A. in chemistry from Rutgers University in 1967, and a Ph.D. in psychology from Clark University in 1977. Since 1975, he has taught at Plymouth State College, currently at the rank of professor. In addition to psychology, he has taught several interdisciplinary courses: in creativity, ecopsychology, and the use of feature films as "case studies." Research areas include: the phenomenology of laughter and emotions, the development of music perception in children and adults, the effects of drama on children's conceptions of death, spiritual and psychological aspects of music (especially the work of Beethoven), near-death, and post-formal/transpersonal theory.

Other interests include gardening, cooking health foods, reading whodunits, improvising at the piano, and songwriting, the last two being the source of his interest in the creative process.

Stephanie Glass-Solomon received her bachelor's degree in dramatic literature from the University of California Berkeley, her master of science in gerontology from the University of Southern California and a master of arts in general psychology from The New School for Social Research. She is a produced playwright as well as having been a full-time faculty member at Antioch University Los Angeles for over 15 years. Solomon has recently coauthored an article in *Generations Magazine* on online education in gerontology and has recently written and performed two one-woman jazz/cabaret shows in her role as an artist and vocalist. She is currently developing a Music Industry Degree Program for Antioch.

Carl Goldberg is the author of 12 books and 150 professional publications. He is editor-for-the-Americas for *The International Journal of Psychotherapy*. He is also on the editorial board of *The Journal for Adult*

Development and book reviewer for *The American Journal of Psychotherapy* and *Psychoanalytic Books*. Dr. Goldberg was formerly Associate Clinical Professor of Psychiatry at Albert Einstein College of Medicine, Associate Clinical Professor of Psychiatry and Director of Group Psychotherapy Training at Mount Sinai Medical School (at Elmhurst), and Associate Clinical Professor of Psychiatry at George Washington University School of Medicine. He has taught child and adolescent development and other clinical and theoretical courses, and directed group therapy programs in several doctoral programs in clinical psychology, at psychoanalytic and psychotherapy institutes, hospitals, and colleges. He has been a director of a comprehensive community mental health center, and a chief psychologist for a psychiatric service in a federal psychiatric hospital.

Carol Hoare is Professor of Human Development and Human Resource Development in the Department of Counseling, Human, and Organizational Studies at The George Washington University, Washington DC. An alumna of Carlow College, the University of North Carolina at Chapel Hill, and The George Washington University, she enjoys university life because it permits her the luxury and joy of being a student. Erik and Joan Erikson are two mentors who, along with her wonderful husband Ray and two terrific now-adult children, Jenny and Ray, continue to teach her and to inspire her work.

John J. McKenna has been affiliated with Trinity College of Vermont in Burlington, for more than 25 years. He currently holds an appointment as Professor of Psychology and is Coordinator of Advising, Curriculum Review, and Program Evaluation for the Graduate Program in Community Mental Health. After 12 years as a monk of the Cistercian Order, he obtained a master's degree in psychology and religion from Andover Newton Theological School. Following doctoral studies in clinical psychology at the University of Vermont, he began a part-time clinical practice for adolescents, adults, and couples. Dr. McKenna's current research focuses on issues at the interface of spirituality and psychology, narrative and constructivist approaches to therapy and theory, feminist critical perspectives, and alternatives to mainstream empirical research methods in psychology. Dr. McKenna has presented on systemic factors in, and prevention of, child sexual abuse, methods of reducing risks of sexual misconduct by clergy and church program staff, variables related to psychosocial adjustment to cancer diagnosis and treatment, and art and meditation as adjunctive methods of healing.

Verbena Pastor was born in Rome. She holds a doctorate in letters from the Università La Sapienza and master of fine arts in writing from

Norwich University where she is an assistant professor in the graduate program. Her academic interests include history, archaeology, propaganda art, and European culture between 1930 and 1950. Her most recent publication is an essay on the sublime in propaganda art (in *JAISA*). Published in September 1999 are her World War II novel *Lumen* (Van Neste Books) and excerpts from *She Was Watching*, her annotated translation of an Italian war diary, in *Italian Americana*.

Ernest Zebrowski, Jr. is professor and chair of the Department of Science Education at Southern University, Baton Rouge. Previously, he held a professorship in physics at Pennsylvania College of Technology, Penn State. He has written a variety of articles in physics and science education, has authored five books, and has been active in promoting science education for the public. Among his publications is *Perils of a Restless Planet: Scientific Perspectives on Natural Disasters*, Cambridge University Press, 1997.

Author Index

Subject Index

A

abstract reasoning skills, 191
achievement, xi
active passivity, 65
adult development, 189
  and creative process, 209
  positive, 168
  postconventional stages of, xv
  progressive, 196
  research, 200
  researchers, 180
adult developmental theory,
  189, 202
adult education,
  informed by adult developmental theory, 190
  programs, 189
  reconceiving, 189
adult liberal education, 203
adult life, American, 197
adult lives, fragmentation in,
  200
adulthood, xi
aesthetic, 153, 223
  appreciation, 195
  concept of, 152
  criterion, 159
  development, 152
  in human experience, 192
  in science, 158
aging, pathological manifestations of, 88
aggressiveness, 94
altered state, 64
altruism, 222
ambiguity, tolerance for, xviii
American Art Therapy Association (AATA), 110
American,

institutions and lower-stage
  development, 200
social context, 119
superego, 120
transcendentalist movement, 4
Andalusian gypsies
antimystical trends, 12
angel, 35, 37
angelic guidance, 70
Angels of Comfort, 62, 64
anxiety, 199
archetypal,
  characters of the psyche, 142
  experience of the night journey, 50
  inspiration, 59
  material, xii
  mental images, 30
archetype(s), 21
  Platonic, 59
Aristotle, 95, 160, 192
Aristotelian perspective, 151
art, 125
  criticism, transpersonal
  model of, 222
  of doing science, 156
  as meditation, 13
  power of, 143
  as proactive, 162
  and science,
    connection between, 165
    as symbolic, 151
  therapists, next generation of,
  123
  therapy, 100, 105, 111
    as ego-supporting, 111
    emerging field of, 110
    field of, 109
    healing power of, 113